SAGE ANNUAL REVIEWS OF DRUG AND ALCOHOL ABUSE

SAGE Annual Reviews of Drug and Alcohol Abuse
Volume 3

ADDICTS and AFTERCARE

Community Integration
of the Former Drug User

BARRY S. BROWN, Editor

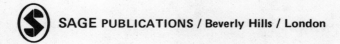 SAGE PUBLICATIONS / Beverly Hills / London

For information address:

 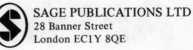

SAGE PUBLICATIONS, INC.
275 South Beverly Drive
Beverly Hills, California 90212

SAGE PUBLICATIONS LTD
28 Banner Street
London EC1Y 8QE

Printed in the United States of America

Library of Congress Cataloging in Publication Data

Main entry under title:

Addicts and aftercare.

(Sage annual reviews of drug and alcohol
abuse ; v. 3)
1. Narcotic addicts--Rehabilitation--United
States--Addresses, essays, lectures. 2. Narcotic
addicts--Rehabilitation--Addresses, essays,
lectures. I. Brown, Barry S. [DNLM: 1. After
care. 2. Drug dependence--Rehabilitation.
3. Self-help groups. W1 SA125TD v. 3 / WM270.3
A224]
HV5825.A648   362.2'93   79-18156
ISBN 0-8039-1148-3
ISBN 0-8039-1149-1 pbk.

FIRST PRINTING

CONTENTS

PART III. MODELS FOR CONTINUING
CARE USING COMMUNITY ORGANIZATIONS

PART IV. HUMAN RESOURCE
ORGANIZATIONS IN CONTINUING CARE

PART V. CLIENT ADVOCACY

FOREWORD

Among the many seemingly intractable problems which face those who provide treatment services to drug users are those of aftercare, or community integration. This volume provides both a theoretical basis for and practical suggestions about providing community integration services and assuring that such services are available to former drug abusers. It is a useful first step for all those working in or interested in the problems of treatment of drug abusers. Like most good volumes reporting on social science research or social problems, the book asks as many questions as it answers.

In all social service programs the problem of providing for the reentry of the person who has received the services into the community at large is a difficult one. The problem in some instances is made both easier and more difficult by the fact that separation from the community at large is often not physical separation. These chapters deal largely with those who have been physically separated, for most of the work has been done in instances of physical separation, such as the separation of the individual who has spent time in a mental institution or who has been in a correctional institution. There is more limited knowledge of how to deal with the person whose unemployment, drug abuse, or alcoholism has left them in fact separated from the community of which they are physically still a part.

The efforts in the mental health and corrections areas are explored and freely borrowed from in various of the chapters in this volume, and similar borrowing is taken from the field of alcoholism. There is less taken from the extensive literature on the multiplicity of employment and training programs of the 1960s and 1970s.

The various chapters not only draw from a variety of other fields but also describe several types of community integration activities: family activities, work activities, the efforts of self-help groups including former users, the use of volunteers, the assistance of advocacy groups, and the use of litigation to enforce community integration rights and responsibilities are all explained. Brown and his colleagues thus provide multiple starting points for those who are concerned with not only treatment but also the prevention of relapse.

In spite of the variety of roles covered and the diversity of areas from which background is drawn in these chapters, community integration for aftercare is an area about which there is little known in the field of drug abuse, and unfortunately, the other areas such as mental health, corrections, and alcoholism, about which more is known, are not themselves overly abundant with success stories.

Perhaps one of the most important areas that this volume opens up is that of using self-help models for community integration. The experience of such a group in Hong Kong is explored and a brief description is presented of all such groups known to be operating in the United States as well as a theoretical discussion of their roles. Self-help groups for drug abuse in this country obviously need to draw from the Alcoholics Anonymous experience, and some have, including those which seem to be enjoying relatively widespread success.

Left unexplored in the area of self-help are two items which those in the field can examine themselves and perhaps look forward to developing further. First is the idea of self-help groups which are focused more on economic adjustment (particularly work place adjustment, finding a job, finding transportation, finding housing, etc.) as opposed to the psychological adjustment self-help groups which are the model for much of what is presented in this volume. Second, the section on self-help groups in this volume, as indeed most of the sections in the volume, focuses primarily on heroin addicts. As the nature of drug abuse changes in this country (or at least the nature of drug abuse treatment, as more and more of those entering treatment seem to be primarily involved with drugs other than heroin), it is possible that problems of self-help in particular may change even more radically in nature.

Self-help groups may become more popular, since frequently those involved in drugs other than heroin also are not as removed from their community as those who are involved with heroin. Thus, problems of treatment of such drug abusers may become more difficult for the treatment system to handle, particularly in locales where those providing treatment services are largely themselves ex-heroin addicts. At the same time, the community integration or aftercare phase of the treatment and rehabilitation process may become one in which increased successes can be enjoyed. If present trends in national statistics continue to show such a shift in drug abuse patterns among those entering treatment, perhaps we can also look forward to greater success rates in the future on the measures of community integration.

The chapters themselves contain a few suggestions for further research, suggestions on action strategies, and discussions of policy implications. In spite of the limited number of direct suggestions, the entire volume is rich with implicit suggestions and ideas for those who wish to do more in the important area of community integration for former drug abusers. For those involved in drug abuse services, this volume will be invaluable in the ideas it offers for action. For those involved in questions of community integration, whether of former drug abusers or of other groups who are outside a general community, this volume also offers much. For both groups as well as for the many others with related interests, *Addicts and Aftercare* is a volume to be consulted often for its many insights, not one merely to be skimmed or read rapidly and then put on the shelf.

> —*Carl Akins, Ph.D.*
> *Executive Director*
> *National Association of State Alcohol and*
> *Drug Abuse Directors (NASADAD)*

INTRODUCTION

BARRY S. BROWN

Increasingly, service delivery programs have come to view the task of rehabilitation as incomplete unless steps are taken to guarantee that former clients not only leave the program with appropriate coping skills, but that they demonstrate the capacity to employ those skills in the community. For many, it is no longer enough to work only in the treatment center to prepare the client for the community; it is also essential that an effort be made to prepare the community to receive and support the former client as a community member. With any one client such effort may involve activities ranging from a periodic posttreatment follow-up to explore that client's adjustment to the community to the coordination of a variety of community agencies in order to meet the special needs of the exiting client. Nor do such efforts need to be restricted to the concerns of the individual client. Activities may be undertaken to change law and/or policy that inappropriately restricts the former client's ability to relate to the extratreatment community.

Activities of these kinds fall under the heading of aftercare, or community integration. Here, and indeed throughout this volume, the terms aftercare and community integration will be used almost interchangeably to describe those activities undertaken at the end of, or more typically as an extension of, the formal treatment process—activities designed to make the community an active ally in the rehabilitation process. Such activities are intended to allow the former client to remain problem-free in the community. As will be detailed in the pages that follow, work in this area is considerably farther advanced in mental health, alcoholism, and corrections than has been the case in the related field of drug abuse. While others will describe the nature and impact of programs in these areas, it will be useful here to explore the rationale used to support the development of aftercare, or community integration, programs and the reasons why the growth of that movement may have been comparatively limited in the drug abuse field.

DIFFERING AFTERCARE CONCERNS IN
MENTAL HEALTH AND CORRECTIONS

In those fields where the primary effort to effect rehabilitation occurs within institutional settings removed from normal community life, the need to structure and pursue client reentry would seem apparent. Clearly, the need for the deinstitutionalization of mental health and correctional clients has stimulated aftercare efforts in both those fields. Indeed, in the comparatively recent history of both mental health and corrections there has been an emphasis on locating postinstitutional treatment programming close to the community setting in which the individual will eventually be fully involved. The community mental health center, the day and night care centers, the halfway house, and the work release program all speak to the need for a graduated disengagement from treatment programming and treatment settings. In fact, one could argue that in too many instances emphasis has been placed almost wholly on disengagement from treatment and that a corresponding engagement with the extratreatment community has been assumed, but far less actively pursued. Thus, it can be seen by planning and treatment staff as important to move the mental health client from 24-hour supervised hospital care to a day care program that does not force the client to adhere to a structured pattern of recreational time, social interactions, and/or institutional work. However, staff may not attach similar importance to working with the client to develop a use of leisure time in the community, to aid in the forming of new social networks, or to pursue with the client the capacity of his/her employment to allow for further growth and achievement in the community. Indeed, the mental health field has lately been charged with creating ex-patient ghettoes, in part as a consequence of its efforts to deinstitutionalize without adequate preparation of client or community for each other.

Nonetheless, spurred by efforts to reduce recidivism and a need for deinstitutionalization, the mental health field has acted increasingly, if uncertainly, to go beyond strategies of disengagement and to explore techniques for actively supporting and structuring community integration. Initiatives begun by Sanders et al. (1967) and Fairweather et al. (1969) in their work with mental health clients have guided a host of similar efforts to develop community aftercare programs.

The field of corrections may be characterized as having an even larger need to develop effective techniques of community integration. While recidivism in the field of mental health is viewed as unfortunate, it is not viewed as posing the threat to society that criminal recidivism does. Community reentry programs become key since virtually all correctional clients return to the community, and community acceptance of recidivism is unthinkable. However, whereas the reentry programs to be structured on behalf of mental health clients may be expected to put a premium on client concerns and give little weight to community protection, the aftercare programs developed in association with corrections are weighted very differently. Parole, which remains the core system of correctional aftercare, is at least as much a system of supervision as it is of support. The parole officer is charged with a responsibility for the protection of society that no mental health aftercare worker need share.

THE INFLUENCE OF MENTAL HEALTH AND CORRECTIONAL PROGRAMMING

It is interesting to consider prospects for aftercare in the field of drug abuse in the light of these conflicting aftercare concerns in the mental health and corrections fields. Drug abuse programming may be fairly characterized as rooted in both of these fields. It is less than 15 years since the country's major drug abuse treatment center had bars on its windows and drew the vast bulk of its clients from correctional institutions.

Recent studies show that the majority of recent drug abuse clients also have made an investment in criminal careers prior to having become addicted (Hayim et al., 1973; McGlothlin et al., 1978; Nurco and DuPont, 1976; Voss and Stephens, 1973; Weissman et al., 1976). Thus, the field of drug abuse—and administrators in that field—can be expected to share some of the concerns, if not the techniques, of correctional rehabilitation.

Consequently, it is hardly surprising that elements of community protection and client supervision will find their way from correctional efforts to drug abuse rehabilitative efforts. Indeed, one of the three most widely accepted goals of drug abuse treatment, that of reduction in criminality, would seem to reflect a major concern with community safety. As described by Sells (1979), it has been argued by some that the other two most frequently cited goals, reduction in drug use and increase in employment, similarly reflect the overweening concern with social control that has marked the recent development of drug abuse rehabilitation.

In fact, it seems fair to say that the goals reflect nothing so much as the effort to serve two masters. By virtue of the population served, if not the origins of its rehabilitative programs, the drug abuse field is appropriately enmeshed in issues of public safety and concern; and by virtue of the aggressive efforts of ex-addict and nonaddict clinicians who dared suggest that rehabilitative efforts owing more to mental health than to corrections could be effective, there developed an ever larger involvement with the drug abuse client as the legitimate *and increasingly central* focus of rehabilitative activity (Jaffe, 1979). Thus, the concern with reduction in drug use and employment can be fairly interpreted not simply as reflecting the need to guarantee continued protection to the community of nonusers, but as reflecting too the effort to grant to the individual the right and the dignity of career choice rather than relegation to a drug abuse career and its accompanying promise of incarceration and/or death. Moreover, as the drug abuse client comes increasingly to be the nonopiate user—and, some might argue, as the drug abuse client comes to be increasingly female and white—the effort to provide treatment in keeping with mental health goals and technology may be expected to increase.

The technology of drug abuse treatment thus appears to reflect an investment in issues of both community safety and individual opportunity. In a significant number of methadone programs, clients are expected to yield a urine sample (under observation lest he/she attempt to pass something inappropriately) for use in monitoring client performance. While these demands have been relaxed somewhat over the years, the use of urine surveillance remains a significant check on client behavior. That technique would seem well suited to efforts at understanding and containing the client's antisocial behavior. More significantly, it can be reasoned that the imposition of a frequent, unscheduled, and observed program of urine samplings can only find application with a population that can be "legitimately" designated as deviates whose behavior could pose a threat to the larger society. Consider whether we are as likely to impose urine surveillance on clients abusing sedative/hypnotic/tranquilizing drugs. Those substances pose a significant threat, but only to the individual. In the same sense, one wonders whether the therapeutic community's application of haircuts and confrontations could be relevant to any population that is not viewed, and does not view itself, as "properly" cut off from the mainstream of society by virtue of its inappropriate behavior.

Again, urine surveillance and haircuts represent only one aspect of the treatment provided the addict-client. Moreover, just as urine surveillance has been deemphasized in methadone programs, haircuts have come to be more largely verbal than physical in nature as well as becoming less common in whatever form. More importantly, there has been increasing effort to expand the role of individual and group counseling, to emphasize individual growth and the use of additional program supports to develop the coping skills believed essential to seizing on community opportunity. In short, there has been a growing emphasis on mental health techniques and a concomitant deemphasis on techniques implying derogation and control. In the recent development of its technology, as in the recent course of its ideology, drug abuse service delivery has increasingly emphasized client growth and deemphasized issues of community safety. The influence on the development of aftercare programming of aspects of that technology and the influence of the addict-client it is designed to serve will be explored next.

IMPEDIMENTS TO DRUG ABUSE AFTERCARE

Given the significant emphasis on community adjustment, whether from the standpoint of corrections or mental health, one can rightly question why there has been relatively little emphasis on aftercare or community integration in the drug abuse field. In the succeeding chapters my colleagues will outline issues and efforts in the area of drug abuse aftercare; I will restrict my comments only to those concerns that appear to have influenced the development of drug abuse aftercare. The impediments to the development of aftercare programming can be considered in their relation to (a) client characteristics, (b) the nature of the treatment process, and (c) the characteristics of drug abuse treaters.

Client Characteristics

Both the characteristics of the addict-client and the perception of that client can be seen as having significantly influenced the development of drug abuse treatment generally. On the one hand, addiction is *not* generally seen as the consequence of significant psychological problems

(Robins, 1979). Consequently, the role of treatment has been to provide to the client opportunities to develop the social and coping skills necessary for him/her to assume a differing life-style. Aftercare strategies based on increasing the capabilities of individuals recovering from psychological disturbance have little relevance for persons seen as differing from the norm in life-styles and values only. It seems fair to say that a general view of the addict-client has been that if he/she is given the necessary tools, e.g., job skills, the individual will be equipped to make his/her way in the world.

Indeed, in terms of perceived characteristics, the addict-client is seen, whether realistically or romantically, as already possessing great capabilities in terms of the demands of the straight world. He/she is seen as effectively manipulative in interpersonal situations and as capable of committing considerable energy and intelligence to maintaining a difficult life-style. Moreover, the addict is viewed by some as among the most competent and highly regarded individuals in the community in which the individual initiates heroin use (Feldman, 1969).

Thus, drug abuse aftercare efforts may be seen as having been slowed by a view of the addict-client as an individual having little need for community-based psychological supports. At the same time, given the increasing emphasis on individual growth as opposed to community protection, any effort to structure a parole-like aftercare that would smack heavily of supervision and control could be justified only with addict-clients exiting from the criminal justice system. Nonetheless, it is instructive that aftercare systems directed at criminal justice clients, which have used major elements of control (urine surveillance) in the context of more usual client supervision (parole), have proven effective in terms of the common goals of drug abuse treatment (McGlothlin, 1977). Again, it should be emphasized that the trend has been away from control-oriented drug abuse aftercare—largely as a consequence of increasing clinical influence over drug abuse treatment, as opposed to the influence of public administrators acting on behalf of community safety.[1] That trend is stimulated further by the increasing numbers of nonaddict clients who have emerged as a concern to the drug abuse field.

The Treatment Process

Just as the characteristics ascribed to the most usual drug abuse client—the inner-city addict—can be seen as having slowed the development of aftercare systems, so too aspects of the treatment forms directed at that client may be seen as having similarly restricted such development. Here it will be useful to explore further aspects of the two dominant forms of drug abuse treatment—methadone maintenance and the therapeutic community. It should be noted that methadone maintenance and the therapeutic community are regarded here as the major forms of drug abuse treatment not in terms of the numbers of clients each has been able to attract, but in terms of the extent to which those modalities have exerted an influence on the delivery of services throughout the field of drug abuse treatment.

Methadone maintenance treatment, and outpatient treatment generally, do not involve the issues of deinstitutionalization that have plagued the mental health and correctional fields. The client is a part of the community from day of program entry to day of exit. The effort to encourage changes in behavior takes place in the context of a community living in which the success of the client's attempts to achieve change can be gauged on a near daily basis and refined as necessary just as frequently. Moreover, this in-program treatment is likely to entail efforts to allow the client to address the adequacy of his/her adjustment to the family and to the work world. However, other areas of community life, which may be equally essential to client change, are unlikely to be addressed in the context of in-program treatment and, even if addressed, will almost certainly not become subject to posttreatment follow-up and assistance as necessary. Areas of such concern could include clients' use of leisure time, the forming of new social networks, the obtaining of welfare and other benefits, securing adequate housing, the acquisition of legal assistance, etc.

While some would suggest a relationship between the reliance on methadone and relatively limited attention to community adjustment, this would imply that drug-free outpatient programs pay more attention to issues of community integration than do methadone programs. In fact, there is no support for such thinking. Rather, it appears that the logic of concentrating, if not restricting, treatment to the clinic setting is rooted firmly in psychiatric tradition.

That tradition encourages an effort to see and work with clients in office settings. As has been discussed above, the client is thereby aided to understand and explore mechanisms for modifying his/her inappropriate behaviors. Activity in the community to implement change is then a subject of office discussion, but the activities themselves are left to the client's initiative. Again, this traditional view of therapy/counseling and of the setting appropriate to its conduct, accords well with a view of the addict-client as an essentially competent, striving individual engaged in an inappropriate life-style.

The therapeutic community involves effort to invest the client in a sequence of graduated responsibility-taking in conjunction with various counseling and educative/vocational experiences which include an emphasis on eventual living-out. Nonetheless, it seems fair to view the therapeutic community as both indebted to the psychiatric tradition and as continuing to bear relation to it. Thus, in the therapeutic community the client is enabled to "grow" sufficiently such that he/she can assume responsibilities for acting on his/her own behalf in the extratreatment community. With the exception of vocational issues there is little, if any, consistent effort to structure the outside community in conjunction with the client. In the logic of the typical therapeutic community treatment program, the client is graduated through a series of life experiences which permit him/her eventually to undertake new roles and behaviors first within the residential setting, and finally in the outside community. That change is effected with a great deal of initial support and direction, a support and direction that are tapered off the closer the client gets to graduation from treatment.

That emphasis on graduation highlights a further difference between methadone and therapeutic community program that also has consequences for program-supported aftercare efforts. While therapeutic community programs make use of a more or less formal graduation *from* treatment (although the client typically continues to have ties to the treatment setting), the methadone program has traditionally viewed addiction as a chronic, relapsing disorder. Thus, staff of the methadone program must act as if the clients are being prepared for continuing prosocial functioning in the community, while believing that some significant number of those clients can be confidently expected to return. The return to treatment may be regrettable, but does not constitute the failure experience that it does for the therapeutic community. In fact, the thought may be father to the deed as rates of return of methadone maintenance clients significantly exceed rates of return of therapeutic community clients (Simpson et al., 1978a).

Thus, maintaining the client in the community is clearly an appropriate goal for the therapeutic community, and one toward which programmatic activity can be seen as appropriately structured; for the methadone program, the client's posttreatment drug-free functioning in the community is a laudatory, but problematic, goal. Not surprisingly, therapeutic community programs emphasize a continuing relationship between former clients and program such that the program may provide continuing support to the former client, while methadone programs emphasize their receptiveness to the former client if and when he/she relapses. In both instances the former client is expected to come to the treatment setting to obtain needed assistance.

Characteristics of Drug Abuse Treaters

Complicating this picture further are the actors on whom effective treatment relies. Fully 30% of all treatment staff involved in drug abuse programming are affiliated with the field of medicine, i.e., are physicians, psychiatrists, or nurses. Indeed, 61% of all degreed professional drug abuse treatment staff, i.e., all degreed staff other than social workers, psychologists, vocational specialists, and lawyers, are affiliated with the medical profession (NIDA, 1978).[2] Given that these actors are likely to be in positions of significant influence, if not administrative control, over programs, it seems probable that their accustomed technology will play an important role in program functioning. Inasmuch as that technology emphasizes the client coming to the treater and the resolution of problems in a treatment setting, it appears likely that the impact of this actor will be to encourage still more the restriction of service delivery to the program setting.

The other major—and in many respects even more significant—actor in the treatment process is the nondegreed professional counselor, or more specifically and more typically the nondegreed ex-addict professional counselor. To an extent unknown in other treatment fields, drug abuse has employed the successful products of its systems not in any token or charitable manner, but in force and with a belief that these counselors are best equipped to deal with the realities of the drug abuse clients' lives. In a display of programmatic harmony atypical for methadone and therapeutic community programs, there is agreement on the usefulness and importance of the ex-addict counselor. Again, however, whatever that counselor's contribution to client functioning and in-program support and change, one can question the capacity of the ex-addict counselor to negotiate with and for the client in the world outside the treatment setting. Many such counselors have gone from being program clients to becoming counselors (although not necessarily in the same program) with little, if any, time spent in jobs outside the treatment setting and without having had a need to develop a social or community life revolving around the extratreatment community.

Consequently, the ex-addict counselor may be in a weak position to lend assistance to the drug abuse client in terms of enabling his/her adjustment to the community. The ex-addict counselor's strengths appear best suited to forcing a confrontation with differing aspects of the addict life-style, encouraging change in behaviors, and providing an in-program role model and support for such change. The ex-addict counselor's capacity to recognize and remove impediments to community adjustment must be viewed as problematic at best. Indeed, with the increasing appearance of nonopiate drug users and concomitant diminution in the numbers of addict-clients, the ex-addict counselor's capacity to deliver in-treatment services can be expected to be tested severely.

THE NEED FOR AFTERCARE INITIATIVES

A question can be raised as to whether in-treatment efforts are not, in fact, sufficient to induce effective community integration. In terms of the limited goals of treatment suggested above (reduced drug use, reduced criminality, and increased employment/licit income), drug abuse treatment has enjoyed significant, but partial, success. In the most comprehensive follow-up study undertaken and one which explores the impact of all treatment modalities, 68% of clients were found to have experienced problems in terms of either drug use or arrests, and 85% had experienced problems as measured by drug use, arrests, unemployment, and/or return to treatment. Over a three-year period half of all drug abuse clients returned to treatment (Simpson et al., 1978b). This is not to disparage the enormous achievement of drug abuse workers in aiding what are obviously large numbers of persons to return to the community better able to take advantage of opportunities for personal growth and achievement within a framework of prosocial functioning. It is simply to assert that there is the real possibility that our accomplishment in the field of drug abuse can be considerably greater.

It is, of course, the contention of this introduction and of this volume that by paying more attention to issues of community integration—and by taking additional steps to achieve that integration—we can enhance our ability to effect client rehabilitation. As will be described in the chapters that follow, the process of community integration can exist as a last step in the treatment process, or can take effect after formal treatment is completed, thereby constituting a community follow-up designed to carry out those efforts in the community necessary to guarantee and extend the gains of treatment.

These community-oriented efforts do assume that in many instances the client cannot remake his/her community to meet the new life-style adopted, and in no case should have to. As described by Brown and Ashery (1979),

The client is viewed as having had relatively limited experinece in dealing with his/her surroundings as other than a known drug abuser. Various members of the client's community will have had limited opportunity to view him/her as anyone other than a drug user and thief/prostitute/hustler. There is little reason to expect the community's perceptions or expectations to change rapidly. More importantly, there is little reason to believe the client can assume and/or maintain the unfamiliar roles of stable employee, or responsible family member or student either rapidly or with ease. Community resources supportive of the client's changed life-style will need to be located and/or developed on his/her behalf.

There is reason to believe that a concern about, and need to take action regarding community integration has long been felt by treatment staff. A frequent complaint of program staff is that the clients will be "thrown right back into the environment that produced them." Given that concern, it will be program staff's responsibility to examine mechanisms for working to modify that environment and/or the client's response to it. The clear danger is that program staff will rely solely on a technology of in-program counseling not because they feel that technology is sufficient to meet the needs of their clients, but because that technology is one about which they feel knowledgable and with which they are comfortable. In the pages that follow effort will be made to explore techniques designed to go beyond accustomed modes of service delivery to permit return to a community supportive of individual growth and accomplishment rather than to an environment that perpetuates client problems.

Individual chapters will explore both theoretical and practical issues in the delivery of aftercare services. Attention will be paid to the roles potential for treatment staff with special reference to issues of vocational rehabilitation/employment and family therapy. The role of self-help groups in promoting community integration will be explored, and self-help initiatives in this country will be examined, as will a significant initiative with former addicts in Hong Kong. Additional chapters will examine the aftercare activities that can be, and are, assumed by community groups working with former drug users. Finally, the too frequently ignored capacity for advocacy groups to promote the former clients' integration into the community will also be explored.

NOTES

1. Herein lies a considerable dilemma for the planner engaged in drug abuse treatment. Public concern, and an accompanying loosening of the public purse

strings, appear related far more to the danger posed by the addict than to any compassion for his/her condition. Consequently, any increase in public concern is more likely to lead to increased pressures for control than to any escalation of treatment efforts.

2. It should be clear that there is little reason to believe that clinical psychologists or psychiatric social workers, whose professional origins are almost equally embedded in the field of psychiatry, will deviate significantly from a psychiatric view of the client in program.

REFERENCES

BROWN, B. S. and ASHERY, R. S. (1979) "Aftercare in drug abuse programming," in R. L. DuPont, A. Goldstein, J. O'Donnell, and B. S. Brown (eds.) Handbook on Drug Abuse. Washington, DC: NIDA.

FAIRWEATHER, G. W., SANDERS, D. H., MAYNARD, H., and CRESSLER, D. L. (1969) Community Life for the Mentally Ill. Chicago: Aldine.

FELDMAN, H. W. (1969) "Ideological supports to becoming a heroin addict." Journal of Health and Social Behavior 9: 131-139.

HAYIM, G. J., LUKOFF, I., and QUATRONE, D. (1973) Heroin Use and Crime in a Methadone Maintenance Program: An Interim Report. Washington, DC: LEAA.

JAFFE, J. H. (1979) "The swinging pendulum: the treatment of drug users in America," in R. L. DuPont, A. Goldstein, J. O'Donnell, and B. S. Brown (eds.) Handbook on Drug Abuse. Washington, DC: NIDA.

McGLOTHLIN, W. H. (1977) "A follow-up of admissions to the California Civil Addict Program." American Journal of Drug and Alcohol Abuse 4: 179-199.

———, ANGLIN, M.D., and WILSON, B. D. (1978) "Narcotic addiction and crime." Criminology 16: 293-315.

NIDA Executive Report, April 1977 (1978) NIDA Statistical Series F, No. 3. Rockville, MD: NIDA.

NURCO, D. N., and DuPONT, R. L. (1976) "A preliminary report on crime and addiction within a community-wide population of narcotic addicts." Presented at 38th Annual Scientific Meeting of the Committee on Problems of Drug Dependency, Richmond, VA.

ROBINS, L. N. (1979) "Addict careers," in R. L. DuPont, A. Goldstein, J. O'Donnell, and B. S. Brown (eds.) Handbook on Drug Abuse. Washington, DC: NIDA.

SANDERS, R., SMITH, R. S., and WEINMAN, B. S. (1967) Chronic Psychoses and Recovery. San Francisco: Jossey-Bass.

SELLS, S. B. (1979) "Treatment effectiveness," in R. L. DuPont, A. Goldstein, J. O'Donnell, and B. S. Brown (eds.) Handbook on Drug Abuse. Washington, DC: NIDA.

SIMPSON, D. D., SAVAGE, L. J., LLOYD, M., and SELLS, S. B. (1978a) Evaluation of Drug Abuse Treatments Based on First Year Follow-up. Rockville, MD: NIDA.

SIMPSON, D. D., SAVAGE, L. J., and SELLS, S. B. (1978b) Data Book on Drug Treatment Outcomes. Fort Worth, TX: TCU.

VOSS, H. L. and STEPHENS, R. C. (1973) "Clinical history of narcotic addicts." Drug Forum 2: 191-202.

WEISSMAN, J. C., MARR, S. W., and KATSAMPES, P. L. (1976) "Addiction and criminal behavior: a continuing examination of criminal addicts." Journal of Drug Issues 6: 153-165.

PART I

THE CLIENT IN THE COMMUNITY

1

REINTEGRATING STREET DRUG ABUSERS
Community Roles in Continuing Care

J. DAVID HAWKINS

In August 1978 Margaret Mead addressed the members of the American Correctional Association. She reminded them of the failures of juvenile courts, juvenile correctional institutions, and junior high schools. In spite of the good intentions of their founders, she argued, they all have failed because of a common mistake: they sought to remove children from bad social conditions. Her message was that separation, taking people out of the larger society to deal with them, does not address the causes of problems and hence does not solve the problems themselves. To solve social problems, the whole fabric of social life must be rewoven as an integral piece. Dr. Mead urged attention to the interconnected patterns of people's social lives, even in the rehabilitation of society's casualties, outcasts, and criminals.

AUTHOR'S NOTE: Preparation of this chapter was supported in part by the Center for Law and Justice, University of Washington. Research on drug treatment program clients in Seattle reported here was supported by a grant from the Services Research Branch, National Institute on Drug Abuse, U.S. Department of Health, Education, and Welfare.

The author thanks Barry S. Brown, Roger Roffman, and Richard Weatherley for their comments on an earlier draft of this chapter.

Dr. Mead's comments apply to the field of drug abuse treatment. Many treatment efforts have suffered from a kind of misplaced concreteness, which Pittel has called the "myth of addiction as cause" (1977b: 28). Too often we have isolated "drug abuse" as the problem and have focused single-mindedly on its elimination. We have largely failed to attend to the interconnected patterns of social life in which people's drug use patterns are embedded. We have also committed another error of separation. We have created treatment enclaves where we seek to cure abusers in isolation from the larger community. Our treatment programs are taboo places reminiscent of TB sanatoriums visited only by patients, their families where permitted, and a handful of dedicated volunteers. These places are avoided by the unscathed. A few doctors, nurses, social workers, and psychologists, and large numbers of former abusers seek to cure afflicted people out of view in these places. Their efforts have not been very successful.

This chapter explores an approach which broadens the focus of rehabilitation. Reintegrating identified abusers into the larger community is a major thrust of this approach. The approach seeks to return to community groups the responsibility for key elements of the rehabilitation process in hopes of reweaving the warp of drug abusers' lives more tightly to the weft of conventional society. This approach is not new, yet it has been largely ignored in drug treatment.

To provide a foundation for the proposals offered here, current knowledge about drug use and drug abuse is reviewed. This information is used to assess the relevance and adequacy of several theories of deviance. The assessment suggests that combined elements of control and cultural deviance theories can provide empirically supported explanations for drug abuse. Based on these theories, a rehabilitation approach is developed which involves community members as key agents in reintegration steps in continuing care. The strengths and limitations of the approach are discussed.

STREET DRUG USE, DRUG ABUSE, AND OPTIONS FOR SOCIETAL RESPONSE

Street drug use is a pattern of illicit use of drugs supported by societally disapproved activities, such as drug dealing, burglary, pimping, and prostitution (Preble and Casey, 1969; Wesson et al., 1975). When brought to the attention of agents of control, such as law enforcement or medical professionals, street drug users are likely to be viewed and treated as drug *abusers,* whether or not they view their drug use as harmful. Street drug use has become defined as a social problem in this society (Becker, 1963, 1966). The labeling and treatment of street drug users as drug abusers has become a prevalent mode of response.

There are, of course, a number of other possible responses to street drug use. Drugs could be provided to users through official channels to reduce dependence on societally disapproved activities to secure them (Roffman, 1973). Street drug users could simply be dealt with as criminals without providing treatment for drug abuse. Illicit drugs could be legalized. This chapter does not discuss the promise or problems of such alternatives approaches to "the drug abuse problem." The goal here is to explore effective means by which people who have been labeled as street drug abusers can be rehabilitated to more conventionally accepted patterns of living.

DRUG USE: A SOCIAL PHENOMENON

For years ethnographers have emphasized that psychoactive drug use patterns must be understood in their sociocultural contexts (True and True, 1977). Drug use "cannot be understood apart from the web of social relations in which it is implicated" (Goode, 1969: 55). Not only are the effects of psychoactive drugs largely determined by "set" and "setting," but social factors themselves appear to influence patterns of drug use. These factors include social norms and expectations (Cavan, 1966; DeRios and Smith, 1976; DuToit, 1977; MacAndrew and Edgerton, 1969; Harding and Zinberg, 1977; Mizruchi and Perrucci, 1970; Wilkinson, 1970), peer use patterns and peer influence (Abelson et al., 1972, 1973; Dembo et al., 1976; Josephson, 1974; Kandel, 1973, 1974; Ray, 1972; Sorosiak et al., 1976; Spevak and Pihl, 1973; Tec, 1972a, 1972b; Tolone and Dermott, 1975; West, 1975), parental use patterns and parental influence (Cevaline, 1968; Lawrence and Vellerman, 1974; Ray, 1972; Sebald, 1972; Smart and Fejer, 1972; Tec, 1974; West, 1975), and family relationships (Alexander and Dibb, 1975; Harbin and Maziar, 1975), including perceived intimacy (Spevak and Pihl, 1976) and perceived familial disaffection (Dembo et al., 1976; Streit et al., 1974; Streit and Oliver, 1972).

THE SOCIAL CAUSES OF DRUG ABUSE

Like drug use, drug abuse is a social phenomenon. In fact, the very definition of drug abuse is socially determined. People in different social roles define abuse differently. To the law enforcement officer, abuse is all use of illegal psychoactive substances; to the medical practitioner, it is all nonmedical use of psychoactive substances (Liaison Task Panel, 1978). The user's family may recognize abuse when drug use interferes with acceptable patterns of family maintenance and interaction. The drug user may define abuse as a pattern of use which has become associated with a number of "hassles," ranging from problems of obtaining adequate supplies of drugs to problems with the law or family members (Carlson, 1976).

Drug abuse is a pattern of drug use which someone has perceived as troublesome.[1] Because drug abuse is subjective and socially defined, the "causes" of drug abuse include the social processes by which an individual's patterns of living become labeled and treated as drug abuse (Becker, 1963). Drug use patterns alone do not predict whether a person will be treated as a drug abuser. Both interactional and structural factors, including how acceptable one's actions are to others, and how much trouble one causes those in the environment who have the power and inclination to intervene, are also important (Mechanic, 1978: 314).

Intrapersonal theories of drug abuse seek to locate the causes of abuse in inherent physical or psychological characteristics of identified abusers. They do not account for the role of social factors in causing drug abuse. These theories have given rise to current treatment approaches which seek to cure individuals in isolation from their social environments.

Since drug abuse is a social phenomenon, it appears worthwhile to investigate social theories of deviance to better understand it. Those theories which imply practical rehabilitation options for addressing social factors associated with drug abuse are particularly relevant to the purpose of this chapter. Of the social theories of deviance (Empey, 1978), strain, control, and cultural deviance theories appear most useful. They postulate social causes which could be directly addressed in programs seeking to rehabilitate identified street drug abusers.[2] To the extent that these theories are empirically supported, they should provide guides for designing effective treatment and continuing care programs.

SOCIAL THEORIES OF DEVIANCE

Strain theories or "social structural disorganization theories" (Cloward and Ohlin, 1960; Cohen,   1955; Merton, 1937) assume that people are universally socialized to aspire to legitimate culturally approved goals of financial and social success. However, some people who occupy lower-class

positions in society are blocked from attaining success through conformity
by inequalities in opportunity inherent in the social structure. Strain
theories view deviance as a result of an incongruity between people's
desires for legitimate rewards and the means available to achieve them. The
most fully developed strain theories suggest that differential access to
illegitimate social roles leads to different forms of deviance, one of which
is drug abuse (Cloward and Ohlin, 1960). Strain theories imply that
providing legitimate opportunities in the social structure for people to
achieve their goals would largely eliminate deviance and crime. (See Weis,
1977: 15-30, for summaries of the theories reviewed here.)

Like strain theories, *cultural deviance theories* view people as confor-
mists. However, these theories postulate that different subcultures or
social worlds within the larger society have their own cultural values.
Deviance results when an individual conforms to cultural values of a
particular group which are in conflict with those of the dominant social
order (Miller, 1958; Shaw and McKay, 1942; Sutherland and Cressey,
1970). Deviance is indicative of bonding to a group with nonconventional values in a pluralistic society; it is conformity with the expectations
of such a nonconventional group. Differential association theory is a
cultural deviance theory which suggests that criminal behavior is learned in
the process of interacting with others who favor criminal norms or values
over conventional law-abiding values. Differential association theory views
association with delinquent peers as a cause of delinquency (Sutherland
and Cressey, 1970; Linden and Hackler, 1973).

Like strain theories, but unlike cultural deviance theories, *control
theories* assume a consensus of cultural values in society. In contrast to
both strain and cultural deviance theories, however, control theories do
not assume that people inherently desire to conform. People have the
capacity to deviate or conform. Proper socialization leads to conformity,
while inadequate socialization leads to nonconformity with shared societal
values. According to control theorists, proper socialization results in a
strong bond to society and its moral order and makes people susceptible to
both internal moral controls and external social constraints. This bond is
the basis of conformity. Deviance occurs when an individuall's bond to
society is weak or broken (Hirschi, 1969; Nye, 1958; Reckless, 1961;
Reckless et al., 1956; Reiss, 1951). In sum, control theories view deviance
as nonconformity which occurs simply because it is not prevented by
effective social controls (Nye, 1958). "The theory asserts that youngsters
who do not develop a bond to the conventional order because of incomplete socialization feel no moral obligation to conform" (Weis, 1977: 35).

Hirschi (1969) has specified the elements of the social bond as attachment to others, commitment to conventional lines of action, involvement in conventional activities, and belief in the moral order and law.

Because control theories do not posit the existence of subcultures with deviant values within the larger society, they do not recognize bonds to deviant social groups as a source of delinquency. The possible role of deviant friends and companions in the initiation or maintenance of deviance is disregarded (Hindelang, 1973: 487; Sakumoto, 1978).

Strain, control, and cultural deviance theories disagree about the specific causes of deviance. Each would give somewhat different priority to different strategies in rehabilitating street drug abusers. Strain theorists have generally called for dramatic structural changes in the society to achieve a more equitable distribution of power and economic resources, and hence, opportunities. However, they have also inspired more moderate proposals for rehabilitation of specific groups. In the rehabilitation context, strain theories suggest that drug abusers be given opportunities to obtain jobs so that they are no longer blocked from achieving economic success through conventional activities.

Cultural deviance theories suggest that the disorganized communities from which many street drug users come should be reorganized (Shaw and McKay, 1942), that efforts should be made to reorient groups of users to positive activities, or alternatively that conscious efforts should be made to destroy attachments among street drug users.

Control theoeory views socialization as an interactive social process which leads to social bonding and conforming behavior. Thus the theory implies that interactive processes can be effectively used in rehabilitation to create social bonds which prevent drug abuse. Such social bonds could be created by developing strong attachments between individual abusers and conventional members of society and developing commitments to and involvement in conventional activities.

Given the different priorities suggested by the three theories, it is important to determine how well each is supported empirically, if theory is to orient rehabilitation efforts. The most rigorous assessments of these three theories have been conducted in studies of juvenile delinquency and drug use among junior and senior high school students. These studies of one type of deviance (delinquency or drug use among students) may not be generalizable to drug abuse. Drug abusers are likely to be underrepresented in school-attending populations (Johnston et al., 1977). Moreover, street drug abuse is a specific type of deviance associated with identifiable patterns of activities. In most of the delinquency studies, delinquency has been more broadly defined. In Hirschi's (1969: 47) study, for example: "Delinquency is defined by acts, the detection of which is thought to result in punishment of the person committing them by agents of the larger society." Unfortunately, systematic studies of the causes of street drug abuse have never been accomplished. The best available evidence comes from ethnographic studies of street drug users and surveys of treated abusers. However, by comparing results of juvenile delinquency and student drug use surveys with ethnographic accounts about street drug use, it is possible to assess the empirical support for these theories and the resulting implications for rehabilitation.

EMPIRICAL SUPPORT FOR SOCIAL THEORIES OF DEVIANCE

Results of the delinquency research do not support strain theory's contention that lower-class youths seek to attain conventional goals, but finding themselves precluded from doing so, turn to delinquency. After much research, the proposed link between delinquency and social class remains a matter of controversy (see Tittle et al., 1978; Hindelang et al., 1979).

More importantly, research has revealed little empirical support for the causal hypotheses of strain theory. Lower-class youths who seek conventional goals are *less* likely, rather than more likely, to engage in delinquency than other lower-class youths (Hirschi, 1969: 227). Research has failed to support strain theory's contention that an individual's delinquency is caused by blocked opportunities for attainment of economic or status goals encountered by the disadvantaged (Elliott and Voss, 1974; Hirschi, 1969; Linden, 1974; Polk, 1969). Elliott and Voss (1974: 170) report:

> We fail to find any support for Cloward and Ohlin's disjunction hypothesis. According to our data, few youth anticipate failure in their efforts to achieve long-range goals, and the few juveniles who anticipate failure are no more likely to engage in delinquent behavior than youth who anticipate success.

Hirschi (1969: 227) notes:

> The greater one's acceptance of conventional (or even quasiconventional) success goals, the less likely one is to be delinquent, regardless of the likelihood these goals will someday be obtained. . . . It is not true that ambition leads to crime; on the contrary, ambition reduces the chances of crime.

These results do not prove the absence of a relationshhip between social class and deviance. They do suggest, however, that an individual's delinquency or drug abuse cannot be adequately explained in terms of blocked opportunities for attainment of legitimate success goals held by that person.

To the extent that these findings can be generalized, they have important implications for rehabilitation of street drug abusers. They suggest that providing more opportunities for lower-class youth to attain the rewards of the larger society may not be sufficient to significantly reduce deviance unless individuals' commitments to conventional success goals are strengthened. Providing jobs and work opportunities for street drug users or removing barriers to attainment of an education may not, in themselves, reduce the undesirable behaviors associated with street drug use if users do not hold conventional success goals (see Elliott and Voss, 1974: 137). Street drug users may simply not care to give up street crime for the rewards of "straight'" jobs if given a chance. They may be unwilling to make the commitments or engage in the activities necessary to secure coventional goals merely because opportunities are provided. Developing commitments to conventional goals may therefore be an important part of the rehabilitation process.

Surveys on student delinquency and drug use and ethnographic studies of street drug users have found empirical support for both control and cultural deviance theories, in spite of their apparent differences regarding cause. Much of the evidence bearing on these theories is instructive for its implications for drug abuse rehabilitation. The evidence regarding control theory will be considered first.

As operationalized by Hirschi, control theory suggests that deviance results when four elements of the social bond to conventional society are inadequate or missing: commitment to conventional lines of action, involvement in conventional activities, belief in the moral order and law, and attachment to others. The evidence regarding three of these proposed elements is particularly instructive for rehabilitation.[3]

Commitment to Conventional Activities

A number of different measures have been used to assess commitment to conventional activities in studies of delinquency and drug use among students. There is question as to whether some of the measures used should be interpreted as indicating *attachment* to conventional institutions (such as school) or *commitment* to conventional activities.[4] However, this issue need not concern us here. All of these measures have repeatedly been shown to be independently related to delinquency as well as to each other. In sum, even when operationalized using a number of different variables, commitment to conventional activities has been shown to preclude deviant behavior such as delinquency and illicit drug use (Elliott and Voss, 1974: 150; Frease, 1972; Hirschi, 1969; Kelly and Balch, 1971; Sakumoto, 1978). Those who are not committed to conventional lines of action are more likely to engage in delinquency and illicit drug use. These findings are consistent with ethnographic studies of street drug users which suggest that they are not strongly committed to conventional lines of action (Feldman, 1973; Preble and Casey, 1969; Stephens and Levine, 1971; Stephens and McBride, 1976; Sutter, 1966, 1969). The implication for treatment is clear. For rehabilitation to be successful, street drug abusers must make commitments to conventional lines of action which they have not previously done. This is an important element in the bond to conventional society.

Involvement in Conventional Activities

Research has shown that involvement in conventional activities is not, in itself, related to delinquency or drug use (Hirschi, 1969: 90; Elliott and Voss, 1974: 136). Involvement in conventional activities appears to contribute to social bonding and to the reduction or prevention of deviant behavior only if associated with attitudinal commitments to conventional goals (Sakumoto, 1978). This finding reemphasizes the importance of commitment noted earlier and strengthens the argument that provision of job, school, or other opportunities for involvement in conventional activities, without providing mechanisms for generating and maintaining commitments to these activities, is unlikely to lead to successful rehabilitation.

Attachment to Others

Hirschi's (1969) formulation of control theory does not distinguish between attachments to conventional others such as parents and conventional peers and attachments to deviant others. Hirschi argued that any attachment to others would preclude deviance such as delinquency and drug abuse.

However, his own data and other studies have shown, as suggested by cultural deviance and differential association theories, that delinquency and drug use are closely related to the type of people with whom one

associates. Attachment to parents and conventional others appears to
inhibit the likelihood of deviance, while association with delinquent or
drug-using peers is closely related to delinquency and drug-using behavior
(Elliott and Voss, 1974; Kandel, 1973, 1974; Sakumoto, 1978; Weis,
1979).

Delinquency is a peer-supported phenomenon. Delinquent peers are
more closely associated with the initiation and maintenance of delinquent
behavior than predicted by control theory (Hirschi, 1969: 230). Bonds do
exist among peers in deviant social worlds, and these support the perpetua-
tion of delinquent activities (Matza, 1964: 63). Commitments to conventional lines of action, involvement in conventional activities, and attachment to conventional others are important elements of the social bond
which, as specified by control theory, can prevent or reduce deviant
behavior. Yet, association with deviant peers and commitment to deviant
lines of action are important in the initiation and maintenance of deviance.
Control theory must be modified to account for the role of deviant peers
predicted by cultural deviance theory.

This support for cultural deviance theory is buttressed by studies of
street drug users. Ethnographic research suggests that the specialized roles
and activities of street life provide more to street drug abusers than simply
an escape from a world in which they are not bonded. Street drug abusers
become involved in and committed to deviant lines of action. Involvement
in the street life-style can provide identities as competent and powerful
individuals.

> Their behavior is anything but an escape from life. They are actively
> engaged in meaningful activities and relationships seven days a week.
> The brief moments of euphoria after each administration of a small
> amount of heroin constitute a small fraction of their daily lives. The
> rest of the time they are aggressively pursuing a career that is
> exciting, challenging, adventurous, and rewarding. . . . Hustling
> (robbing or stealing), trying to sell stolen goods, avoiding the police,
> looking for a heroin dealer with a good bag, coming back from
> copping, looking for a safe place to take the drug, or looking for
> someone who beat (cheated) (them) among other things. [Preble and
> Casey, 1969: 2]

Addicts are often forced to test themselves against the greatest odds
each day. To sustain his need for drugs and his status on the streets, the
addict must demonstrate over and over again his mastery of the
harsh world in which he lives. To be a "righteous dope fiend"
requires considerable competence in a multitude of job and social

skills, and the addict receives direct proof that he is competent each
time he scores—each time his hustle is converted to the heroin he
craves. Whether or not he is actually addicted, the addict's perceived
need for heroin provides a context in which he can (or must)
repeatedly prove his worth. [Pittel, 1974]

Street drug abusers develop commitments to their deviant life-style; that
life-style provides rewards consistent with its value system.

The fact that both street drug abuse and delinquency appear to contribute to the self-identity of participants as competent and powerful
individuals has important implications for rehabilitation. If street drug
abuse offers rewards, the task of rehabilitation is not simply to create
bonds to the dominant social order, as implied by control theory. Rather,
the task is to replace bonds to a deviant social world and its activities with
stronger bonds to a more conventional social world. This is no small task.
The socialization process which results in social bonding begins at birth
and continues throughout human experience. Reversing the cumulative
effect of a street drug abuser's experiences which led to the present
life-style is not likely to be easy. The prognosis would be much better for
an attempt to establish strong bonds to the conventional order from early
childhood. Nevertheless, there is some evidence which suggests the task
may be possible.

Hirschi (1969: 228) notes that cultural deviance theories assume that
all groups, whether conventional or deviant, are equally able to command
the loyalty and affection of their members, and that deviant groups are as
cohesive as nondeviant groups. However, while research has shown that
associations with delinquent friends are related to delinquency, Hirschi's
efforts to measure the degree of *attachment* in these relationships suggest
that attachments among those in deviant subgroups may not be as strong
as the attachments among those in more conventional groups (1969: 229).
Hirschi found that delinquents were less likely to want to be like and less
likely to admire their delinquent peers than more conventional youth. He
suggests that "the interpersonal relations among delinquents are not of the
same quality of warmth and intensity as those among nondelinquents."

Available information about the relationships among street drug abusers
is anecdotal. However, it also suggests that these associations may not be
characterized by strong interpersonal attachments. Though the enterprise
of securing resources and drugs on the streets depends entirely on informal
connections with dealers, fences, and other users, users must be constantly
wary not to be "ripped off" or turned in by others. The social networks of
the street world include large numbers of people, but may not be charac-

terized by emotional closeness, perceived support, or mutual reciprocity of rights and obligations. Street drug abusers have reported that network members are "associates" rather than "friends," and that interactions among street drug users may even be hostile and threatening (Fiddle, 1976). Street drug abusers may not have strong bonds of attachment to their drug-using peers.[5]

Another indication that the bonds to the deviant subculture of street drug abuse may be vulnerable is the fact that the life career of street drug abusers is a cycle of addiction, withdrawal (abstinence), relapse, and readdiction (Lindesmith, 1947). Users typically experience recurrent difficulties in maintaining their drug use patterns on the streets. When they identity these problems or "hassles" with their drug use, they periodically seek to withdraw from drugs (see Carlson, 1976; Lindesmith, 1965; Waldorf, 1972). They typically enter drug treatment programs or seek assistance from family members or other nondrug-users for a period of time, and remove themselves from the social world and activities of street drug abuse. Users often return to drug use once the "hassles" associated with it have been diminished. Students of street drug abuse have viewed the frequency with which former abusers return to drug use as indicative of the strength of that deviant life-style.

The cycle of withdrawal and readdiction can be viewed in another way. The fact that people periodically withdraw from street life suggests that bonds to that life and to those in it are breakable. Abusers sever these bonds themselves from time to time. Further, treated abusers have consistently shown dramatic short-term decreases in drug use and criminal activities after leaving treatment (see Macro Systems, 1975: 61-62; Mandell and Amsel, 1973; Mandell, Goldschmidt, and Grover, 1973; Systems Sciences, 1975). These changes indicate a weakening of involvements in and commitments to street life. It may be that ex-abusers return to street life after treatment because treatment programs fail to help them replace broken bonds to the street world with stronger bonds to the conventional world. The return to street lives may result from the failure of treatment programs to help clients develop attachments to conventional others, involvement in, and commitment to conventional lines of action, rather than from the strength of ties to street life per se.

A THEORETICALLY GROUNDED
REHABILITATION APPROACH

To summarize, available evidence supports control theory's contention that conformity to the expectations of the conventional social order is ensured by strong bonds of commitment, involvement, and attachment between an individual and that social order.

However, research also suggests that deviance from the expectations of the conventional society is more than an absence of bonds to the conventional order. As predicted by cultural deviance theory, deviance is associated with commitments to, involvement in, and attachments to a deviant subculture. For street drug users, the associations and rewards of street life provide bonds to a deviant social world which ensure conformity with its expectations.

Nevertheless, there is evidence that bonds to the deviant social world of street drug abuse may be somewhat weak and vulnerable. Interpersonal attachments among street drug users do not appear strong. Commitments to the life-style of street drug abuse are sometimes broken. Users withdraw from involvement in the street world from time to time.

When this evidence is pieced together, it suggests a comprehensive approach to rehabilitating street drug abusers. The goal of the approach is to replace bonds to the social world of street drug use with stronger bonds of attachment, commitment, and involvement in the conventional social order. "Curing" identified abusers of physiological dependencies or of psychological problems thought to cause them is not enough. Rather the goal is to bond street drug abusers more strongly to conventional society than they are bonded to street life. Successful rehabilitation must include a series of steps:

(1) Drug abusers must make and maintain commitments to conventional lines of action and to achieving the rewards offered through them.

(2) They must develop skills necessary to attain these rewards in acceptable ways. Without such skills they are likely to fail and return to the streets where their existing skills are rewarded.

(3) They must develop networks of social supports beyond treatment programs to assist in achieving the rewards of straight life and to provide encouragement and reinforcement for involvement in conventional lines of action.

(4) They must become involved in ongoing conventional activities apart from treatment which they find more rewarding than the activities of street life.

If these steps are accomplished, street drug abusers will establish stronger bonds to conventional life than to street life, and as a result, should refrain from patterns of drug use and illegal activity deemed unacceptable in conventional society.

With a few notable exceptions, however, drug treatment programs have failed to consistently assist in all four steps. Specifically, the third and fourth steps have received little attention. These are reintegration steps. In my view, their successful accomplishment requires well-designed continuing care programs in the larger community to follow drug treatment program participation. A brief review of the proposed rehabilitation steps will provide a basis for my suggestions for continuing care.

Developing Commitments to Straight Lives

Street drug abusers are specialists who have developed skills, styles, and interaction patterns for survival on the streets (Hawkins, 1978; Stephens and McBride, 1976). To leave the social world of the streets and enter the straight world, street drug abusers must unlearn or discard their specializations and develop new skills, styles, and identities. They are not likely to succeed in such a total transformation unless they decide to seek the rewards offered through conventional lines of action. If durable change is to occur, drug abusers must make a commitment to new lives during the rehabilitation process. A task of drug treatment programs is to encourage individuals, who may be ambivalent or recalcitrant, to make such commitments. Treatment programs can do this in several ways.

Offering Rewards. Treatment programs offer immediate rewards to people who are uncertain about their commitments to street life without requiring that they have the skills to attain these rewards for themselves. By providing these rewards immediately after a period when the rewards of street life were becoming harder to attain or were accompanied by increasing hassles, treatment programs may present attractive comparisons between straight life and street life.

Even if people enter drug treatment involuntarily, and have no intention of giving up street life over the long run, they are more likely to weigh the choices at this point than when they were successfully functioning on the streets. At this point, they are probably most keenly aware of the drawbacks of street life. Further, by entering treatment they detach themselves to some extent from the roles, activities, and interactions of the streets. Bonds to street life may be particularly weak.

In this context, treatment programs provide people access to economic resources, free medical and dental care, and other benefits without "hustling." Further, they alleviate pressure from the legal system. By providing a "time out" for reconsideration and choice, and by providing a few of the rewards of straight lives, treatment programs seek to encourage clients to make new commitments (see Liaison Task Panel, 1978).

Developing Perceptions of Control. Treatment also appears to encourage clients to perceive that they have the power and personal control
necessary to follow through on decisions to change their lives. Experiments by Glass and Singer (1972) and Seligman (1975) have shown the
importance of perceived control in social functioning. According to Seligman (1975), people must perceive that they can influence outcomes in
order to take control of their actions.

There is evidence that after participation in drug treatment programs,
clients have greater perceptions of internal control and personal responsibility than they did at entry, and that treated clients have greater perceptions of control than nontreated addicts (Cryns, 1974).

Early results of a prospective study of clients from methadone maintenance programs, outpatient counseling programs and therapeutic communities in King County, Washington, indicate similar increased perceptions of control from intake to six-month follow-up, as shown in Table
1.1. Over half the clients saw themselves as very much in control of their
own lives at follow-up, an increase of roughly 20% from intake.[6] While
these changes cannot be directly attributed to treatment, they do suggest
that after treatment clients believe they can follow through on their
choices between street life and straight life.

Encouraging Conversion. Finally, some treatment programs (particularly therapeutic communities) appear to help clients who stay for more
than a few weeks develop temporary commitments to living straight lives,
whatever their intentions at entry. Therapeutic communities encourage
clients to talk and to act as if they were committed to straight lives. They
use the resultant dissonance between such scripted performances and
street values to lead clients to attribute certain characteristics to themselves. Through the process, clients appear to become converted to building new "straight" selves (Wacker and Hawkins, 1978).

TABLE 1.1: **Perceptions of Control[a] at Treatment Entry and Six-Month
Follow-up (N = 177)**

	Very Much	Pretty Much	Not Very Much	Not At All
Entry	31.6%	22.6%	25.4%	20.3%
Follow-up	55.4%	24.3%	15.3%	5.1%
	X^2 = 22.75 Significant beyond .01 level.			

a. How much do you feel like you are in control of what happens to you?"

Reinforcements offered in the treatment context are the means by which treatment programs help ambivalent clients develop commitments to straight lives. While it is important that clients make these commitments during treatment, maintaining the commitments in the larger community beyond the rewards and constraints of treatment is essential. This is a task in which continuing care programs can assist.

Developing Basic Skills

People who have experienced street life will maintain commitments to straight lives only if they are able to attain the rewards promised. To do so they will need to exercise the requisite skills. During their careers on the streets, drug abusers rarely practice or receive reinforcement for using such skills. Thus the skills are largely inhibited, extinguished, or not acquired.

> We can be sure that the majority of former addicts do not possess the countless skills (necessary to navigate straight lives), and we can be sure that they will not acquire them automatically merely because they have learned to refrain from the use of drugs. [Pittel, 1977a: 5]

Ex-abusers need to become proficient in a number of skill areas. They must develop skills to secure and maintain employment (Pittel, 1977b: 6-8), skills in recognizing and coping with high-risk drug relapse situations (Marlatt and Gordon, 1978), skills in building and maintaining supportive social networks, and skills in decision-making, planning, and evaluating long-term consequences of various actions, to name but a few.[7]

Treatment programs can help clients develop many of the basic skills required, though they have not consistently done so. (See, for example, Arkin, 1974; Presnall, 1974; Task Force on Federal Heroin Addiction Programs, 1972.) Yet ultimately these skills must be fully developed in the social contexts of the larger society where they are to be practiced. Efforts to teach people survival skills in treatment settings have generally failed to generate desired outcomes after treatment, both for drug clients in therapeutic communities (Smart, 1976),[8] and for formerly institutionalized mental patients (Fairweather, 1978; Test and Stein, 1978). In contrast, approaches which have tied rewards to performance of skills in actual functioning environments have generally succeeded in helping people develop requisite skills for socially approved survival after treatment (Fairweather et al., 1969). The full development of adaptive skills must take place in the larger community where these skills will ultimately be practiced. Continuing care programs can assist in skills development after ex-abusers leave treatment.

Developing Social Supports

To be successfully bonded to conventional society, street drug abusers must develop strong attachments to conventional others to replace attachments to deviant peers. Social networks can provide emotional, financial, and physical support (see Gans, 1962; Bell and Boat, 1957; Litwak and Szelenyi, 1969; Weiss, 1974). When they do, they are elements of social support systems which serve to improve adaptive competence in dealing with short-term crises and life transitions, as well as long-term challenges, stresses, and privations (Caplan and Killilea, 1976).

Effective support systems provide individuals with feedback about themselves, validation for their expectations of others, and help in dealing effectively with the external world. They help individuals make use of personal strengths; assist with daily living tasks individuals cannot accomplish alone; and provide access to instrumental supports, such as financial help, information, and material goods (Caplan, 1973).

Unfortunely, people's existing social networks do not always provide support in time of need. The absence of supports makes people vulnerable to interpersonal and environmental assaults and a variety of other problems (Cobb, 1976; Cassel, 1976). Some social networks themselves cause problems for network members (Attneave, 1969; Pancoast, 1970). Tolsdorf (1976) has shown that the networks of some psychiatric patients are responsible for creating distress which eventually precipitates mental crises. Interaction patterns in some families also appear to encourage the maintenance of heroin addiction (Harbin and Maziar, 1975; Selden, 1972; Stanton et al., 1978).

Social networks and social support systems have two conceptually distinct components. The primary, informal or personal, component includes those people such as kin, friends, and neighbors with whom an individual has diffuse and affective relationships. The secondary, formal or impersonal, component includes those with whom an individual interacts for specific purposes, and with whom the individual does not maintain affective ties (MacElveen, 1977). A staff person in a drug program, a doctor, or a store clerk are usually secondary members.

Research has shown that people seek assistance from primary social network members more readily than from secondary institutional helpers (Croog et al., 1972; Sussman, 1953). Generally, primary network members are the first line of support. Formal helping organizations such as drug treatment programs are usually contacted only when the primary network is unable to adequately assist (Bergin, 1971).

Research has shown that participation in an *adequate* primary social network can preclude the need for formal treatment. Research on the networks of released mental patients has shown that the absence of a viable network is correlated with return to the mental hospital, and that formation of a network correlates with improved social functioning:

> We believe that this finding can serve as a prognostic indicator for subsequent community performance; i.e., persons with small, poorly connected networks represent an at-risk group requiring added professional support if they are to remain out of the hospital. Conversely, it suggests that social networks can have a preventative and curative role within a community setting. [Sokolovsky et al., 1978: 14]

Just as a social network of deviant peers can reinforce deviant behavior by approving and modeling such behavior (Bandura, 1969; Burgess et al., 1970; Linden and Hackler, 1973: 31-32), integrating drug abusers into durable primary networks of supportive conventional others can increase their chances of maintaining conforming lives after treatment.

With a few notable exceptions,[9] however, drug programs have failed to help clients mobilize durable primary supportive relationships with conforming others following treatment. Continuing care programs can link ex-abusers to primary networks of conventional others and provide ongoing consultation to network members to help them remain viable supports after clients leave treatment.

Becoming Involved in Conventional Activities

Participation in conventional activities must be made more rewarding than street life if commitments to a conventional life-style are to be maintained after treatment (Akers, 1973). Activities which provide a sense of usefulness, competence, belonging, and personal power are likely to be viewed as rewarding (Polk and Kobrin, 1972). Conventional activities with these characteristics can be made structurally available to ex-abusers by continuing care programs.

GOALS OF CONTINUING CARE

Treatment and continuing care are essential components in a process of rehabilitation and reintegration. Rehabilitation begins in treatment programs with development of commitment to change and the skills necessary to bring about change. Reintegration must follow. Ex-abusers need to develop social networks in the larger community which provide social supports for their efforts to live conventional lives. They need to become engaged in roles and activities which provide rewards and a stake in conformity. To complete the task of reintegration, continuing care must achieve the following goals:

(1) Assist clients to refine skills necessary for attaining the rewards of conventional lives through actual exposure and practice in the larger community.

(2) Assist clients to become involved in activities which provide perceptions of usefulness, competence, belonging, and personal power.

(3) Strengthen attachments to conventional others by assisting former abusers to develop primary supportive social networks of conventional others where these do not exist, and by assisting primary networks to function effectively as social supports.

(4) Assist ex-abusers to maintain perceptions of personal control and responsibility for their own lives.

CHARACTERISTICS OF CONTINUING CARE PROGRAMS

To successfully achieve these goals, continuing care programs should have four general characteristics.

Consultation Approach

The consultation approach has been used increasingly in recent years in the mental health field (Altrocchi, 1972; Caplan, 1970; Cherniss, 1977; Dworkin and Dworkin, 1975; Gartner and Riessman, 1972; MacLennan et al., 1975; Woody, 1975). In traditional consultation models, the goal is to help consultees arrive at their own solutions to problems at hand (Schien, 1977; Woody, 1975). Continuing care programs should assist in enhancing the competence and autonomy of ex-abusers through use of a consultation approach to explore alternative paths for reintegration (Altrocchi, 1972: 477-480; Caplan, 1970: 28-30).

However, consultative arrangements should be broadened in continuing care. Members of ex-abusers' primary social networks should themselves be engaged as collaborators and consultants, participating with ex-abusers in planning, taking initiative for, and carrying out plans of action aimed at reintegration. Staff of continuing care programs should provide consultation directly to the primary social support people in the network and minimize their direct services to clients. Social network members and community volunteers should become the agents of reintegration. This "collaborative consultation" approach (Feldman, 1978) can maximize the potential for creating strong primary attachments between ex-abusers and conventional others.

The collaborative consultation model appears appropriate for continuing care for several reasons. First, continuing care programs which rely on traditional service delivery models are not likely to lead to development of strong primary relationships between ex-abusers and conventional community members. In traditional models of service delivery, there is a status inequality between paid staff and clients. Interactions take place at specified times and in specified locations (often in staff offices). They often focus on rehabilitation issues deemed important by staff. These structural and interactional characteristics are not likely to facilitate development of equality and mutuality in relationships between staff and clients. Yet mutuality is an important characteristic of supportive primary relationships:

> [Mutuality is] a critical variable that may differentiate the help-giving relationship of a natural helper from that of a paid counselor. . . . Mutuality . . . provides the broad framework for meaningful help giving and receiving. . . . Mutuality, then, in the natural helper-helpee relationship . . . implies a depth relationship based upon doing, feeling, and sharing with one another . . . experientially, mutuality appears to contain such dimensions as acceptance, spontaneity, availability, followup, outreach, willingness to receive as well as give help, commonality of experience and equality of status. [Patterson and Twente, 1972: 38-69]

By engaging primary network members as collaborative consultants, the structural impediments to mutuality which exist in traditional relationships between paid service providers and clients can be minimized. Primary relationships should be enhanced over time. The approach provides the opportunity for ex-abusers to increasingly contribute in mutual sharing and exchange in the network. This can, in turn, further strengthen network attachments and ex-abusers' perceptions of control and responsibility.

The collaborative consultation model has merit for a second reason. A formal service delivery model is unlikely to be capable of spontaneously providing support and assistance as needed (Graziano, 1969). Service agencies must have institutional rules for service delivery. These include criteria for what services will be provided, to whom, and under what conditions. Besides making apparent the inequality of the relationship between service provider and client, these rules inherently limit the flexibility of services to meet people's needs as they develop. Compared with primary networks in which people interact on a routine basis, formalized service organizations have a limited capacity for individualized assistance. This is true whether the need is for a $5 loan, for assistance in getting to work when one's car is broken down, or for consultation when one has just had a disagreement with a supervisor. Attending to these small needs as they emerge can make the difference between adequate coping with the everyday difficulties of a new life-style and surrendering to mounting frustrations. It is unlikely that a formal service model, even if well coordinated with other service agencies, can directly address these needs as they emerge. Service organizations will more likely be called in after situations have reached crisis proportions when ex-abusers' commitments to the struggle to maintain a new life are wavering or gone.

For these reasons, in the models explored later in this chapter, community volunteers and primary network members are the major agents of continuing care. Staff move back into consultative roles. Their responsibilities are limited to administration and management; recruitment and selection of community volunteers; recruitment, selection, and needs assessment with program participants; and training and consultation to community volunteers and to natural network members.

Using staff as consultants to community volunteers and network members who have routine contact with the target population has been shown effective and cost-efficient in aftercare programs for former mental patients. An experimental study conducted by Weinman and Kleiner (1978: 151) linked mental health clients with community "enablers" to develop specific community living skills. Two conditions were compared: providing staff consultation to the "enablers" and making staff directly available to clients rather than to the "enablers." The former arrangement was most effective:

> The results have shown that patients in the enabler-centered condition [staff consultation to the enabler] are superior to their counterparts in the patient-centered condition [staff consultation to the patient] in psychiatric status and comparable to them on the other outcome measures. Thus, enablers trained by professional staff can provide services to patients that generate even more favorable outcomes than professional staff services [provided directly to clients].

Community Support and Participation

Continuing care efforts must be supported by the larger community organizationally, financially, and through direct involvement of community people as new members of ex-abusers' primary social networks. Reintegration requires the active participation of members of the groups into which ex-abusers are to become integrated. This involvement has been largely missing in drug treatment programs, reflecting a dominant trend in social programs in the last century:

> Increased urbanization and industrialization in society have been accompanied by increased professionalism concentrated in formal agencies charged with responsibilities for solving social problems. . . . Professionally staffed agencies have failed to have significant impact on the social problems. Furthermore, these agencies and their programs have tended to become "disengaged" from the community, or at best are peripheral to the mainstream of community life. They have not functioned as a central part of the life of the community. [Pink and White, 1973: 29]

Reintegration requires building enduring bonds between former abusers and conventional members of society. These can be created only if members of the larger community actively reach out to reattach ex-abusers. Community members must come to view ex-abusers as part of the community, though they have violated its expectations, rather than as "outsiders" (King, 1969: 218-219). Community acceptance and support have been shown to be the best predictors of the social functioning of former mental patients in board and care facilities (Segal and Aviram, 1978).

The reintegration models explored below stress coordination and integration of independent collaborating actors, rather than program control or supervision of the "ill" or "deviant." Such models require active community support and participation in continuing care.

Attractive and Relevant Services

Continuing care should be so attractive that ex-abusers want to participate voluntarily after an orienting exposure. Yet extraneous incentives for participation should be minimized. Drug *treatment* programs will of necessity continue to use legal and other pressures to encourage clients to develop initial commitments to changing their lives. However, to the extent possible, *continuing care* participation should not be a means to shorten or avoid prison time, a condition of parole, or a way to secure welfare benefits. These extraneous incentives encourage cynical attempts to "game" one's way through the program. Continuing care should focus on providing people who have made commitments to change during treatment with skills, structural opportunities, and social supports for reintegration to the larger community, so that their commitments can be maintained.

While attempts at minimizing extraneous incentives for participation in continuing care will undoubtedly limit the number of former abusers willing to participate, failure to do so can jeopardize the community support necessary both for the success and existence of these models of continuing care. Including cynical participants can quickly lead to the disillusionment of community volunteers and to political problems with community groups whose participation and cooperation are essential in the proposed models (King, 1969: 219).

Some will argue that limiting continuing care to those already committed to change ensures program success and, in essence, makes continuing care superfluous. This is the implicit view of treatment programs which help clients break addictions and develop a desire to live new lives, but provide little assistance in the process of reintegration. Yet as those who have tried to stop smoking know, commitment to change itself does not guarantee change. The continuing care models explored here assume that, even for the committed, skills, structural opportunities, and supports can make the difference between successful reintegration and a disillusioned return to the life of street drug abuse.

How can people be encouraged to participate voluntarily if legal pressures and other external incentives are removed? Some who have implemented aftercare programs for ex-abusers believe the task is impossible:

> The main obstacle has been presented by the patients themselves. Most of them do not have sufficient motivation and stability to use the service of a community agency. Many need an active reaching-out service, and others need involuntary supervision. [Maddux et al., 1971]

On the other hand, the failure of aftercare programs to maintain client participation may stem from their inordinate emphasis on formal counseling and their relative inattention to providing services to meet clients' specific and tangible needs (Pittel, 1977b: 25). The best hope for getting ex-abusers to participate voluntarily in continuing care is to make the services offered relevant and directly useful in assisting them to maintain new lives.

Further, financial, social, and psychological barriers to participation must be minimized. Community or government financial support for continuing care programs will be required to minimize financial barriers and to provide financial rewards for participation in some of the activities outlined. Social and psychological barriers can be decreased by separating continuing care from existing drug treatment programs and by making continuing care services available noncategorically to anyone. Many clients leaving drug treatment want to establish their independence from treatment programs. They do not want to be reminded of the dependence and stigma associated with treatment for drug abuse. They may not wish to associate with former abusers (NIDA, 1978: 12; see also King, 1969: 56). Importantly, once they have withdrawn from drugs and become committed to establishing more conventional patterns of living, their needs for skills, opportunities, and social supports may be quite similar to those of others seeking reintegration to the larger society, whether former alcoholics, former mental patients, ex-convicts, or others who have managed to escape stigmatizing processing and labels (Pittel, 1977a: 21). Pittel has argued convincingly that continuing care services need not be categorically limited to drug abusers (1977a: 21). Continuing care programs open to anyone who desires assistance in reintegration may help minimize the stigma of participation for ex-abusers, encourage voluntary participation, provide opportunities for making new acquaintances not from the drug culture, and broaden the base of potential community and funding support.

Transition from Treatment

The move from treatment to continuing care can be facilitated by a transitional period during which clients participate in both programs. As noted above, ex-abusers often feel a need to assert their independence following treatment. Exposing them to the services available in the continuing care program during a transition period can help minimize resistance to participation after leaving treatment. If the continuing care program is adequately designed, exposure during treatment can make clients aware that a useful noncoercive resource is available. This exposure can also facilitate development of primary relationships with people from the continuing care program. Such relationships are likely to encourage continued participation in the program.

Participation in continuing care can begin once clients' drug use is under control (e.g., once clients have been stabilized on methadone, completed detox, or remained abstinent in a therapeutic community for a minimum of perhaps a month). Clients should have expressed or demonstrated commitment to new lives. Behavioral evidence of this commitment is desirable, but clients should not be required to "prove themselves" without assistance in the larger community prior to admission. The decision regarding participation should be based on mutual agreement of the client, staff of the treatment program, and staff of the continuing care program.

Some conflicts between treatment program staff and continuing care staff during this transition period should be anticipated. It is likely that disagreements over therapeutic approaches and the sequence and timing of rehabilitation steps will emerge in individual cases, even if staffs share a general model of rehabilitation and reintegration. These disagreements can be particularly devastating to clients exposed to differing sets of expectations and demands from the staffs of two programs. It will be essential to establish routine and frequent communications between staffs of the treatment and continuing care programs. A common rehabilitation plan and an acceptable division of responsibility should be hammered out in each case if this transitional arrangement is to succeed.

Individually Tailored Services

It is essential that continuing care activities be tailored to meet the specific needs of each former user. Continuing care programs must develop a number of intervention models and a needs assessment process for determining appropriate involvement for each entering participant.

At entry, continuing care staff and each new participant should assess the participant's existing skills and opportunities and the availability of potentially supportive conventional others in his or her primary social network. An assessment should be made of the ex-abuser's skills and opportunities to enter work or other activities which can provide experiences of usefulness, competence, belonging, and personal power. The existing social network should be assessed to determine who is likely to contribute to a return to drug dependence or street life and who is likely to support the participant's efforts to develop new living patterns. Additionally, the network should be assessed to identify opportunities for reciprocity and mutuality (e.g., opportunities for the ex-abuser to help others in the network). Finally, the network should be assessed to identify possible housing arrangements with supportive people not likely to contribute to relapse. Based on these assessments, a range of continuing care interventions may be appropriate. Several models are outlined below.

MODELS FOR CONTINUING CARE

Consultation to Existing Networks

Some former abusers already have primary social networks with the potential to provide social support.[10] Yet even where primary network members are available, former abusers may not know how to use these people as constructive supports. Further, network members may not know how to provide support in such a way that it contributes to maintenance of the new life-style, rather than creating pressures to return to drug use. Stanton and his colleagues (1978: 3) cite increasing evidence that many street drug abusers maintain close ties with their families of origin. Yet the patterned relationships between abusers and their families often contribute to relapse and drug addiction (1978: 3). Thus, when potential primary support people are available, it is important to involve them in consultative relationships during continuing care. The goal of consultation is to help them support the ex-abusers' new life, rather than add stress or contribute to relapse. Two examples of this approach are collaborative consultation and network assemblies.[11]

Collaborative Consultation. During needs assessment interviews, the ex-abuser and continuing care staff may identify a number of concrete needs, whether for housing, financial assistance, child care, a job, emotional support, or assistance in getting to work. In the collaborative consultation model, the ex-abuser identifies a person in his or her network who best knows how to meet such needs or is most likely to be able to help. This may be an employer, spouse, friend, coworker, neighbor, or other individual. The ex-abuser invites that person to a consultation session. Client, network person, and staff review the need to be addressed or skill to be developed. The ex-abuser and network member, with staff serving as a consultant, then outline a plan for meeting the need which they subsequently implement in the community. This approach enables network members to function effectively as social supports by engaging them in tangible collaborative tasks with the ex-abuser. Further, collaborative consultation introduces the network member to a staff person who will remain available as a consultant as needed by the support person. Collaborative consultation sessions can be repeated sequentially with network members as needed throughout reentry to build a strong network of primary social supports with consultation back-up.

Network Assemblies. A more ambitious approach is the mobilization of an ex-abuser's social network during the reentry phase. Assemblies of network members invited by the ex-abuser seek to develop concrete plans to ensure the successful integration of the ex-abuser into the larger community, and to identify the specific social support roles network members will play in the process (Speck and Attneave, 1973). According to Speck and Attneave, network assemblies progress through a clearly recognizable sequence of phases. Staff take facilitation roles during network assemblies to help ensure progress through this sequence. Responsibility for developing and implementing plans rests with the ex-abuser and network members. Again, through the process, staff can offer an ongoing consultative relationship to network members who will compose the primary support system after treatment. Network assemblies have already been used effectively in reentry planning for therapeutic community clients.[12]

Formation of Primary Social Supports

A substantial proportion of ex-abusers leaving treatment will need more assistance in reintegration than can be provided by their existing social networks. Some will not have potential supports in the form of nondrug-using friends, adult living partners, or others with whom they can share information and resources in time of need. As noted by Stanton and his colleagues (1978: 27), some may also be overdependent on relationships with parents, which must be replaced by "stable nondrug-related relationships outside the family."

People without available supports may be particularly likely to return to the associative network of street drug users and to relapse to drug abuse. An interviewer in a drug treatment followup study summarized this process after interviewing several hundred clients:

> A lot of people I talked to who started using again said they wanted to stay clean but they couldn't. They didn't like being alone, and they were afraid to meet new people, especially straight people. They'd rather be with drug users than alone. Once they get together with their drug-using friends, it's hard to stay clean. [See also Stanton et al., 1978: 7].

Just as a viable social network can support adjustment to a straight life, reentry to a drug-using network can precipitate return to the drug life. A followup of 156 therapeutic community clients in Seattle showed that of those abstinent during treatment, 34% had relapsed to heroin or other illegal opiate use at the end of six months. Of those who relapsed, 69%

reported, in response to an open-ended question, that they used heroin the first time after leaving treatment because they were with friends who were using. In essence, they reported their use as a response to informal social pressure from peers. Only 25% who relapsed to opiates indicated that their use was a response to problems or stress.[13] For those leaving residential treatment programs, at least, return to opiate use is often closely associated with attempts to reestablish social connections of some type following treatment.

When the networks of ex-abusers do not provide adequate social supports, community resources must be mobilized. The goal is to develop primary attachments between the ex-abuser and conventional others who can provide such supports. To be durable, these attachments must be characterized by emotional closeness and perceived emotional support, and by mutuality and reciprocity of rights and obligations. The new relationships should be diffuse, rather than limited to a specialized content. They will differ in this respect from relationships of self-help groups which revolve around a particular shared experience such as drug addiction or alcoholism (Caplan, 1973). In short, the goal of community resource mobilization is to create new friendships in the full sense of the word.

Creating new friendships between strangers is not an easy task, yet several integrative models are available.

Activities Model. The activities model is most applicable for those former abusers who are neither attached to strong supportive primary networks nor engaged in conventional activities, such as jobs, which make them feel useful, competent, powerful, and part of something important. It is a companionship model with an important variation. In this model, former abusers and new "straight friends" (community volunteers) seek out and become involved in participatory activities, screened and selected for their potential to provide the ex-abuser with a meaningful role. The key characteristic of the model is its attempt to achieve the attachment, commitment, and involvement elements of the social bond simultaneously.

In the activities model, former abusers entering continuing care are introduced to a "straight friend" by continuing care staff. This first meeting should include time for socialization among the three, such as dinner together. The goal is "to break the ice" so that the ex-abuser and straight friend feel somewhat comfortable with one another and have a base for future conversations. After this first meeting, the straight friend and ex-abuser will continue the relationship, while the staff person is available on a consultation basis. The model differs from other companionship approaches in the following steps.

Following the first meeting, the straight friend and ex-abuser attend a small group session of three to five companion pairs, facilitated by staff. During this session, each straight friend is responsible for presenting to the group a brief description of one or more activities the companions may wish to undertake together. Ultimately, each activity presented should require active participation, though initially, passive activities, such as spectator sports, movies, or observations of more active roles, may be included to help companions become more comfortable with each other and to minimize performance anxieties of the ex-abusers.

After the initial session, the activities presented should hold at least the potential for a sense of usefulness, competence, belonging, and personal power through participation. Further, they must be potentially open to these new participants. Activities such as working with children, which are likely to be closed to recent drug abusers, should not be included. Nevertheless, a wide range of activities can be included. Job or employment opportunities can be explored through this vehicle, as can involvement in political campaigns, civic and political groups and councils, volunteer service organizations, environmental groups, and religious groups.

After the activities are presented, participants discuss them and each pair of companions decides on the most appealing for a reconnaissance visit. At this time, participants also discuss ground rules for the visit. The straight companion and the ex-abuser will visit the activity site together during the next week with four basic questions in mind: (1) Is this interesting to me? (2) Is it important; is it worth putting effort into? (3) Could I add or contribute anything? (4) Could my participation make a difference or be important?

Following the visit, companions discuss the experience with each other and subsequently rejoin their small groups to present the activity and their reactions to it. At the conclusion of these discussions, each pair decides whether to follow up on the activity visited, or to visit another activity. The decision should be based on the ex-abuser's answers to the four questions outlined above. If the ex-abuser answers all affirmatively, then the activity should be pursued. If most or all the answers are negative, then another activity should be tried. Companions continue to visit activities and debrief with their small groups until an activity is found which meets all the criteria.

Returning to group sessions for debriefing has several benefits. First, it broadens the range of each ex-abuser's straight acquaintances. It provides a self-help support group where anxieties and fears about involvement in straight activities can be shared and discussed. It exposes ex-abusers to a

range of activities for possible involvement. Finally, it can also create
incentive to find an activity of interest. Ex-abusers looking for the "per-
fect" activity may be more susceptible to chiding from fellow clients to
look harder for the positive aspects of possible activities than from straight
friends thought to be naive about the comparative rewards of the street
life which the program seeks to replace. To the extent that the small
groups become ongoing support groups, participants may wish to continue
to meet regularly beyond the activity selection phase.

Once companions have found an acceptable activity, they can begin to
plan their involvement. This may require strategizing, making appropriate
contacts, and going through the requisite steps of gaining access, including
getting training in some cases. In other instances, entry may require
nothing more than an expression of interest. However, in all cases, the
companions will need to plan ways to develop the ex-abuser's involvement
in a role which provides a sense of usefulness, competence, belonging, and
personal power.

Depending on the activity selected, the ex-abuser and straight friend
may participate together. They may, for example, become crisis-line telephone volunteers or active in civic groups, neighborhood councils, or
campaigns focusing on issues of interest to the ex-abuser such as redlining,
community health promotion, or law enforcement practices in certain
neighborhoods. In other instances, such as when the activity is a paid job,
the nature of the activity itself may preclude the full involvement of the
straight friend, but she/he should remain involved in planning and assessment with the ex-abuser to ensure that the ex-abuser's participation is
aimed at meeting the criteria outlined.

The model's applicability to a broad range of activities is a key characteristic. It allows flexibility to meet particular needs of individual ex-
abusers. After treatment, many former abusers are able to secure jobs, but
these are often mundane. The model can be used to involve working
ex-abusers in free-time activities which meet the criteria and thus provide
positive self-concept in spite of mediocre jobs. More ambitious programs
can use the model to attack the world of work itself. Additionally, the
model can help develop meaningful activities and attachments which
maintain positive self-identity over the short run, even for those having
difficulties securing work.

The key elements of the model are summarized below:

(1) The ex-abuser is responsible for determining whether an activity is
    worth pursuing based on assessment of its ability to meet the four
    criteria. If activities cannot be found which meet these criteria, it is

unlikely that the ex-abuser will become committed to them and bonded to conventional society.

(2) The approach builds attachments between straight friends and ex-abusers by providing them common tasks. In many instances, they will be entering contexts unfamiliar to both. Facing a new environment together should increase their sense of commonality and hence their attachments to each other.

(3) The straight friend is not in a position of control. Rather she/he assists the ex-abuser to make decisions about what activities will be important, useful, and worthwhile, and assists the ex-abuser in making specific plans for involvement. The straight friend seeks to function as an ally and friend, rather than as a teacher or counselor.

(4) Small group sessions provide self-help supports and encouragement for ex-abusers without relying exclusively on relationships among ex-abusers as the basis for forming new attachments and commitments to conventional society.

(5) Participation provides opportunities for ex-abusers to learn and practice decision-making, planning, and assessment skills in real contexts with the assistance of role models who possess such skills.

Several issues must be addressed in implementing the activities model. First is the question of organizational sponsorship and involvement of community participants. A wide range of community groups could be involved. Individual groups might wish to sponsor such a program as a project. The model could be implemented by community mental health clinics, civic or fraternal organizations, chamber of commerce chapters, other business groups, religious organizations, or ACTION volunteers. The sponsoring organization would influence the types of activities included. A project sponsored by a chamber of commerce or business group might target jobs and establish a program in which straight friends and ex-abusers initially visited work sites to learn about the nature of jobs performed and ultimately worked toward meaningful job placements for the ex-abusers. A project sponsored by action volunteers might focus on involvement in neighborhood development, community organizing, or other public interest activities.

Alternatively, a number of community groups could become involved in a coordinated program. Again, members of these groups could participate as straight friends. However, sponsorship by several groups would likely broaden the range of activities to which companion pairs could gain initial access. This would be especially likely if members of cosponsoring groups paved the way for visits from companion pairs to organizations in which they were involved. This cosponsorship model would increase opportunities for linking ex-abusers to activities matching their needs, capabilities, and interests.

In any case, to guarantee success, it would be important to adhere closely to the model. The program could quickly lose its effectiveness if it became simply a recreational activities program or a more traditional companionship program.

The vulnerability of the model indicates the importance of attention to several other implementation issues. First, staff functions and responsibilities should be clearly defined, and staff should be well-trained to perform them. Staff would provide a personal link between the drug treatment program and a straight friend. Staff would recruit ex-abusers, explain the program, and introduce them to straight friends in a shared social context. This is an important function. A companion program implemented by Wolf and his associates (see Chapter 9) has had to overcome ex-abusers' apprehensions about signing up to spend time with straight strangers. Secondly, staff would screen volunteers and train those straight friends selected. They would provide regular consultation to straight friends to discuss progress, difficulties, and possible solutions. After making initial introductions, staff would not provide direct services to ex-abusers. Finally, staff would facilitate small group sessions. This would provide an opportunity to monitor progress of companion pairs and to check for adherence to and problems in the activities model. It would provide independent data for use in consultation with straight friends, and an opportunity to ensure that straight friends were fulfilling their commitments to participation.

Given these staff responsibilities, staff must understand the assumptions and activities of the model. Further, they must be skilled in small group facilitation, sufficiently at ease with both ex-abusers and straight volunteers to win their involvement, and skilled in the consultation role (Altrocci, 1972; Caplan, 1970; Mannino et al., 1975; Signell and Scott, 1972).

A second issue in implementating the model is recruitment and selection of straight friends. While people may be drawn from a wide range of community groups, only those with certain characteristics should be selected. Straight friends should have: (1) an ability to listen empathetically, (2) willingness to respond promptly to need, and (3) demonstrated capacity to care about others as evidenced in informal interactions in their own natural settings (Collins and Pancoast, 1976: 68). Research conducted by the Partners Program in Denver (Pryor, 1979: personal communication) suggests that volunteers who do not view themselves as particularly power-ful, have good self-concepts, and are characterized by an external locus of control make the most effective "senior partners" in a companionship program for juvenile offenders. Such people are less likely to try to force change in others. Straight friends who approach the companionship rela-tionship with the intention of establishing a new friendship rather than "saving" an ex-abuser are, ultimately, the most likely to be effective in developing enduring social bonds. Recruiting and screening volunteers for these characteristics will be one of the most important steps in the project. The personal characteristics of volunteers will largely determine the success or failure of the program. Thus, staff should not hesitate to contact references of volunteers for candid assessments of their skills and characteristics.

Volunteers must also make adequate time commitments. The Friends Program in Concord, New Hampshire, provides some guidelines for "senior friends" in a delinquency prevention companionship program. The pro-gram requires that volunteers make a one-year commitment to spend at least five hours per week with a "junior friend." Three-fourths of those who volunteer find, during orientation, that the program requires more time than they can commit. However, these people can participate as volunteers in supplemental support activities. To succeed, this model requires extensive interaction between straight friends and ex-abusers, and it is important to secure adequate commitments from straight friends in advance, even if this limits the size of the program.

Methods of recruiting volunteers are also important. It may be desirable to recruit straight friends through informal word-of-mouth processes rather than through public announcements. Less formal recruitment pro-cesses can help protect the privacy of ex-abuser participants, and may help prescreen community volunteers. Where such processes do not produce enough volunteers, media campaigns, volunteer recruitment programs coordinated with the United Way, or other methods may be necessary. In this case more rigorous screening and training procedures will be required.

Three sources of volunteers should be considered in addition to com-munity groups such as businesses, clubs, and civic organizations. First are former drug abusers who have succeeded in establishing new lives. These people are intimately familiar with the obstacles ex-abusers face and the rationalizations they make. They know the street world and its language. They can make excellent straight friends for the most skeptical and hesitant ex-abusers. However, caution is in order. The history of drug abuse treatment is replete with stories of ex-addict paraprofessional counselors who relapsed to street drug use (Deitch, 1974).[14] Ex-abusers selected as straight friends should have a history of productive nondrug-dependent involvement in the larger community and meet the selection criteria outlined earlier. Volunteers who meet these criteria may be particularly effective consultants to staff and straight friends when problems are encountered in companionship relationships.

People who share the same socioeconomic, ethnic, and cultural backgrounds as ex-abusers should also be recruited. Weinman and Kleiner (1978: 141) selected "community enablers" from working-class populations for an aftercare project with former mental patients:

> The enablers' advantage in working as social change agents lay in their sharing of common socioeconomic backgrounds with the patients, communicating with them in a down-to-earth manner, and spending long periods of time assisting them with daily living activities. Typically, the enablers . . . had time on their hands, and a desire to be useful. They had a high school education or less, with no particular training or experience in dealing with mental patients. Some had worked as nurses' aides, and a few had an interest in people with mental problems because of mental illness in their own families.

The effectiveness of Weinman and Kleiner's project suggests the desirability of recruiting straight friends from low-income community areas and socioeconomic groups. People who have experienced social, economic, and cultural pressures conducive to street drug abuse and have managed to escape that life-style can provide strong, realistic role models for ex-abusers. These straight friends and their ex-abuser companions may develop strong attachments through participation in shared new experiences offered in the activities model.

Professionals, such as nurses, social workers, or treatment practitioners, who respond to calls for help from friends and neighbors on a voluntary basis in their nonworking lives should also be recruited. Such professional volunteers have been effecitvely used as crisis counselors in the prevention of suicide (Collins and Pancoast, 1976: 67-69). While few may be able to commit the time required for the program, those who can are likely to be particularly effective straight friends, because of their skills in working with people in helping capacities and their ability to help others in a personal nonprofessional role as neighbor or friend. It may, however, be beneficial to provide a special training component for professional volunteers to ensure that they function as helping friends, rather than as counselors or therapists, to their ex-abuser companions.

Once volunteers are selected, they should be oriented to the program and trained. Weinman and Kleiner (1978: 158) write:

> The effective utilization of indigenous community members requires that professional staff assume a training function. They should train the community members to help (the client) deal with the requirements of daily living. . . . The role of the community member is to exert a significant influence on the social behavior of (clients) so that it more closely approximates standards which are acceptable to the community. To help them perform this role effectively, professional staff should focus on helping the enablers establish interpersonal relationships with (clients) that enhance cohesion and resolve conflict.

Alley and Blanton (1978) provide a comprehensive list of resources relevant to training community volunteers.

Survival Skills and Recreational Companionship Models

Community volunteers who cannot commit the time required in the activities model can be used in less ambitious companionship approaches which provide supplemental services in continuing care. However, by themselves, these approaches are unlikely to be adequate to meet the reintegration goals of continuing care.

One component would assist ex-abusers in developing specific rudimentary skills for minimal functioning. Some ex-abusers will need assistance in learning to open checking and savings accounts, to shop to conserve resources and ensure good nutrition, to use public transportation, and the like. When natural network members cannot be identified to assist in these tasks through the collaborative consultation process, community volunteers can accompany ex-abusers to the locales where these skills are used to assist in learning and practicing them.

This is an inexpensive and effective model for ensuring that rudimentary survival skills are developed (Weinman and Kleiner, 1978). The focus is on development of specific behavioral competencies (Stein and Test, 1978: 49). Most importantly, the model again provides a vehicle for involving community members in the reintegration process.

However, the model's utility as a bonding strategy for ex-abusers may be limited. Few ex-abusers are likely to need prolonged assistance in developing rudimentary skills in shopping, handling money, and the like (Pittel, 1979: personal communication). Companionship relationships based on providing such skills may, therefore, be short-lived. Additionally, this approach may have limited potential for development of diffuse reciprocal friendships between companions.

Community volunteers can also assist ex-abusers in finding nondrug-related ways to use leisure time. Recreational activities could be shared by companion pairs discussed here once rudimentary skills were learned. Shared recreational activities could facilitate development of more durable friendships. However, companionship programs which focus primarily on helping people learn to use leisure time may hold limited promise for ensuring successful reintegration unless they also concentrate on engaging ex-abusers in activities which provide perceptions of usefulness, competence, personal power, and a sense of belonging (Polk and Kobrin, 1972: 5). By themselves, recreational programs have not been particularly effective in juvenile delinquency prevention and remediation (Dixon and Wright, 1974; Romig, 1978).

Home Placements

Community volunteer families can provide living arrangements for ex-abusers. These arrangements are appropriate for those who have no other adult with whom to live or for those whose available living partners are drug users or family members likely to create stress and contribute to drug relapse.

A diversity of home environments, ranging from roommates of the same age to intact nuclear family units, could be developed. Matching the ex-abuser and a home environment could provide arrangements more responsive to specific needs than possible in halfway houses or other group-living situations.

Polak (1978: 127) has summarized the strength of the home placement approach in community mental health:

Carefully selected individuals without formal training take on responsibilities usually carried out by professional staff. The family sponsors tend to quite naturally treat clients in their home as guests. They orient themselves more to the strengths and positive features of the clients than to their pathology, and are much less likely than . . . professionals to view all client behavior in an illness framework. . . . Home sponsors are warm, outgoing healthy people who are rich in life experience. We provide little in the way of formal training, focusing instead on encouraging sponsor families to utilize their already existing skills. . . . Sponsor families provide a clear model of healthy individual and family behavior which can be generalized to the client's [own life].

There is evidence from the mental health field that the home placement approach can reduce the need for further formal treatment. Weinman and Kleiner (1978) found significantly greater recidivism (rehospitalization) when former patients lived independently (22%) than when they lived in the homes of community enablers (4%).

Additionally, the home placement approach can build lasting attachments between volunteer families and clients placed with them. Two-thirds of the clients in Weinman and Kleiner's study who were not rehospitalized, continued to reside in the home placement for at least 24 months after the 12-month demonstration project. Polak (1978: 132) writes:

> Clients admitted to private homes often develop meaningful personal attachments to one or more members of the sponsoring family. In several instances, the client has adopted the sponsor family as part of his own extended family. The private home system . . . provides a social setting which encourages the development of personal relationships.

If experiences with home placements can be generalized to ex-abusers, they may offer ongoing primary social supports, reduce community members' prejudices toward ex-abusers, and in turn enhance the self-esteem of ex-abusers seeking to build new lives (Weinman and Kleiner, 1978: 156-157).

However, the home placement model involves risks and questions. Both legitimate and unfounded prejudices regarding possible "rip-offs" and drug use in the home may limit the number of adequate home placements to be found. Further, the model may have limited utility for ex-abusers. It is likely to be most appropriate for younger ex-abusers who have not yet established families of their own outside their parents' homes. Finally, well-trained staff would be required for screening volunteer families, for matching ex-abusers with appropriate families, and to provide *on-call* consultation on a 24-hour basis. This model of continuing care should be explored in small carefully controlled demonstration projects prior to attempting more general implementation.

College Dorm Placement

This model would provide living arrangements in college dormitories for ex-abusers who want to complete educational credentialing. The model has been used successfully in the "Residence Release Program" at the University of Washington. State and federal prisoners who qualify are released early to pursue a degree. Participants live together on one floor of a university dormitory and are subject to spot-check urinalysis, sign-in/sign-out requirements, and restrictions on travel. Even with these restrictions, participants are able to pursue their educations and develop friendships with other students (Morrell, 1978: personal communication).

A similar program could be established for people leaving drug treatment. The program would be enhanced by sponsorship and participation of campus groups, including fraternities, sororities, religious organizations, public interest groups, and sports clubs. These groups could offer introductions to and involvement in their activities, using the activities model outlined earlier. In this case, straight friends would be volunteer students from these organizations. Again, a small staff would be required for administration and consultation. Coordination with campus schools and departments, such as the School of Social Work, could provide needed professional services and administrative support, while further integrating the program into the campus community.

Implementing such a program would require attention to restrictions and regulations. Those in the Resident Release Program appear necessary to minimize college administrators' concerns about the "contaminative effect" of ex-convicts on other students. Yet similar regulations could severely limit voluntary participation of ex-abusers. Nevertheless, the success of the Resident Release Program suggests that the model be explored, given its potential to offer opportunities and attachments to new networks of nonabusers.

Community Employment Models

Perhaps the most ambitious and promising continuing-care approaches would combine interactive and structural strategies while focusing on employment. Work is central in defining roles and identities in this society. It can provide a sense of successful accomplishment, contribution, and participation, as well as tangible financial rewards. Thus, employment has great potential for providing a stake in conformity.

If work is to meet this goal, however, it must meet the criteria outlined earlier. The work should be perceived as important; it should provide an opportunity to develop and exhibit competence; it should offer opportunities to contribute and be useful; and it should provide a sense of participation and belonging (Polk and Kobrin, 1972). It is difficult to find jobs open to ex-abusers which provide such opportunities. Community groups can play a major role in developing such work opportunities with and for ex-abusers. In addition to the activities model presented earlier, several models appear promising.

Community Lodges. Community lodges pioneered by Fairweather and his associates have demonstrated effectiveness as mental health aftercare programs. They have been shown less expensive and more effective in reducing recidivism than traditional community aftercare programs (Fairweather et al., 1969). Lodges are independent, democratically run residential units which are also self-supporting cooperative business enterprises. (Lodges discussed by Fairweather and his colleagues developed financially successful janitorial and gardening services.) Staff serve only as consultants to the lodges after an initial set-up and transition period.

The community lodge model is somewhat similar to the business enterprises of Synanon and Delancey Street (Hampden-Turner, 1977), with a major exception. The lodges do not depend upon a single authoritarian or charismatic leader. Members are themselves responsible for decision-making and for the success of their cooperatively owned, cooperatively run enterprise.

By providing employment opportunities and living arrangements with others seeking to establish new lives, community lodges can offer incentives and supports for a new live. Participants are responsible for all aspects of a business, including administration and management, contracting, purchasing, pricing, and production of marketable products or services. These tasks can provide inherent satisfactions for people with a wide range of interests and skills. Additionally, the success of the enterprise depends upon the contribution of all members. As a result, structural arrangements (the reward system of the business) and interactional arrangements (peer pressure to do one's part) encourage a stake in conformity.

To succeed, community lodges must be self-supporting. Members must have reason to establish and enforce standards for performance to prevent lodges from becoming "dope houses" or crash pads. If the very survival of the organization depends on members' conforming participation, they will have greater reason to ensure such conformity from one another. Lodges should not be publicly subsidized, though financial assistance will be necessary to start them.

Though financially self-sufficient, lodges will require community support and involvement. Sponsorship by a respected community organization, such as a private corporation or group of business people (Rotary, Kiwanis, chamber of commerce, etc.), can be especially helpful. The sponsoring group can groom the environment to minimize political problems likely to be encountered and to help secure initial funding. Group members can collaborate with founding lodge participants to identify a marketable product or service to be produced. They can provide needed assistance and consultation in establishing and maintaining the business. Skills in contracting, setting up books, purchasing, marketing, and a host of other tasks will be required in the new business. The expertise of community business people should be mobilized to help lodge members develop these skills. Similarly, labor unions may be enlisted to provide training and apprenticeship certification to lodge members, should the lodge engage in trades such as renovation of privately owned buildings. Again, these approaches can create attachments between ex-abusers and conventional others, while providing commitment to and involvement in conventional activities offering a stake in conformity.

Nonresidential Participant-Run Businesses. The model outlined above can be used in establishing nonresidential cooperatively run businesses as well. In Seattle, the Central Breakthrough Maintenance Program established a continuing care employment program for ex-abusers called CADRE, using CETA funds to pay salaries of the ex-abusers. The CADRE program was a speakers/resource bureau for community organizations concerned with drug-related problems. In the program, professionals participated as consultants to CADRE staff after an initial training and orientation period. The ex-abusers on CADRE's staff were responsible for planning and carrying out the organization's work. They responded to requests for assistance from community groups, collaboratively dividing responsibilities for research and presentations. In addition to providing speakers to schools, community groups, and clubs, they participated in planning sessions with businesses interested in establishing alcoholism and drug treatment programs for their employees.

Other possibilities for employment of ex-abusers can be created in noncategorical continuing care programs themselves. Ex-abuser participants can be hired as community "enablers" to assist those with less rudimentary survival skills, such as former mental patients. Ex-abusers can help these people learn how to shop, take public transportation, open checking and savings accounts, and otherwise function in the community. Providing paid employment in such helping roles can help former abusers see themselves as useful and competent people. Programs based on similar principles have trained and used high-risk adolescents and adjudicated delinquents as tutors for primary school children (National Commission on Resources for Youth, 1974).

Neighborhood-Based Employment Programs. In a number of communities across the country, local citizens' groups, nonprofit organizations, schools, community action agencies, and neighborhood planning councils have used HUD and DOL monies to take initiative for developing youth employment programs to meet specific needs of the local community. These programs recognize that the job market for youth, as for ex-abusers, is extremely limited. Therefore, they focus on developing training and work opportunities in growth industries that may offer permanent jobs and opportunities for advancement, while simultaneously meeting community needs. Programs have been established to train low-income minority youth as solar technicians and place them in private industry in California, to offer paid jobs to former juvenile offenders in Michigan winterizing neighborhood homes, and to offer employment and on-the-job training in neighborhood recycling projects in California, Michigan, and Washington, DC. Local groups can use the same principles for developing work training and employment opportunities for ex-abusers in continuing care programs.

Such programs can be made especially relevant to community needs and effective in ensuring the integration of ex-abusers if they provide roles for community members and ex-abuser participants in planning and decision-making. The Neighborhood Planning Councils of Washington, DC provide a model of neighborhood-based, democratically run public employment programs, which seek to simultaneously address the needs of the community and employees through collaborative, participatory decision-making (Seldman, 1977: 22-26).

STRATEGIES AND PROSPECTS FOR
COMMUNITY INVOLVEMENT

All the models presented here have stressed the active involvement of community members in reintegrating ex-abusers. Active community participation is an element generally missing from rehabilitation programs for ex-abusers. How can business groups, community mental health clinics, universities, Kiwanis clubs, and ACTION volunteers be engaged in the task of reintegrating street drug abusers? Will members of these groups take ex-abusers into their homes, be seen in public places with them, introduce them to their friends, and make them part of their social networks? Not unless they somehow come to own the problem as their responsibility.

If this is to happen, professionals and paraprofessionals concerned with the rehabilitation of drug abusers must take the initiative. They must become entrepreneurs for community involvement and responsibility in continuing care, approaching community groups and convincing them of the need to participate in planning and developing programs. Professionals should not simply design and implement new programs which include opportunities for community volunteers. Rather, the very process of program development should be one of collaborative consultation among professionals, members of community groups, and ex-abusers whom the programs will serve (Caplan and Grunebaum, 1967).

Community groups must participate from the start in developing and appraising models, and realistically assessing the abilities of their members to implement them. Ultimately, community organizations should provide the administrative umbrella for programs, funds for program operation, and most importantly, personnel to carry out programs activities. Community members will come to feel ownership of the problem and the programs aimed at resolving it only if they assume such responsibility.

In addition to securing community involvement, a collaborative consultation process for planning and developing continuing care can, itself, provide ex-abusers with meaningful and rewarding activities and linkages to conventional others (Toch et al., 1975).

The collaborative consultation model is not without risks. Conflict can provide power, knowledge, and self-esteem (Alinsky, 1946) just as collaboration can (Feldman, 1978). Ex-abusers may try to gain control over the planning process by attacking those who have ignored them for years. They could easily antagonize community collaborators and lose their participation. Throughout the process, emphasis must be on the goals of creating new vehicles for integrating, rather than on condemning existing institutions for their failure to meet human needs. Professional collaborators will have to continually consult and mediate to ensure this focus.

At the other extreme, there is a risk of tokenism in collaborative consultation. Ex-abusers or community members may be coopted by professionals who appear to have expertise others do not (Gartner and Riessman, 1972: 285-286). This risk must be recognized and avoided. Care must be exercised to provide both groups with information, without usurping their decision-making power in the planning and development process.

These potential problems underscore the importance of the staff of the continuing care program. Roffman (1965) has shown that innovative social programs staffed with personnel from traditional programs may, over time, become increasingly similar to the traditional institutions in which the staff previously worked. To the extent that continuing care staff are drawn from the ranks of treatment programs, this "regression" toward the direct service models used in existing drug treatment programs may occur. This potential problem should be recognized from the outset, and the collaborative consultation model continually reinforced. Periodic involvement of outside consultants familiar with collaborative consultation may help prevent deterioration of the model over time.

All the models we have outlined can be abused. It is easy to imagine scenarios in which former abusers take advantage of opportunities to rip off those attempting to assist or those they are supposed to be helping. One such incident, even a single relapse or serious offense by a partici- pating ex-abuser, can quickly jeopardize essential community support. The risks can be minimized by screening ex-abusers, by careful recruitment and training of community participants, by close adherence to the funda- mental principles of creating structural opportunities and primary social supports, and by providing readily available consultation and support to participating community members and groups (King, 1969: 219). Yet ugly incidents are inevitable. It will be important to develop realistic expecta- tions with participating community groups from the beginning. They should prepare for failures even as they labor to achieve success. Only if they can learn not to give up in the face of failure will the reintegration models proposed here succeed. The alternative is dismal:

> Deprived children placed in foster homes, the mentally ill returning to their families, the probationer or ex-prisoner in lodgings, can all impose considerable strain upon those with whom they live and upon the local community in which their homes are set. Unless they cannot be merely tolerated but accepted and actively helped, their own state may become worse than ever, whilst a disillusioned com- munity turns back to the barren expedient of isolation. [King, 1969: 217]

CONCLUSION

Theoretically supported models for continuing care have been pro- posed. These models require the active participation of community groups and individuals in reaching out to reintegrate former street drug abusers into conventional society. In the models, community members work directly with ex-abusers to (1) develop skills for social functioning in environments where they will be practiced; (2) create and find opportuni- ties for participation in conventional activities which provide a sense of usefulness, competence, personal power, and belonging; and (3) provide primary social supports for maintaining straight lives. In these models, staff act primarily as consultants and supports to community members who are the agents of reintegration.

What are the prospects for success? Clearly, if community participation cannot be secured, these models will fail. Even if it can, a number of questions remain to be answered. They include:

(1) Can sufficient numbers of ex-abusers be motivated to make commitments to conventional lives to justify continuing care reintegration programs?

(2) Are street drug abusers psychologically capable of establishing strong healthy bonds to conventional others, or are they somehow incapable of such attachments?

(3) Can opportunities for rewards from conventional activities be provided for former abusers, or is the combination of economic constraints and social prejudices so strong that ex-abusers cannot be reintegrated without major structural reforms?

(4) Can community volunteers function as collaborators and companions, rather than as experts or teachers who try to exert control when they find situations ambiguous or threatening?

(5) Will the creation of structural opportunities and social supports be adequate to encourage ex-abusers to maintain straight lives in the face of the familiar rewards of street life?

Hopefully, well-designed and well-implemented programs could generate favorable answers to such questions. But this hope must be empirically tested. Controlled experimental projects should be mounted to assess the effectiveness of the community integration approach to drug abuse rehabilitation.

A final comment is in order. Even if the models explored here prove effective in assisting in the reintegration of street drug abusers, they will do little to change the broader social order in which street drug abuse is embedded. Until basic socialization institutions are themselves restructured to provide all with a stake in conformity, new outsiders will emerge to replace the few reintegrated.

If the roots of crime lie far back in the foundations of our social order, it may be that only a radical change can bring any large measure of cure. Less unjust social and economic conditions may be the only way out, and until a better social order exists, crime will probably flourish and society continue to pay the price. [Healy et al., 1935: 222]

NOTES

1. This definition purposely omits the element of "compulsion" common in other definitions of drug abuse for two reasons. First, it is difficult to define. Is a

daily martini before dinner, a daily glass of wine with dinner, or a daily methadone dose compulsive? One's response is likely to vary depending on the dysfunctional consequences one perceives associated with such patterns of use. Secondly, drug use need not be compulsive to have dysfunctional consequences and to be considered drug abuse by some. Drinking before driving may be considered drug abuse, though not associated with an element of compulsion. It can be viewed as abuse because of the likelihood of associated driving accidents. It might be more appropriate to define abuse in terms of dysfunctional consequences associated with drug use and to omit reference to compulsive aspects. But there is also a problem with the concept of dysfunctional consequences as definitive of drug abuse. Perceptions of dysfunctional consequences are themselves subjective and vary with individuals. For this reason, drug abuse is defined here as a pattern of drug use which has been successfully labeled as drug abuse. To the extent that an individual has changed or been forced to change actions as a result of personal or social definitions of his or her behavior as drug abuse, that individual is considered a drug abuser. Hence, the person who enters treatment for drug use problems is defined by the fact of entering treatment as a drug abuser. This definition does not provide clear criteria for recognizing drug abuse in the specific drug-taking behaviors of individuals. It may lead to confusion regarding use of the terms drug use and drug abuse in the text. The term drug abuse is used when referring to someone whose drug use has been successfully labeled as drug abuse.

2. It is beyond the scope of this chapter to review all available social theories of deviance. (Reviews can be found in Empey, 1978: NIJJDP, 1977.) I have selected strain, control, and cultural deviance theories because these theories appear to be the most scientifically adequate with direct implications for designing rehabilitation interventions for individuals. Other social theories, such as labeling (Becker, 1969; Lemert, 1967, 1969) and radical (Schur, 1973) theories question the efficacy of intervention with identified deviants. Their perspectives are valuable and can, in fact, guide critiques of the proposals offered in this chapter. However, my purpose in this chapter is to explore the possibilities for successful intervention with identified drug abusers, and for this purpose strain, social control, and cultural deviance theories have greatest relevance.

3. Hirschi (1969) asserts that absence of belief in the conventional moral order has an independent effect on delinquency. However, the items used by Hirschi to measure beliefs are the same attitudinal items used in the analysis of attachment (Sakumoto, 1978: 18). Because of the methodological problems in attempting to measure beliefs using survey techniques, the evidence regarding this proposed element of the bond is not discussed here (see Sakumoto, 1978: 18).

4. Researchers have not been consistent in the selection, scaling, and interpretation of commitment indicators. They have sought to distinguish between the impact of performance variables and variables indicating attachment to school. Some have used the performance measures as indicative of commitment to conventional activities (Hirschi, 1969; Sakumoto, 1978) while others have included apparent indicators of commitment to conventional activities (such as time spent on homework outside school) along with indicators of attachment (such as liking school) in developing scales (Elliott and Voss, 1974).

5. It is likely that there are organized forms of deviance which are supported and maintained by strong attachments among participants and strong beliefs in

nonconventional values. So-called Mafia families come to mind as examples. The argument here is that street drug abuse and adolescent delinquency do not share such characteristics.

6. Responses from 156 clients in this study followed up six months after leaving therapeutic communities (TCs) were consistent with these results. When asked in an open-ended question to name the most important influences leading to improvement since entering treatment, 32% of the respondents said that decisions or actions they had taken for themselves had been most helpful. No other answer was consistently given by more than 15% of the respondents. Similarly, when asked about the importance of a number of specific possible influences including treatment, family, and job opportunities on posttreatment functioning, 74% responded that "changes or decisions (I) made on (my) own "had helped a lot." In comparison, 53% said their families had "helped a lot," and 40% said treatment had "helped a lot." When asked in an open-ended question how the treatment program had helped them most, 48% of the former TC clients said it had helped them to take control of their own lives. No other answer was consistently given by more than 10% of the respondents. Apparently, these clients had come to view themselves as controlling their own lives.

7. See Pittel, 1978, for results of a comprehensive needs assessment survey which identified skills and resources needed by ex-abusers leaving treatment programs.

8. According to Smart (1976), those therapeutic community clients who become treatment practitioners themselves are likely to succeed after treatment. Apparently, the skills taught in therapeutic communities are best suited to preparing clients to function in similar social contexts, i.e., other treatment programs.

9. See Callan et al., 1975; Stanton, 1978; and the discussion of alumni associations in this book.

10. To illustrate, a study of 156 therapeutic community clients in Seattle found 47% living with some other adult in the larger community (parents, spouse/lover, or friend) six months after leaving treatment. Of these, only 14% (10) reported that the people they lived with used illegal drugs other than marijuana and hashish. Further, 64% (101) reported they had friends they tried to see regularly, and 62% (97) that they had at least one or more "close friends." Only 20% (20) of those who regularly saw friends reported that these friends used drugs other than marijuana, hashish, or alcohol. (Interestingly, only 13% of the sample reported having friends they had made in the therapeutic community, indicating the extent to which people separate themselves from treatment and those they knew there when they leave.)

Other results of the study also indicated the availability of supports to these former clients. Seventy percent (110) reported having found a new place to live since treatment. Of these, 65% (72) reported getting help finding it, and of these, 77% (56) said they got help from friends, coworkers, and family, while only 15% (11) got help from a secondary source such as a social service agency or treatment program. The remainder received help from "associates."

Fifty-six percent (87) of the clients reported having found a job since treatment. Of these, 56% (49) reported getting help in finding it. Sixty-nine percent (34) of those who got help were helped by friends, coworkers, or family, while only 16% were helped by a secondary source such as an employment service or treatment program.

Forty-five percent (70) of the clients had borrowed money and paid it back following treatment. Of these, 86% (60) had borrowed from friends, coworkers, or family members. Only 7% (5) reported borrowing from a secondary source such as a finance company or bank. The remainder borrowed from "associates."

These figures suggest that it is not unreasonable to expect as many as half the people leaving residential treatment programs to have primary social network members who can act as social supports for establishing a more conventional life-style.

11. A third approach, structural family therapy (Stanton, 1978), appears more appropriate during treatment than continuing care because it focuses specifically on eliminating pathogenic behaviors from family interaction patterns. Importantly, however, the ultimate goals of structural family therapy are similar to those we have outlined. Stanton and his colleagues (1978: 27) write: "Specifically, the addict must a) cease his dependence on drugs; b) achieve some measure of separation from his parents, typically by leaving home; c) be seen by parents, himself, and the community as successful in some activity such as work or school; d) achieve stable nondrug-related relationships outside the family." The continuing care models proposed in this paper are focused on achieving the last two goals.

12. See Callan et al., 1975: 19-25 for a more detailed description of this process.

13. These data are from the Center for Addiction Services evaluation study in Seattle on which the author collaborated and are reported here for the first time. The CAS evaluation study was supported by a grant from the Services Research Branch, National Institute on Drug Abuse, U.S. Department of Health, Education, and Welfare.

14. See Alley and Blanton (1978: 257-262) for an annotated bibliography on issues in using ex-addicts as service providers in drug rehabilitation programs.

REFERENCES

ABELSON, H., COHEN, R., and SCHRAYER, D. (1972) Public Attitudes Toward Marijuana. Part I. New Jersey: Response Analysis Corporation.

——— and RAPPAPORT, M. (1973) Drug Experience, Attitudes and Related Behavior Among Adolescents and Adults. New Jersey: Response Analysis Corporation.

AKERS, R. L. (1973) Deviant Behavior: A Social Learning Approach. Belmont, CA: Wadsworth.

ALEXANDER, B. K. and DIBB, G. S. (1975) "Opiate addicts and their parents." Family Process 14: 499-514.

ALINSKY, S. D. (1946) Reveille for Radicals. Chicago: Univ. of Chicago Press.

ALLEY, S. and BLANTON, J. (1978). "Paraprofessionals in mental health: an annotated bibliography from 1966 to 1977." Berkeley: Social Action Research Center.

ALTROCCHI, J. (1972) "Mental health consultation," in C. Eisdorfer and S. Golann (eds.) Handbook of Community Mental Health. New York: Appleton-Century-Crofts.

ARKIN, S. M. (1974) "Public employment and other elements in addict rehabilitation." Presented at the 1974 annual meeting of the National Association for the Prevention of Addiction to Narcotics.

ATTNEAVE, C. (1969) "Therapy in tribal settings and urban network intervention." Family Process 8 (September): 192-210.

BANDURA, A. (1969) Principles of Behavior Modification. New York: Holt, Rinehart and Winston.

BECKER, H. S. (1963) Outsiders. New York: Free Press.

——— (1966). "Introduction," pp. 1-31 in H. S. Becker (ed.) Social Problems: A
Modern Approach. New York: John Wiley.

——— (1969) "Deviance and the response of others," pp. 585-589 in Cressey and
Ward (eds.) Delinquency, Crime, and Social Process. New York: Harper and Row.

BELL, W. and BOAT, M. D. (1957) "Urban neighbors and informal social relations."
American Journal of Sociology 62: 391-398.

BERGIN, A. E. (1971) "The evaluation of therapeutic outcomes," in A. E. Bergin
and S. L. Garfield (eds.) Handbook of Psychotherapy and Behavior Change: An
Empirical Analysis. New York: John Wiley.

BURGESS, R. L., BURGESS, J. M., and ESVELDT, K. C. (1970) "An analysis of
generalized limitation." Journal of Applied Behavior Analysis 3 (Spring): 39-46.

CALLAN, D., GARRISON, J., and ZERGER, F. (1975) "Working with the families
and social networks of drug abusers." Journal of Psychedelic Drugs 7(1): 19-25.

CAPLAN, G. (1970) The Theory and Practice of Mental Health Consultation. New
York: Basic Books.

——— (1973) Support Systems and Community Mental Health. New York: Human
Sciences Press.

——— and GRUNEBAUM, H. (1967) "Perspectives on primary prevention: a review."
Archives of General Psychiatry 17: 331-346.

CAPLAN, G. and KILLILEA, M. (1976) Support Systems and Mutual Help. New
York: Grune and Stratton.

CARLSON, K. (1976) "Heroin, hassle and treatment: the importance of perceptual
differences." Addictive Diseases: An International Journal 2(4): 569-584.

CASSEL, J. (1976) "The contribution of the social environment to host resistance."
American Journal of Epidemiology 104: 107-123.

CAVAN, A. (1966) Liquor License: An Ethnography of Bar Behavior. Chicago:
Aldine.

CEVALINE, G. E. (1968) "Drug use on high school and college campuses." Journal
of School Health 38: 638-646.

CHERNISS, C. (1977) "Creating new consultation programs in community mental
health centers: analysis of a case study." Community Mental Health Journal 13:
133-141.

CLOWARD, R. A. and OHLIN, L. E. (1960) Delinquency and Opportunity: A
Theory of Delinquent Gangs. New York: Free Press.

COBB, S. (1976) "Social support as a moderator of life stress." Psychosomatic
Medicine 38(5): 300-311.

COHEN, A. K. (1955) Delinquent Boys: The Culture of the Gang. New York: Free
Press.

COLLINS, A. H. and PANCOAST, D. L. (1976) Natural Helping Networks: A
Strategy for Prevention. Washington DC: National Association of Social Workers.

CROOG, S. H., LIPSON, A., and LEVINE, S. (1972) "Help patterns in severe illness:
the roles of kin networks, non-family resources and illness: the roles of kin
networks, non-family resources and institutions." Journal of Marriage and the
Family 35(February): 32-41.

CRYNS, A. G. (1974) "Personality characteristics of heroin addicts in a methadone treatment program: an exploratory study." International Journal of the Addictions 9(2): 255-266.

DEITCH, D. (1974) "The end of the beginning: dilemmas of the paraprofessional in current drug abuse treatment." Unpublished manuscript.

DEMBO, R., SCHMEIDLER, J., and KOVAL, M. (1976) "Demographic, value and behavior correlates of marijuana use among middle class youth." Journal of Health and Social Behavior 17(June): 177-187.

DeRIOS, D. and SMITH, D. E. (1976) "Using or abusing: an anthropological approach to the study of psychoactive drugs." Journal of Psychedelic Drugs 8(3): 263-266.

DIXON, M. C. and WRIGHT, W. E. (1974) "An evaluation of policy related research on the effectiveness of juvenile delinquency prevention programs." Nashville, TN: George Peabody College for Teachers.

DuTOIT, B. (1977) Drugs, Rituals and Altered States of Consciousness. Rotterdam: A. A. Balkema.

DWORKIN, A. L. and DWORKIN, E. P. (1975) "A conceptual overview of selected consultation models." American Journal of Community Psychology 3: 151-159.

ELLIOTT, D. S. and VOSS, H. L. (1974) Delinquency and Dropout. Lexington, MA: Lexington Books.

EMPEY, L. T. (1978) American Delinquency: Its Meaning and Construction. Homewood, IL: Dorsey.

FAIRWEATHER, G. (1978) "The development, evaluation, and diffusion of rehabilitative programs: a social change process," pp. 295-308 in L. I. Stein and M. A. Test (eds.) Alternatives to Mental Hospital Treatment. New York: Plenum.

———, SANDERS, D. H., MAYNARD, H., and CRESSLER, D. L. (1969) Community Life for the Mentally Ill: An Alternative to Institutional Care. Chicago: Aldine.

FELDMAN, H. (1973) "Street status and drug users." Society 10: 32-38.

FELDMAN, R. E. (1978) "Collaborative consultation: a process for joint professional-consumer construction of primary prevention programs." Unpublished manuscript.

FIDDLE, S. (1976) "Sequences in addiction." Addictive Diseases, 2(4): 553-567.

FREASE, D. E. (1972) "The schools, self-concept and juvenile delinquency." British Journal of Criminology 12: 133-146.

GANS, H. L. (1962) The Urban Villagers. New York: Free Press.

GARTNER, A. and RIESSMAN, F. (1972) "Changing the professions," in R. Gross (ed.) The New Professionals. New York: Simon and Schuster.

GLASS, D. and SINGER, J. (1972) Urban Stress: Experiments on Noise and Social Stressors. New York: Academic Press.

GOLDENBERG, I. I. and KEATINGE, E. (1973) "Businessmen and therapists: prejudices against employment," pp. 92-112 in H. H. Liebowitz (ed.) Vocational Rehabilitation of the Drug Abuser, Vol. 4. Washington DC: Youth Projects, Inc.

GOODE, E. (1969) "Multiple drug use among marihuana smokers." Social Problems 17: 50-56.

GRAZIANO, A. M. (1969) "Clinical innovation and the mental health power structure: a social case history." American Psychologist 24: 10-18.

HAMPDEN-TURNER, C. (1977) Sane Asylum: Inside the Delancey Street Foundation. New York: William Morrow.

HARBIN, H. T. and MAZIAR, H. M. (1975) "The families of drug abusers: a literature review." Family Process 14: 411-431.

HARDING, M. and ZINBERG, N. E. (1977) "The effectiveness of the subculture in developing rituals and social sanctions for controlled drug use," in B. DuToit (ed.) Drugs, Rituals and Altered States of Consciousness. Rotterdam: A. A. Balkema.

HAWKINS, J. D. (1978) "Some suggestions for self-help approaches with street drug abusers." Unpublished manuscript.

HEALY, W., BRONNER, A., and SHIMBERG, M. (1935) "The close of another chapter in criminology." Mental Hygiene 19: 208-222.

HINDELANG, M. J. (1973) "Causes of delinquency: a partial replication and extension." Social Problems 20(4): 471-487.

———, HIRSCHI, T., and WEIS, J. G. (1979) "Correlates of delinquency: the illusion of discrepancy between self-report and official measures." Unpublished manuscript.

HIRSCHI, T. (1969) Causes of Delinquency. Berkeley: Univ. of California Press.

JOHNSTON, L. D., BACHMAN, J. G., and O'MALLEY, P. M. (1977) Drug Use Among American High School Students. Rockville, MD: National Institute on Drug Abuse.

JOSEPHSON, L. (1974) "Trends in adolescent marijuana use," in E. Josephson and E. E. Carroll (eds.) Drug Use: Epidemiological and Sociological Approaches. New York: John Wiley.

KANDEL, D. (1973) "Adolescent marijuana use: role of parents and peers." Science (September): 1067-1069.

——— (1974) "Inter- and intragenerational influences on adolescent marijuana use." Journal of Social Issues 30(2): 107-135.

KELLY, D. H. and BALCH, R. W. (1971) "Social origins and school failure." Pacific Sociological Review 14(October): 413-430.

KING, J. (1969) The Probation and After-Care Service. London: Butterworths.

LAWRENCE, T. S. and VELLERMAN, J. D. (1974) "Correlates of student drug use in a suburban high school." Psychiatry 37(May): 129-136.

LEMERT, E. (1967) Human Deviance, Social Problems, and Social Control. New York: Prentice-Hall.

——— (1969) "Primary and secondary deviation," pp. 603-607 in Cressey and Ward (eds.) Delinquency, Crime, and Social Process. New York: Harper and Row.

Liaison Task Panel on Psychoactive Drug Use Misuse (1978) Report to the President's Commission on Mental Health.

LINDEN, E. W. (1974) "Interpersonal ties and delinquent behavior." Ph.D. dissertation, University of Washington.

LINDEN, E. W. and HACKLER, J. C. (1973) "Affective ties and delinquency." Pacific Sociological Review 16: 27-46.

LINDESMITH, A. (1947) Opiate addiction. Bloomington: Principia Press.

——— (1965) The Addict and the Law. Bloomington: Indiana Univ. Press.

LITWAK, E. and SZELENYI, I. (1969) "Primary group structures and their functions: kin, neighbors, and friends." American Sociological Review 34: 465-481.

MacANDREW, C. and EDGERTON, E. (1969) Drunken Comportment: A Social Explanation. Chicago: Aldine.

MacELVEEN, P. M. (1977) "Social networks," in D. Longo and R. Williams (eds.) Clinical Practice in Psychosocial Nursing: Assessment and Intervention. New York: Appleton-Century-Crofts.

MacLENNAN, B. W., QUINN, R. D., and SCHROEDER, D. (1975) "The scope of community health consultation," in F. V. Mannino, B. W. MacLennan, and M. F.

Shore (eds.) The Practice of Mental Health Consultation (DHEW, No. (ADM) 74-112). Washington, DC: U.S. Government Printing Office.

Macro Systems (1975) "Three year follow-up study of clients enrolled in treatment programs in New York City." Unpublished manuscript.

MADDUX, J. F., BERLINER, A., and BATES, W. F. (1971) Engaging Opioid Addicts in a Continuum of Services: A Community Based Study in the San Antonio Area. Behavioral Science Monograph #71-7. Texas Christian University Press.

MANDELL, W. and AMSEL, Z. (1973) "Status of addicts treated under the NARA program (HMS 142-72-37). Department of Mental Hygiene, School of Hygiene and Public Health, Johns Hopkins University (Reprinted by Executive Office of the President, Special Action Office for Drug Abuse Prevention).

MANDELL, W., GOLDSCHMIDT, P., and GROVER, P. (1973) Interdrug Final Report: An Evaluation of Treatment Programs for Drug Abusers, Vol 2: Summary. Baltimore: Johns Hopkins Univ. Press.

MANNINO, F. V., MacLENNAN, B. W. and SHORE, M. F. (1975) The Practice of Mental Health Consultation (DHEW No. (ADM) 74-112). Washington, DC: U.S. Government Printing Office.

MARLATT, G. A. and GORDON, J. R. (1978) "Determinants of relapse: implications for the maintenance of behavior change." Seattle: University of Washington Alcoholism and Drug Abuse Institute, Technical Report 78-07.

MATZA, D. (1964) Delinquency and Drift. New York: John Wiley.

MECHANIC, D. (1978) "Alternatives to mental hospital treatment: a sociological perspective," pp. 309-320 in L. I. Stein and M. A. Test (eds.) Alternatives to Mental Hospital Treatment. New York: Plenum.

MERTON, R. K. (1937) "Social structure and anomie." American Sociological Review 3(October): 672-682.

MILLER, W. B. (1958) "Lower-class culture as a generating milieu of gang delinquency." Journal of Social Issues 14(Summer): 5-19.

MIZRUCHI, E. H. and PERRUCCI, R. (1970) "Prescription, proscription, and permissiveness: aspects of norms and deviant drinking behavior," in G. L. Maddox (ed.) The Domesticated Drug: Drinking Among Collegians. New Haven, CT: College and University Press.

National Commission on Resources for Youth (1974) New Roles for Youth. New York: Citation Press.

NIDA (1978) "Nonresidential self-help organizations and the drug abuse problem: an exploratory conference" (DHEW No. (ADM) 78-752). Washington, DC: U.S. Government Printing Office.

NIJJDP (1977) Preventing Delinquency: A Comparative Analysis of Delinquency Prevention Theory. Vol. 1 of 9. Washington, DC: Office of Juvenile Justice and Delinquency Prevention, U.S. Department of Justice.

NYE, F. I. (1958) Family Relationships and Delinquent Behavior. New York: John Wiley.

PANCOAST, D. L. (1970) "Boarding home providers for released mental hospital patients." Unpublished manuscript.

PATTERSON, S. and TWENTE, E. (1972) "Utilization of human resources for mental health." Lawrence, KA: Univ. of Kansas School of Social Welfare.

PINK, W. T. and WHITE, M. F. [eds.] (1973) Delinquency Prevention: A Conference Perspective on Issues and Directions. Portland: Regional Research Institute.

PITTEL, S. M. (1974) "Addicts in wonderland: sketches for a map of a vocational frontier." Journal of Psychedelic Drugs 6: 231-242.

——— (1977a) "Addict aftercare: essence or afterthought." Presented at University of Washington Alcoholism and Drug Abuse Institute's Fourth Annual Summer Conference, Seattle, WA.

——— (1977b) Community Support Systems for Addict Aftercare. Walnut Creek, CA: Pacific Institute for Research and Evaluation.

——— (1978) Addict Aftercare Needs and Services. Walnut Creek, CA: Pacific Institute for Research and Evaluation.

POLAK, P. R. (1978) "A comprehensive system of alternatives to psychiatric hospitalization," pp. 115-137 in L. I. Stein and M. A. Test (eds.) Alternatives to Mental Hospital Treatment. New York: Plenum.

POLK, K. (1969) "Class strain and rebellion among adolescents." Social Problems 17: 214-224.

POLK, K. and KOBRIN, S. (1972) Delinquency Prevention Through Youth Development. Youth Development and Delinquency Prevention Administration, U.S. Department of Health, Education, and Welfare.

PREBLE, E. and CASEY, J. J. (1969) "Taking care of business: the heroin user's life on the streets." International Journal of the Addictions 4(1): 1-24.

PREBLE, E. and MILLER, T. (1977) "Methadone, wine, and welfare," in R. Weppner (ed.) Street Ethnography: Selected Studies of Crime and Drug Use in Natural Settings. Beverly Hills: Sage Publications.

PRESNALL, L. F. (1974) "The employment and training of exdrug users: a three way intersection." Presented at the 1974 Annual Meeting of the National Association for the Prevention of Addiction to Narcotics.

RAY, O. S. (1972) Drugs, Society, and Human Behavior. St. Louis: C. V. Mosby.

RECKLESS, W. (1961) The Crime Problem. New York: Appleton-Century-Crofts.

———, DINITZ, C. S., and MURRAY, E. (1956) "Self concept as an insulator against delinquency." American Sociological Review 21: 744-746.

REISS, A. J. (1951) "Delinquency as failure of personal and social controls." American Sociological Review 16: 196-207.

ROFFMAN, R. A. (1973) "Heroin and social welfare." Social Work 18(1): 22-32.

——— (1965) "The Federal pre-release guidance center: operating strategies and mandate." MSW thesis, University of Michigan.

ROMIG, D. (1978) Justice for Our Children: An Examination of Juvenile Delinquent Rehabilitation Programs. Lexington, MA: D.C. Heath.

SAKUMOTO, K. N. (1978) "Attachment to delinquent friends: peer influences and delinquent involvement." M.A. thesis, University of Washington.

SCHUR, E. M. (1973) Radical Nonintervention: Rethinking the Delinquency Problem. Englewood Cliffs, NJ: Prentice-Hall.

SEBALD, H. (1972) "The pursuit of 'instantness' in technocratic society and youth's psychedelic drug use." Adolescence 7: 343-350.

SEGAL, S. P. and AVIRAM, U. (1978) The Mentally Ill in Community-Based Sheltered Care: A Study of Community Care and Social Integration. New York: John Wiley.

SELDEN, N. E. (1972) The Family of the Addict: A Review of the Literature. International Journal of the Addictions 7: 79-107.

SELDMAN, N. (1977) "Neighborhood planning council." Communities: Journal of Cooperative Living 25: 22-26.

SELIGMAN, M. P. (1975) Helplessness: On Depression, Development, and Death. San Francisco: Freeman.

SHAW, C. R. and McKAY, H. D. (1942) Juvenile Delinquency and Urban Areas. Chicago: Univ. of Chicago Press.

SIGNELL, K. A. and SCOTT, P. A. (1972) "Training in consultation: a crisis in role transition." Community Mental Health Journal 8: 149-160.

SMART, R. G. (1976) "Outcome studies of therapeutic community and halfway house treatment for addicts." International Journal of the Addictions 11(1): 153-159.

——— and FEJER, D. (1972) "Drug use among adolescents and their parents: closing the generation gap in mood modification." Journal of Abnormal Psychology 70: 153-160.

SOKOLOVSKY, J. and COHEN, C. (1978) "Personal networks of ex-mental patients in a Manhattan SRO hotel." Human Organization 37: 5-15.

SOROSIAK, F. M., THOMAS, E., and BALET, F. (1976) "Adolescent drug use: an analysis." Psychological Reports 38: 211-221.

SPECK, R. V. and ATTNEAVE, C.L. (1973) Family Networks: Retribulization and Healing. New York: Behavioral Publications.

SPEVAK, M. and PIHL, R. O. (1976) "Nonmedical drug use by high school students: a three year survey study." International Journal of the Addictions 11(5): 755-792.

STANTON, M. D. (1978) "Some outcome results and aspects of structural family therapy with drug addicts," in D. Smith, S. Anderson, M. Buston, T. Chung, N. Gottlieb, and W. Harvey (eds.) A Multicultural View of Drug Abuse: The Selected Proceedings of the National Drug Abuse Conference 1977. Cambridge, MA: Schenkman.

———, TODD, T. C. HEARD, D. B., KIRSCHNER, S., KLEIMAN, J. I., MOWATT, D. T., RILEY, P., SCOTT, S. M., and VANDEUSEN, J. M. (1978) "Heroin addiction as a family phenomenon: a new conceptual model." American Journal of Drug and Alcohol Abuse 5(2).

STEIN, L. I. and TEST, M. A. (1978) "An alternative to mental hospital treatment," pp. 43-55 in L. I. Stein and M.A. Test (eds.) Alternatives to Mental Hospital Treatment. New York: Plenum.

STEPHENS, R. and LEVINE, S. (1971) "The street addict role: implications for treatment." Psychiatry 34: 351-357.

——— and McBRIDE, D. C. (1976) "Becoming a street addict." Human Organizations 35(1): 87-93.

STREIT, F., HALSTED, D. L., and PASCALE, P. J. (1974) "Differences among youthful users/non-users of drugs based on their perceptions of parental behavior." International Journal of the Addictions 9(October): 749-755.

STREIT, F. and OLIVER, H. G. (1972) "The child's perception of his family and its relationship to drug use." Drug Forum 3: 283-289.

SUSSMAN, M. B. (1953) "The help patterns for the middle class family." American Sociological Review 18(February): 22-28.

SUTHERLAND, E. H. and CRESSEY, D. R. (1970) Principles of Criminology. New York: J. B. Lippincott.

SUTTER, A. G. (1966) "The world of the righteous dope fiend." Issues in Criminology 2: 177-222.

——— (1969) "Worlds of drug use on the street scene," in D. R. Cressey and D. A. Ward (eds.) Delinquency, Crime, and Social Process. New York: Harper and Row.

Systems Sciences, Inc. (1975) "Follow-up of ex-clients of the District of Columbia's narcotic treatment administration programs, 1970-1973." Unpublished manuscript.

Task Force on Federal Heroin Addiction Programs (1972) Introduction to Treatment and Rehabilitation. (Reprinted in Grassroots, May 1974, supplement: 14-19.)

TEC, N. (1972a) "The peer group and marijuana use." Crime and Delinquency 18: 298-309.

——— (1972b) "Socio-cultural context of marijuana." International Journal of the Addictions 7(4): 655-669.

——— (1974) "Parent-child drug abuse: generational continuity or adolescent deviancy." Adolescence 9(35): 351-364.

TEST, M. A. and STEIN, L. I. (1978) "Training in community living: research design and results," pp. 57-74 in L. I. Stein and M. A. Test (eds.) Alternatives to Mental Hospital Treatment. New York: Plenum.

TITTLE, C. R., VILLEMEZ, W. J., and SMITH, D. A. (1978) "The myth of social class and criminality." American Sociological Review 43(5): 643-656.

TOCH, H., GRANT, J. D., and GALVIN, R. T. (1975) Agents of Change: A Study in Police Reform. Cambridge, MA: Schenkman.

TOLONE, W. L. and DERMOTT, D. (1975) "Some correlates of drug use among high school youth in a midwestern rural community." International Journal of the Addictions 10(5): 761-777.

TOLSDORF, C. C. (1976) "Social networks, support and coping: an exploratory study." Family Process 15: 407-417.

TRUE, W. R. and TRUE, J. H. (1977) "Network analysis as a methodological approach to the study of drug use in a Latin city." in R. S. Weppner (ed.) Street Ethnography. Beverly Hills: Sage Publications.

WACKER, N. and HAWKINS, J. D. (1978) "Verbal performances and addict conversion: toward a linguistic understanding of the successes and failures of therapeutic communities." Unpublished manuscript.

WALDORF, D. (1972) Careers in Dope. Englewood Cliffs, NJ: Prentice-Hall.

WEINMAN, B. and KLEINER, R. J. (1978) "The impact of community living and community member intervention on the adjustment of the chronic psychotic patient," pp. 139-159 in L. I. Stein and M.A. Test (eds.) Alternatives to Mental Hospital Treatment. New York: Plenum.

WEIS, J. G. (1977) "Comparative analysis of social control theories of delinquency," in Preventing Delinquency: A Comparative Analysis of Delinquency Prevention Theory. Vol. 1 of 9. National Institute for Juvenile Justice and Delinquency Prevention, Office of Juvenile Justice and Delinquency Prevention, Law Enforcement Assistance Administration, U.S. Department of Justice.

——— (1979) "Peer influence and delinquent behavior." Unpublished manuscript.

WEISS, R. S. (1974) "Parents without partners as a supplementary community," in R. S. Weiss (ed.) Loneliness. Cambridge, MA: MIT Press.

WESSON, D. R., SMITH, D. E., and LERNER, S. E. (1975) "Streetwise and non-streetwise polydrug typology: myth or reality?" Journal of Psychedelic Drugs 7: 121-134.

WEST, H. J. (1975) "Adolescent drug attitudes: a seven year study on marijuana and LSD." Dissertation Abstracts International 35(9-A): 5944.

WILKINSON, R. (1970) The Prevention of Drinking Problems. Alcohol Control and Cultural Influences. New York: Oxford Univ. Press.

WOODY, R. H. (1975) "Process and behavioral consultation." American Journal of Community Psychology 3: 277-285.

2

THE CLIENT AS FAMILY MEMBER
Aspects of Continuing Treatment

M. DUNCAN STANTON

In recent years, the importance of the family in the genesis, maintenance, and alleviation of drug problems has received increasing recognition. A number of literature reviews (Harbin and Maziar, 1975; Klagsbrun and Davis, 1977; Salmon and Salmon, 1977; Seldin, 1972; Stanton, 1978c, 1979a) and over 370 related papers (Stanton, 1978a) have emerged. People in the field have come to realize that unless one takes an extreme genetic or sociological view of addiction, drug problems develop within a family context and most addicts are not isolates who have no primary ties. In other words, problems that arise in addicts' lives can usually be linked to the interpersonal forces and relationships that surround them. Such forces come to bear both during treatment and into the future—they are an integral part of the continuity of care. While it is not disputed that many other factors (e.g., environmental, physiological, economic, conditioning, and genetic) can also be critical, family variables have to assume a position of salience in the arena of addictive symptomatology.

SOME BASIC CONCEPTS

Before proceeding to the specifics of addiction, it is important to provide some conceptual clarification vis-á-vis the family and the role of symptoms within it. A major problem which has existed both in the drug abuse area and in the larger field of mental health, has been the simplistic view of the family which has predominated. Except for consideration of the early developmental years, the family has been viewed as a more or less inert influence which, at worst, can bring additional "stress" on the symptomatic member. However, its importance in symptom *maintenance* has generally gone unrecognized. In instances where the family *is* mentioned, discussion has usually been couched in, for example, mother-addict or father-addict dyads, or of the characteristics of some people as individuals; the concept of the family as a *system* of people composed of the members *and* their interactions has rarely been applied. Such individually and dyadically oriented concepts are not really in tune with what we have learned about families over the past 20-25 years.

Related to the above is the role of the symptom per se within the family system. A symptom can be seen as a particular kind of behavior which functions as a homeostatic mechanism regulating family transactions (Jackson, 1965) i.e., it maintains the dynamic equilibrium among the members. It is a communicative act which serves as a sort of contract between two or more members and often occurs when a person is "in an impossible situation and is trying to break out of it" (Haley, 1973: 44). The person is locked in a sequence or pattern with the rest of his family or significant others and cannot see a way to alter it through nonsymptomatic means (Stanton, 1979b). More specifically, the symptom may help, for instance, in the labeling of a member as helpless and incompetent and, therefore, unable to leave home. It might serve as a problem which unifies the family and keeps it intact, much as a catastrophe unites people who experience it together. Similarly, it might function as a beacon light, drawing the attention of other members to the symptom bearer and away from their own difficulties. These are just a few of the functions which a symptom can serve within a family homeostatic system.

Lennard and Allen (1973) have emphasized how, in order for drug abuse treatment to "take hold," the social context of the abuser much be changed. Applying this to the family, one could assert, as have Bowen (1966), Haley (1962), and others, that in order for the symptom to change, the *family system* must change. Conversely, treatment which changes an individual has to also be affecting his interpersonal system. However, if broader system change (rather than change primarily in the individual) does not occur, the chances for prolonged cure are reduced, for there can be considerable pressure on the "improved" symptomatic member to revert to the old ways. This idea has important implications for the way in which drug abuse treatment is approached.

It is helpful to consider symptoms as they fit into the family life cycle. Most families encounter similar stages as they progress through life, such as birth of first child, child first attending school, children leaving home, death of a parent or spouse, etc. These are crisis points, which, although some times tough to get through, are usually weathered without inordinate difficulty. On the other hand, symptomatic families develop problems because they are not able to adjust to the transition. They become "stuck" at a particular point. Like a broken record, they repetitively go through the process without advancing beyond it. An example is the family which repeatedly goes through the addiction/readdiction cycle. Another is the family of the youthful schizophrenic who will not let him leave home, but keeps him in a role of being incompetent—even when he palpably demonstrates his capabilities (Haley, 1973).

Sometimes different symptoms are interchangeable. A specific symptom may not always be as important as the fact that the bearer has *some* kind of problem. If, for example, the symptom serves as a rallying point, then being thrown in jail might serve as effectively to mobilize the family as would taking an overdose. In such a case, the apparent dissimilarity of these two behaviors becomes academic, for they are functionally equivalent.

The discussion thus far has dealt with events and behaviors that often lie outside the purview and experience of most treaters; the actions of family members other than the symptom bearer are rarely or only occasionally observed within the context of most conventional treatment settings. When the larger system actually is encompassed, we must make a conceptual leap into new ways of thinking about symptoms such as substance abuse. Such a view is radically different from and discontinuous with individually or intrapsychically oriented cause-and-effect explanations. It is a new orientation to human problems. Einstein stated that the theory to which we subscribe determines what we see, and it is hoped that through application of this different perspective, the reader will be better able to understand the material to follow.

ADDICT FAMILY PATTERNS AND STRUCTURES

It is not the purpose of this chapter to discuss the extensive body of demographic, psychosocial, and interactional literature which has accumulated on the families of drug abusers. This has been done in the aforementioned reviews. Instead, a brief overview will be given on the predominant patterns and structures which have emerged from the body of existent research. Their relevance for treatment will also be noted. Emphasis here and throughout the chapter will be on findings with families in which a member shows heavy, compulsive drug use rather than occasional or experimental use. Usually such people have been referred to as "addicts."

Family of Origin

Drug misuse appears initially to be an adolescent phenomenon. It is tied to the normal, albeit troublesome, process of growing up, experimenting with new behaviors, becoming self-assertive, developing close (usually heterosexual) relationships with people outside the family, and leaving home. Kandel et al. (1976) propose from their data that there are three stages in adolescent drug use and each has different concomitants. The first is the use of legal drugs, such as alcohol, and is mainly a social phenomenon. The second involves use of marijuana and is also primarily peer influenced. The third stage, frequent use of other illegal drugs, appears contingent more on the quality of the parent-adolescent relationship than on other factors. Thus, it is concluded that more serious drug misuse is predominantly a family phenomenon.

The importance of adolescence in the misuse of drugs becomes more apparent when family structure is considered. The prototypic drug abuser family—as described in most of the literature—is one in which one parent is intensely involved with the abuser, while the other is more punitive, distant and/or absent. Usually the overinvolved, indulgent, overprotective parent is of the opposite sex. Sometimes this overinvolvement even reaches the point of incest (Cuskey, 1977; Ellinwood et al., 1966; Wellisch et al., 1970). Further, the abusing offspring may serve a function for the parents, either as a channel for their communication, or as a disrupter whose distracting behavior keeps their own fights from crystallizing. Conversely, the addict may seek a "sick state" in order to position himself, childlike, as the focus of the parents' attention. Consequently, the onset of adolescence, with its threat of losing the adolescent to outsiders, heralds parental panic. The family then becomes stuck at this developmental stage and a chronic, repetitive process sets in, centered on the individuation, growing up and leaving of the "identified" patient (Alexander and Dibb, 1975; Cannon, 1976; Huberty, 1975; Noone and Reddig, 1976; Reilly, 1976). The use of drugs is a paradoxical solution to the dilemma of staying or leaving, for it allows a certain level of competence (e.g., hustling) within a framework of incompetence, i.e., it is *pseudo-individuation* (Stanton et al., 1978). It is also consonant with the frequent substance abuse which parents in many of these families show. In addition, much as the behavior of the young schizophrenic keeps his family together by giving them a problem to focus on and thus avoiding parental dissension or separation, the use of drugs can have adaptive consequences (Davis et al., 1974; Haley, 1973). This can extend even into adulthood, and there is evidence that the majority of drug addicts maintain close family ties up to age 30 and, in many cases, beyond (see Stanton et al., 1978, for a review of these studies).

Based upon the literature and upon their own studies, Stanton et al. (1978) have presented a conceptual model for heroin addiction as a cyclical (vs. linear) family homeostatic process. Although the model has a number of components and covers many facets of the addictive process, the central thesis is as follows:

> Heroin addiction can be thought of as part of a *cyclical process* involving three or more individuals, commonly the addict and his two parents. These people form an intimate, interdependent, interpersonal system. At times the equilibrium of this interpersonal system is threatened, such as when discord between the parents is amplified to the point of impending separation. When this happens the addict becomes activated, his behavior changes, and he creates a situation that dramatically *focuses attention upon himself*. This behavior can take a number of forms. For example, he may lose his temper, come home high, commit a serious crime, or overdose on drugs. Whatever its form, however, this action allows the parents to shift focus from their marital conflict to a parental overinvolvement with him. In effect, the movement is from an unstable dyadic interaction (e.g., parents alone) to a more stable triadic interaction (parents and addict). By focusing on the problems of the addict, no matter how severe or life-threatening, the parents choose a course that is apparently safer than dealing with long-standing marital conflicts. Consequently—after the marital crisis has been successfuly avoided—the addict shifts to a less provocative stance and begins to behave more competently. This is a new step in the sequence. As the addict demonstrates increased competence, indicating that he can function independently of the family—for example by getting a job, getting married, enrolling in a methadone program or detoxifying— the parents are left to deal with their previously unresolved conflicts. At this point in the cycle marital tensions increase and the threat of separation arises. The addict then behaves in an attention-getting or self-destructive way, and the dysfunctional triadic cycle is again completed. [pp. 161-162]

It should be emphasized that in the above paradigm all three (or more) members play a part. Each contributes a piece of the action and any one of them can behave in such a way as to initiate the cycle or take it to the next phase. To break the model down into its separate components (e.g., "weak father," "overprotective mother," or "wastrel son") is to overlook their individual, but interdependent, contributions.

Family of Procreation

Concerning marriage and the family of procreation, it has generally been concluded that the (usually heterosexual) dyadic relationships that addicts become involved in are a repetition of the nuclear family of origin, with roles and interaction patterns similar to those seen with the opposite-sex parent (Harbin and Maziar, 1975; Seldin, 1972; Taylor et al., 1966; Wold and Diskind, 1961). In a certain number of these marriages both spouses are addicted, although it is more common for one or neither of them to be drug dependent at the beginning of the relationship (Fram and Hoffman, 1973; Wellisch et al., 1970). If the marital union is formed during addiction, it is more likely to dissolve after methadone treatment than if initiated at some other time (Africano et al., 1973). Also, nonaddicted wives tend to find their husbands' methadone program to be more satisfactory than do addicted wives (Clark et al., 1972). Equally important, the rate of marriage for male addicts is half that which would be expected, while the rate for multiple marriages is above average for both sexes (O'Donnell, 1969). Chein et al. (1964), Scher (1966), and Stanton et al. (1978) have noted how parental permission is often quite tentative for the addict to have a viable marriage. Although he attempts flight into marriage, there is often a certain pull or encouragement for him to go back. Consequently, he usually returns home, defeated, to his parents.

Family Factors Which Neutralize
Treatment for Addiction

From the early papers (e.g., Berliner, 1966-1967; Hirsch, 1961; Mason, 1958; Wolk and Diskind, 1961) to the present, many writers have attested to the importance of the family in the maintenance of addiction. Not only is the drug taking of one member often overlooked by relatives, it is frequently either openly or covertly encouraged (Harbin and Mazier, 1975; Klagsbrun and Davis, 1977; Seldin, 1972; Stanton, 1979; Wellisch and Kaufman, 1975). Further, in addition to supporting the drug-taking pattern, the family may actually work to sabotage those treatment efforts which begin to succeed in reducing or eliminating it. Examples of this have been commonly reported in the literature, such as the wife of the recovering alcoholic who buys him a bottle of liquor for his birthday, or the parent of the heroin addict who gives him money to purchase drugs. Thus the family is crucial in determining whether or not someone *remains* addicted.

Addicts who are married or are living with a spouse-type partner are involved in at least two intimate interpersonal systems—that of the "marriage" and that of the family of origin. Since more time is spent in the marital context, this system would appear to be more influential in maintaining the drug pattern. A number of writers (e.g., Gasta and Schut, 1977; Wellisch et al., 1970) have emphasized the importance of drugs in many such relationships, and Hejinian and Pittel (1978) give data indicating that while addicts' spouse-type partners generally voice strong support for the abuser's abstinence, there is also evidence for an unconscious collusion to remain addicted. However, Stanton et al. (1978) have underscored the interdependence between the marital couple and one or both of their respective families of origin. In line with the observations of Chein et al. (1964) and Scher (1966), they have observed that a "rebound" effect often occurs from marital quarrels, resulting in the addict returning to his parents. These authors also note that couples therapy often stresses the marriage and brings on another rebound, so that treatment has to begin by including both systems; the key is to start with the parental-addict triad and move more toward the family of procreation in accordance with parents' readiness to "release" the addict (Stanton and Todd, 1978; Stanton et al., 1978).

THE FAMILY AND POSTTREATMENT ADJUSTMENT

A number of studies have been performed on the relationship between posttreatment adjustment and the effectiveness, as a support system, of the client's family. Concerning the research on nondrug clients, there has been some inconsistency, but the most common findings for posthospital adjustment indicate better prognosis if the client: (a) lives with his/her family of procreation rather than family of origin, (b) occupies a central (rather than peripheral) position in the family, and (c) lives in an intact family (Dintiz et al., 1961; Ferber et al., 1967; Freeman and Simmons, 1963; Kowalewski, 1972; Mannino and Shore, 1974; Meyer and Borgatta, 1959; Miller, 1967).

Pertaining to drug abuse, Vaillant (1966b) found that a high percentage of heroin addicts returning to New York City from the drug program at Lexington, Kentucky, went to live either with their mothers or a female blood relative; the rate of readdiction in this group was also very high. Thompson (1973) noted a similar pattern. Zahn and Ball's (1972) data with Puerto Rican addicts indicated that cure was associated with living with one's spouse, while noncure tied in with living with one's parents or relatives. Stanton et al. (1978) observed that prognosis was better for addict families in which the parents were most easily able to release the addict to spouse or outsiders during the course of treatment.

One aspect of this topic which has rarely been dealt with in the literature has to do with the potential benefits of reaching new stages in the family life cycle. It is this author's clinical impression, for instance, that when some addicts reach the point of parenthood, i.e., have their own children, they respond appropriately to the additional responsibility and cease or reduce their drug taking; the parental role takes precedence. A somewhat more chagrining variation on this theme is when they give one or more of their children to their parents as a means of "buying" freedom (Boszormenyi-Nagy and Spark, 1973; Stanton et al., 1978). Along these lines, the change sometimes appears to generate from the other end, with the addict's parents accepting their new role as grandparents (without necessarily adopting a grandchild); as a consequence they may ease the pressure on their own drug-addicted offspring to remain in an infantile or immature role.

While much of the above discussion has dealt with ways in which the family can neutralize the treatment effort, family involvement can also prove beneficial (Dell Orto, 1974). The inherent leverage of significant others can be used to help the drug abusing member *overcome* his problem, rather than serving as a force which *maintains* it. To this point, Eldred and Washington (1976) found in interviews with 158 male and female heroin addicts that the people the patients thought would be most helpful to them in their attempts to give up drugs were the members of their families-of-origins or their in-laws; second and third choices were an opposite sex partner and the patient himself or herself. Further, Levy (1972) indicated in a five-year follow-up of narcotic addicts that patients who successfully overcame drug abuse most often had family support.

FAMILY SERVICES

Data from a recent survey of 2,012 drug treatment facilities by Coleman and Davis (1978) indicate that the majority of our nation's drug programs provide some kind of family services—in many cases family or marital therapy—as at least one part of their therapeutic armamentarium.

This section will discuss several of these, with particular emphasis on the growing field of family therapy.

Family and Marital Therapies

In a sense almost any kind of family treatment has a built-in continuity-of-care component. This is because, by engaging the interpersonal system of the identified patient (IP) in treatment, one is in effect bringing a major facet of the outside environment into the office. Conversely, by working with this natural system *in vitro,* one is extending one's treatment directly to the outside world (*in vivo*). In other words, if such a system is changed, then the environment of the client is changed.

There are real problems in molding family approaches to therapy to fit the treatment modalities which have historically been predominant in the drug abuse field. Schwartzman (1975, 1977a, 1977b; Schwartzman and Kroll, 1977) has stressed some of these points repeatedly, as have Berliner (1966-1967) and others. Part of the problem stems from the conceptual gulf that divides family treatment from the others. Nonfamily approaches tend either to try to replace the family or ignore it. For instance, in its purest form, the therapeutic community (TC) is orthogonal to family approaches in its operations. Its ethos holds that family relationships are destructive influences which are to be avoided; hence a substitute family is formed from the members of the community. In contrast, a family perspective leads to the view that the TC is too divorced from the "real" world, and that upon graduation or discharge the client will reencounter the same, unchanged forces he left when he entered. Consequently, and partly because of the high rates of either early dropouts from inpatient settings or readdiction following discharge (cf., Berliner, 1966-1967), it does seem reasonable to consider alternative approaches to treating addictive problems.

The other predominant mode is pharmacological substitution (e.g., methadone). With this approach the family is not considered, and the emphasis is more on the physiological aspects of the addiction. Family variables lie pretty much outside its purview. They are not so much intentionally condemned as they are simply not considered.

The crux of the problem, and the point at which family and the other two approaches are antithetical, lies with the way in which nonfamily treatments can serve to *reinforce the family structure and status quo.* Both of them function to keep the IP in his designated "sick" role; the individual rather than the family is seen as the problem. Methadone maintenance, at least initially, can serve to perpetuate the problem by palpably sanctioning the idea that the IP is handicapped and unable to be drug-free. Such an idea would be more credible if it were not for the plethora of articles and studies documenting how the family goes through a crisis when the IP gets better. As for the TC, it has been noted in the literature how addict families often show great tolerance for any treatment program which continues to keep the "patient" label on the addict. This is particularly true in tightly structured, drug-free communities, where the IP is treated as a "junkie" even when he is off drugs. Once again, his family role and structure are, however unintentionally, reinforced.

A related issue has to do with responsibility. In most conventional drug treatments a person becomes symptomatic, is handed over to the therapeutic agency, treated, and then (usually) returned to his family and environs. From the family's view, this is "black box" therapy because they are usually not directly involved. They are also therefore absolved of any responsibility for its success or failure. This happens even though the client is someone they have raised, and even though they may function, consciously or not, in ways which undercut the efforts of the agency. His reentry is with the understanding that he is to adopt a different role and level of functioning, but the family (or for that matter, the community) has not been prepared to receive this new, changed, member. Thus, the old forces, patterns, and pressures again take hold. The sad part of this scenario is not only that cure is impeded, but the well-meaning and hard-working agency is left feeling responsible for the failure.

It might seem from the above that a straw man has been set up and knocked down. To some extent this is true. Many treatment programs combine family approaches with other modalities. However, it is hard to do this without making certain concessions which are not conducive to effecting family change. For example, even *discussing* adjustments in methadone dosage with the family is a form of "buying into" the idea that the IP is a handicapped person who needs his (legally sanctioned) drugs. Further, even if the family meets with the IP for treatment at the TC, they are seeing him amidst a group of peers who are problem-prone and "incompetent," thus making it harder for him to be viewed as normal. In short, there is a need to closely scrutinize our service delivery systems to insure that their operational models help them to alleviate rather than perpetuate the problems they are charged with correcting.

Relevant Studies. The literature on family treatment for drug problems has been reviewed extensively elsewhere (Stanton, 1978c) and will not be dealt with at length here. Many different approaches have been used, including: conjoint marital therapy, group marital therapy, marital-behavioral contingency contracting, family contingency contracting, training in parenting and postnatal child care, parents groups, concurrent parent and adolescent groups, siblings groups, family mediation, familization treatment, multiple family therapy, and social network intervention. The most common type has been conjoint family therapy and this has been based upon a number of theoretical systems, such as the psychodynamic, family systems, structural, strategic, problem-centered, and personalistic viewpoints. Most of the work has been performed within the context of an overall drug treatment program which includes other concurrent modes, for example inpatient group therapy or methadone maintenance.

Some of the studies have not provided continuing care in the usual sense in that they (a) have been outpatient based; (b) have terminated treatment at hospital discharge, even if it only lasted a few sessions (Bartlett, 1975); (c) have admitted part or all of the family to an inpatient program, but did not continue past discharge (Catanzaro, 1973); or (d) have been time-limited (Funk, 1974; Reilly, 1976; Wunderlich, Lozes and Lewis, 1974). In others, family treatment has been provided only during the inpatient stay, with continuing care given in the form of individual counseling (e.g., Hendricks, 1971). This is in contrast to programs such as that of Weisman et al. (1969) in which brief inpatient care, which included family treatment, was continued via postdischarge family therapy.

Of the 56 papers on family approaches to treatment for drug problems reviewd by Stanton (1978c), very few provided outcome data. In fact, only 26 made even the slightest mention of the efficacy of their treatment. While all discussed to some extent their treatment techniques, only four included comparisons with other treatments or with control groups. Wunderlich et al. (1974) studied the effects of short-term group therapy given separately for court-referred, drug-abusing adolescents and their parents. The control group was composed of court-referred, nondrug adolescent cases who went to other agencies. On follow-up, the drug group stayed in school longer, had dramatically lower recidivism rates for arrests, and generally showed less social maladjustment than the controls. Hendricks (1971) found in a one-year follow-up of narcotics addicts who had participated in inpatient multiple family groups that 41% were still free of illegal drugs, compared to 21% among patients who had not received this treatment; since subjects were not randomly assigned to treatment groups, these results must be viewed with caution. In a four-six-month follow-up, Ziegler-Driscoll (1977) compared addicts receiving brief structural therapy with controls who did not receive it and found no difference as to the number of patients abstinent from all drugs and alcohol. This study should not be considered a good test of treatment effects by most standards, however, because it was meant to be exploratory and (a) the therapists had never done family therapy before, (b) the supervisors were unfamiliar with the patient population, (c) the overall therapeutic milieu was hostile to the study, and (d) the methodology of the study was generally not conducive to getting or keeping families in treatment. In a later paper Ziegler-Driscoll (1978) reported that the therapists became more competent with later cases and that certain subgroups of the treated sample did appear to profit from family treatment relative to comparable subsamples of the control group. A third outcome study (Stanton, 1978d; Stanton et al., 1979) compared three randomly assigned family treatment modes for heroin addicts on methadone with clients who received methadone and individual counseling. A major finding from six-month posttreatment follow-ups was that the ratio of days free from (a) nonopiate illegal drugs, (b) all illegal drugs, (c) illegal opiates, and (d) all illegal drugs and alcohol, was 1.4 to 2.7 times as great (depending on the particular dependent variable) for those receiving structural family therapy (Minuchin, 1974) than for the nonfamily group.

Social Network Intervention

A form of intervention related to family therapy has been developed by Ross Speck and associates (Speck and Attneave, 1973). It has been termed "social network intervention" or "family network therapy" and is a problem-focused approach which addresses the client within the context of his family and total interpersonal field. The idea is to mobilize the social forces which impinge on him and put them to work to deal with the problem. Groups of from 30 to 200 are gathered, including immediate family, grandparents, relatives, personal friends, neighbors and even work associates. Effort is devoted to restructuring these systems, especially where they are dysfunctional, and concentrating energy on alleviating the problem. This is a kind of "retribalization." Often, locating a job or living quarters for the client is a primary goal. Several of these large meetings may be held, scheduled weeks, or even months, apart. Speck and Attneave describe a case in which the approach was used with an amphetamine addict. Callan et al. (1975) have used it with drug addicts within a therapeutic community, although they did not extend the meetings beyond discharge. All in all, social network intervention can be considered one of the more innovative approaches to establishing continuing post-treatment supports for client and family.

Families Anonymous

In 1971 a self-help group called Families Anonymous (FA) was established to aid families in dealing realistically with drug problems in one or more of their members (sometimes families with other symptoms, such as behavior problems, are enrolled as well). Families Anonymous has established over 100 chapters across the nation. Its major theme is to shift the participants' emphasis from the drug abuser to the self as a person who has his or her own (legitimate) difficulties (Brown and Ashery, 1978; Families Anonymous, 1971). It attempts to relieve family members' anxiety and guilt and guide them toward finding help outside the family. Although it was not conceived as an aftercare organization, its effects can certainly extend to posttreatment support of a drug-using member.

FA shares many principles with its sister organization, Al-Anon. Both apply the same 12 steps in guiding members' behavior. Both also apply principles similar to those of family treatment, even though the philosophies differ. For instance, "loving detachment" requires change in nonsubstance-abusing members. The "group sharing" that occurs is in many ways similar both to multiple family therapy and group therapy. FA's power, then, may lie not only in its espoused philosophy, but also in the operations it recommends, e.g., maintaining some distance from the IP and ceasing to be overnurturant. It has certainly been a welcome addition to the drug treatment scene.

Additional Considerations

There are a number of factors which should be kept in mind when considering the role of the family within and beyond the treatment effort. Some of these are presented here.

Family Involvement. One of the biggest problems noted in the literature is the difficulty in getting families to become involved either in the treatment or the continuing care program for drug addicts. Fathers have been noted to be particularly resistant. The families appear defensive and afraid of being blamed. A considerable amount of time and energy—the kind Berliner (1966-1967) terms "reaching-out casework"—may be needed to recruit them as part of the treatment and posttreatment process. When such steps are taken, recent indications are that success can be achieved in this endeavor, depending on the commitment, type of approach, and innovation of the recruiter (see Stanton, 1978c for a review of these studies).

The other side of this coin has to do with the extent to which families are knowledgable of the services available to them. There does appear to be a need for better dissemination of information about available facilities, especially at the local level. Chambers (1977) has data indicating that half the families for whom drug-related treatment is indicated are either unaware of existent resources or find them unacceptable.

Crises and Administrative Flexibility. Much of the writing in this field has spoken to the frequent occurrence of family crises at the point when the drug-abusing member improves or goes off drugs. Such crises can take many forms, such as the parents splitting up, his/her spouse becoming depressed, or a sibling developing problems. These difficult times require that treatment personnel have the flexibility to respond immediately, before events progress too far. For example, they must be able to meet with members in the evening, or make home visits. Consequently, it is incumbent upon the administrative arm of the facility to also be flexible and, through its procedures, better enable its treaters to respond quickly and without undue encumbrance.

Multiple Family Relationships. Several of the family service or treatment activities discussed thus far—such as multiple family therapy, Families Anonymous, or parents groups—can have effects which extend well beyond their specific settings. Through them, parents and families come in contact with other parents and families, and the stage is set for a multifamily support system. In fact, Ziegler-Driscoll (1977) noted that participants in "relatives" groups, which took place following inpatient discharge, developed a certain cohesiveness, tended to keep in touch outside the group, and helped each other through crises. In a sense, such groups can serve to alter a facet of the community within which their members reside, thereby establishing a new community-based support system.

Drug Subculture and Conditioning. The addict who "cleans up" is usually subjected to pressure from peers, pushers, and acquaintances in the drug subculture to return to his habit. Conditioning to the paraphernalia and setting itself can also occur. These influences can be very strong. However, there are indications in the literature and in this author's own experience that if change has been effected in the family system, the pull from such factors can be resisted. With effective treatment the family can be a source of strength in helping the addict to stay off drugs. For example, we (Stanton et al., 1978) have seen parents take charge of intercepting calls from "junkie" contacts and actively work to support their offspring and shield them from their old ways. This sort of turn-around can fortify the "withstanding" process long enough for the prior relationships and learned patterns of behavior to lose their potency.

Such action by the family can also facilitate the IP's reintegration into the community. Not only can the family serve as a barrier to the reestablishment of earlier practices, it can provide encouragement and support for the development of alternative activities or work/school commitments. This can occur either through their giving explicit, unambiguous permission for or actively engaging in locating and establishing alternative activities.

A MODEL

Some years ago, Berliner (1966-1967) described an integrated continuing care program which included "pre-admission counseling services to families, concurrent treatment of family problems, post-hospital treatment services to patient and family members, and a controlled evaluation of results" (p. 83). In the present section, a brief outline will be proffered of another model for family intervention which is aimed at reintegration of the IP into the community. The model is not as comprehensive as Berliner's in some respects, putting more emphasis on the family and less emphasis on some of the other services discussed elsewhere in this volume. It is based on this author's sense of what works best, judging both from the literature and from personal experience. Some of the components have been described elsewhere (Haley, 1979; Stanton and Todd, 1978). The primary goal is to provide the reader with guidelines as to where (and to some extent how) family services—especially treatment—can be most strategically and effectively applied.

If it is accepted that drug addiction is a family phenomenon (Stanton, 1978b; Stanton et al., 1978), a single, basic ground rule applies: *Under no circumstances should any facet of the program reinforce the notion that the addict is incompetent or handicapped.* To do this only sanctions and rigidifies the dysfunctional family system, thereby thwarting beneficial change. Services which ignore this tenet are doing the client, his family, and society no favors.

Second, steps taken in the service plan should be directed toward, or at least performed with a keen awareness of ways in which the family addictive cycle can be changed or halted. As mentioned above, this cycle includes the sequential behaviors of all members—not just the addict. The continuing care program should be designed to directly intervene in and change the family process surrounding this cycle (Stanton, 1978b, 1978c; Stanton et al., 1978).

Inpatient and Residential Treatment

In contrast to the practices of many in the field, the position taken here is to try to avoid residential or hospital admission. This is because, first, alternative actions are possible which may succeed in preventing it, such as family crisis therapy (Langsley et al., 1971). Second, as with schizophrenia (Haley, 1973), experience has shown that people may do well within the treatment setting, but suffer rapid relapse upon discharge to family and community. In the drug field, a high percentage of clients in such programs drop out prematurely, so that the most motivated ones (those with the most outside support?) are retained; this unfortunate trend can be seen as indirect support for the importance and power of significant others vis-á-vis the symptom. Third, hospitalization tends to perpetuate a family pattern which interferes with effective cure. It stabilizes the family in its old ways—a sort of "marking time"—and prevents real change. As mentioned before, drug addict families are often quite accepting of any treatment program which continues to keep the "patient" label on the addict, so that the mere presence in such a program is sufficient, in many cases, to keep the family dysfunctionally stable.

In situations where commitment to a residential or hospital setting has actually occurred, the treater must consider carefully if he actually has the leverage to effect family change. For example, it might not be auspicious to try to make family interventions when he does not, say, have control over the detoxification process. More prudently, he should wait until the addict returns home and the family system has a more direct influence (Stanton et al., 1978). Even if he was engaged with the family prior to admission, he might consider terminating at that point and rejoining them after discharge.

Family Treatment

Space does not permit more than a superficial coverage of family treatment variables here. Rather than discussing specific techniques and therapeutic moves, the material below pertains primarily to the structure of the therapy.

Case Control. The person who treats the family must have primary administrative control of the case (Davis, 1978; Gasta and Schut, 1977; Haley, 1979; Stanton and Todd, 1978). For example, he must be allowed to decide or permit changes in medication (e.g., methadone) dosage. Otherwise, he can easily be undermined by the client and members of his family and played off against his fellow treaters. In addition, such control allows him to deal more effectively with crises.

Number and Spacing of Sessions. The existent evidence indicates that, rather than undertaking prolonged treatment with regular interviews over years, the therapy should be time limited. It should follow a pattern of intense involvement and rapid disengagement (Haley, 1979; Reilly, 1976; Stanton and Todd, 1978). Contracts for, say, 8-12 sessions should be made with families; these can be extended to 20 sessions with recontracting, but rarely more unless the family wants to make a new contract for other problems. It is probably best to space final sessions further apart, e.g., 2-6 weeks. "Innoculatory" follow-up sessions should be scheduled over the months following termination in order to insure the continuation of positive change and monitor continuity of care. Such a system also seems to make families less hesitant to take the initiative in reengaging in treatment, since they know they are not committing themselves to interminable therapy if they do contact the treater.

Caseload. Families with severe drug problems can be very difficult to treat. They are often demanding, draining, and skillful at organizing resistance. It therefore seems advisable to limit one's caseload for this kind of work to three or four cases at a time, particularly while learning the techniques. As one develops expertise, the caseload can be enlarged (Stanton and Todd, 1978).

Family Support Systems

In addition to individual family intervention within a continuing care paradigm, there is also room for ancillary support systems. Some of these will be briefly mentioned.

Multiple Family Therapy and Parents Groups. In most cases where these have been used, they have been applied instead of, rather than in conjunction with, conjoint therapy for the individual family. Few data exist on a combination approach, and such an approach has the inherent danger that the two efforts will end up working at cross-purposes—especially if handled by different treaters. Nonetheless, these modes do have the potential for providing support groups for drug-using families which extend both into the community and over time. They can ease the difficulty and challenge faced by individual families confronted with the possibility of slipping back into the readdiction cycle.

Families Anonymous. Berenson (1976), in his work with substance abusing families, has noted that the treater often cannot, alone, provide the constant and necessary support these families require. He advocates that they develop ties to FA or Al-Anon to aid them in coping with crises and in maintaining whatever beneficial change has occurred. Again, while not primarily designed for aftercare, these organizations can serve the additional function of community based support systems of the sort which are ongoing and responsive.

Acculturation and Family Support. A topic deserving of more attention is the relationship between drug addiction, immigration, and parent-child cultural disparity. Based on his data, Vaillant (1966a) discovered that the rate of addiction among first generation residents was three times that of immigrants; offspring of immigrants who were born in New York City were at greater risk for addiction than either their parents or offspring born in the former culture. Noting the abnormal dependence of addict mothers on their children, he suggested that (a) immigrant parents are under the additional strain of having to cope with their new environment; (b) parental migration may be correlated with parental instability; and (c) "the immigrant mother, separated as she often is from her own family ties, may be less able to meet the needs of those dependent on her and yet experience greater than average difficulty in permitting her child mature independence" (p. 538). It might be added that immigrant parents are also faced both with the "loss" of the family they left in their original culture, plus their own possible feelings of guilt or disloyalty for having deserted these other members. If so, such families are an important target group for direct intervention and continuing support. This area needs further investigation, but it does appear that the development of community support systems is indicated in order to replace the lost extended family and previous culture. Efforts could be aimed specifically at enlisting the aid of fully acculturated families whose cultural/ethnic background is the same as that of the target group. This is an aspect of continuing care which also holds considerable potential for primary prevention of drug problems.

REFERENCES

AFRICANO, A., FORTUNATO, M., and PADOW, E. (1973) "The impact of program treatment on marital unions in a methadone maintained patient population." Proceedings of the 5th National Conference on Methadone Treatment 1: 538-544.

ALEXANDER, B. K. and DIBB, G. S. (1975) "Opiate addicts and their parents." Family Process 14: 499-514.

BARTLETT, D. (1975) "The use of multiple family therapy groups with adolescent drug addicts," in M. Sugar (ed.) The Adolescent in Group and Family Therapy. New York: Brunner/Mazel.

BERENSON, D. (1976) "Alcohol and the family system," in P. Guerin (ed.) Family Therapy: Theory and Practice. New York: Gardner.

BERLINER, A. K. (1966-1967) "Narcotic addiction, the institution and the community." International Journal of the Addictions 1-2: 74-85.

BOSZORMENYI-NAGY, I. and SPARK, G. M. (1973) Invisible Loyalties. New York: Harper and Row.

BOWEN, M. (1966) "The use of family therapy in clinical practice." Comprehensive Psychiatry 7: 345-374.

BROWN, B. S. and ASHERY, R. S. (1978) "Aftercare in drug abuse programming," in R. L. Dupont, A. Goldstein, and J. O'Donnell (eds.) Handbook on Drug Abuse (National Institute on Drug Abuse publication). Washington, DC: U.S. Government Printing Office.

CALLAN, D., GARRISON, J., and ZERGER, F. (1975) "Working with the families and social networks of drug abusers." Journal of Psychedelic Drugs 7: 19-25.

CANNON, S. R. (1976) Social Functioning Patterns in Families of Offspring Receiving Treatment for Drug Abuse. Roslyn Heights, NY: Libra Publications.

CATANZARO, R. J. (1973) "Combined treatment of alcoholics, drug abusers and related problems in a family residential center." Drug Forum 2: 203-212.

CHAMBERS, C. (1977) "Trends and projections," in L. G. Richards and L. B. Blevens (eds.) The Epidemiology of Drug Abuse: Current Issues. (NIDA Research Monograph No. 10). Washington, DC: U.S. Government Printing Office.

CHEIN, I., GERARD, D., LEE, R., and ROSENFELD, E. (1964) The Road to H. New York: Basic Books.

CLARK, J. S., CAPEL, W. C., GOLDSMITH, B. M., and STEWART, G. T. (1972) "Marriage and methadone: spouse behavior patterns in heroin addicts maintained on methadone." Journal of Marriage and the Family 34: 496-501.

COLEMAN, S. B. and DAVIS, D. I. (1978) "Family therapy and drug abuse: a national survey." Family Process 17: 21-29.

CUSKEY, W. (1977) An Assessment of the Clinical Efficacy of the Mabon Parents Demonstration Project. (Report prepared for the Services Research Branch, National Institute on Drug Abuse). Philadelphia: Cuskey, Ipsen & McCall Consultants, Inc.

DAVIS, D. I. (1978) "Forum: family therapy for the drug user: conceptual and practical considerations." Drug Forum 6: 197-199.

———, BERENSON, D., STEINGLASS, P., and DAVIS, S. (1974) "The adaptive consequences of drinking." Psychiatry 37: 209-215.

DELL ORTO, A. E. (1974) "The role and resources of the family during the drug rehabilitation process." Journal of Psychedelic Drugs 6: 435-445.

DINTIZ, S. et al. (1961) "Psychiatric and social attributes as predictors of case outcome in mental hospitalization." Social Problems 8: 322-328.

ELDRED, C. A. and WASHINGTON, M. N. (1976) "Interpersonal relationships in heroin use by men and women and their role in treatment outcome." International Journal of the Addictions 11: 117-130.

ELLINWOOD, E. H., SMITH, W. G., and VAILLANT, G. E. (1966) "Narcotic addiction in males and females: a comparison." International Journal of the Addictions 1: 33-45.

Families Anonymous (1971) A Guide for the Family of the Drug Abuser. Torrance, CA.

FERBER, A., KLIGLER, D., ZWERLING, I., and MENDELSOHN, M. (1967) "Current family structure: psychiatric emergencies and patient fate." Archives of General Psychiatry 16: 659-667.

FRAM, D. H. and HOFFMAN, H. A. (1973) "Family therapy in the treatment of the heroin addict," pp. 610-615 in Proceedings of the 5th National Conference on Methadone Treatment 1. National Association for the Prevention of Addictions to Narcotics.

FREEMAN, H. and SIMMONS, O. (1963) The Mental Patient Comes Home. New York: John Wiley.

FUNK, M. J. (1974) "Recidivism rate following a volunteer communication program for families with juvenile drug offenders." Journal of Voluntary Action Research 3: 26-30.

GASTA, C. and SCHUT, J. (1977) "Planned detoxification of addict marital pairs: diagnosis and treatment strategies." Presented at the meeting of the National Drug Abuse Conference, San Francisco, May.

HALEY, J. (1962) "Whither family therapy." Family Process 1: 69-100.

——— (1973) Uncommon Therapy. New York: W. W. Norton.

——— (1976) Problem Solving Therapy. San Francisco: Jossey-Bass.

——— (1979) Young Eccentrics: The Therapy of Mad Young People. In press.

HARBIN, H. T. and MAZIAR, H. M. (1975) "The families of drug abusers: a literature review." Family Process 14: 411-431.

HEJINIAN, C. L. and PITTEL, S. M. (1978) "Can marriage survive addiction and treatment?" Presented at the National Drug Abuse Conference, Seattle, Washington, April.

HENDRICKS, W. J. (1971) "Use of multifamily counseling groups in treatment of male narcotic addicts." International Journal of Group Psychotherapy 21: 84-90.

HIRSCH, R. (1961) "Group therapy with parents of adolescent drug addicts." Psychiatric Quarterly 35: 702-710.

HUBERTY, D. J. (1975) "Treating the adolescent drug abuser: a family affair." Contemporary Drug Problems 4: 179-194.

JACKSON, D. D. (1965) "The study of the family." Family Process 4: 1-20.

KANDEL, D. B., TREIMAN, D., FAUST, R., and SINGLE, E. (1976) "Adolescent involvement in legal and illegal drug use: a multiple classification analysis." Social Forces 55: 438-458.

KLAGSBRUN, M. and DAVIS, D. I. (1977) "Substance abuse and family interaction." Family Process 16: 149-173.

KOWALEWSKI, N. H. (1972) "A follow-up study of patients of a psychiatric day hospital for the purpose of planning a follow-up service." Social Service Review 46: 457.

LANGSLEY, D. G., MACHOTKA, P., and FLOMENHAFT, K. (1971) "Avoiding mental hospital admission: a follow-up study." American Journal of Psychiatry 127: 1391-1394.

LENNARD, H. L. and ALLEN, S. D. (1973) "The treatment of drug addiction: toward new models." International Journal of the Addictions 8: 521-535.

LEVY, B. (1972) "Five years after: a follow-up of 50 narcotic addicts." American Journal of Psychiatry 7: 102-106.

MANNINO, F. V. and SHORE, M. F. (1974) "Family structure, aftercare and post-hospital adjustment." American Journal of Orthopsychiatry 44: 76-85.

MASON, P. (1958) "The mother of the addict." Psychiatric Quarterly Supplement 32 (Part 2): 189-199.

MEYER, H. and BORGATTA, E. (1959) An Experiment in Mental Patient Rehabilitation. New York: Russell Sage.

MILLER, D. (1967) "Retrospective analysis of post-hospital mental patients' worlds." Journal of Health and Social Behavior 8: 136-140.

MINUCHIN, S. (1974) Families and Family Therapy. Cambridge, MA: Harvard Univ. Press.

NOONE, R. J. and REDDIG, R. L. (1976) "Case studies in the family treatment of drug abuse." Family Process 15: 325-332.

O'DONNELL, J. A. (1969) Narcotic Addicts in Kentucky. Washington, DC: U.S. Government Printing Office.

REILLY, D. M. (1976) "Family factors in the etiology and treatment of youthful drug abuse." Family Therapy 2: 149-171.

SALMON, R. and SALMON, S. (1977) "The causes of heroin addiction: a review of the literature. Part II." International Journal of the Addictions 12: 937-951.

SCHER, J. (1966) "Patterns and profiles of addiction and drug abuse." Archives of General Psychiatry 15: 539-551.

SCHWARTZMAN, J. (1975) "The addict, abstinence and the family." American Journal of Psychiatry 132: 154-157.

――― (1977a) "Addict abstinence and the illusion of alternatives." Ethos 5 (2): 138-150.

――― (1977b) "Systemic aspects of abstinence and addiction." British Journal of Medical Psychology 50: 181-186.

――― and KROLL, L. (1977) "Methadone maintenance and addict abstinence." International Journal of the Addictions 12: 497-507.

SELDIN, N. E. (1972) "The family of the addict: a review of the literature." International Journal of the Addictions 7: 97-107.

SPECK, R. V. and ATTNEAVE, C. L. (1973) Family Networks. New York: Pantheon.

STANTON, M. D. (1978a) "The family and drug misuse: a bibliography." American Journal of Drug and Alcohol Abuse 5: in press.

――― (1978b) "Forum: family therapy for the drug user: conceptual and practical considerations." Drug Forum 6: 203-205.

――― (1978c) "Family treatment of drug problems: a review," in R. L. Dupont, A. Goldstein, and J. O'Donnell (eds.) Handbook on Drug Abuse. (National Institute on Drug Abuse publication). Washington, DC: U.S. Government Printing Office.

――― (1978d) "Some outcome results and aspects of structural family therapy with drug addicts," in D. Smith, S. Anderson, M. Buxton, T. Chung, N. Gottlieb, and W. Harvey (eds.) A Multicultural View of Drug Abuse: The Selected Proceedings of the National Drug Abuse Conference–1977. Cambridge, MA: Schenkman.

——— (1979a) "Drugs and the family." Marriage and Family Review 2 (2).

——— (1979b) "Family therapy: systems approaches," in G. P. Sholevar, R. M. Benson, and B. J. Blinder (eds.) Treatment of Emotional Disorders in Children and Adolescents. New York: Spectrum.

——— and TODD, T. C. (1978) "Structural family therapy with heroin addicts," in E. Kaufman and P. Kaufmann (eds.) The Family Therapy of Drug and Alcohol Abusers. New York: Gardner.

———, HEARD, D. B., KIRSCHNER, S., KLEIMAN, J. I., MOWATT, D. T., RILEY, P., SCOTT, S. M. and VAN DEUSEN, J. M. (1978) "Heroin addiction as a family phenomenon: a new conceptual model." American Journal of Drug and Alcohol Abuse 5 (2).

STANTON, M. D., TODD, T. C., and Associates (1979) The Family Therapy of Drug Addiction. In press.

TAYLOR, S. D., WILBUR, M., and OSNOS, R. (1966) "The wives of drug addicts." American Journal of Psychiatry 123: 585-591.

THOMPSON, P. (1973) "Family of the addict explored." The Journal (Addiction Research Foundation, Toronto) 2: 8.

VAILLANT, G. E. (1966a) "Parent-child cultural disparity and drug addiction." Journal of Nervous and Mental Disease 142: 534-539.

——— (1966b) "A 12-year follow-up of New York narcotic addicts: III Some social and psychiatric characteristics." Archives of General Psychiatry 15: 599-609.

WEISMAN, G., FEIRSTEIN, A., and THOMAS, C. (1969) "Three-day hospitalization: a model for intensive intervention." Archives of General Psychiatry 21: 620-629.

WELLISCH, D. D., GAY, G. R., and McENTEE, R. (1970) "The easy rider syndrome. a pattern of hetero- and homosexual relationships in a heroin addict population." Family Process 9: 425-430.

WELLISCH, D. and KAUFMAN, E. (1975) "Family therapy," in E. Senay, V. Shorty, and H. Alksne (eds.) Developments in the Field of Drug Abuse. Cambridge, MA: Schenkman.

WIKLER, A. (1973) "Dynamics of drug dependence." Archives of General Psychiatry 28: 611-616.

WOLK, R. L. and DISKIND, M. H. (1961) "Personality dynamics of mothers and wives of drug addicts." Crime & Delinquency 7: 148-152.

WUNDERLICH, R. A., LOZES, J., and LEWIS, J. (1974) "Recidivism rates of group therapy participants and other adolescents processed by a juvenile court." Psychotherapy: Theory, Research and Practice 11: 243-245.

ZAHN, M. and BALL, J. (1972) "Factors related to the cure of opiate addiction among Puerto Rican addicts." International Journal of the Addictions 7: 237-245.

ZIEGLER-DRISCOLL, G. (1977) "Family research study at Eagleville Hospital and Rehabilitation Center." Family Process 16: 175-189.

——— (1978) "Family treatment with parent addict families," in D. Smith, S. Anderson, M. Buxton, T. Chung, N. Gottlieb, and W. Harvey (eds.) A Multicultural View of Drug Abuse: The Selected Proceedings of the National Drug Abuse Conference–1977. Cambridge, MA: Schenkman.

3

THE FORMER ADDICT IN THE WORK PLACE

The process of drug abuse rehabilitation is not valued as complete, either by staff or by clients, unless the acquisition of paid employment has been achieved. That employment is seen as essential to permitting the consequences of rehabilitation to remain significant and of long duration. For all of us, employment represents not only our means of support, but a significant investment of our physical and emotional energy. Working is taken as a basic fact of life; however, it is also an area in which competition exists and in which each person will be essentially on his/her own. That is why it is quite essential that this area be addressed for and by the client from the time treatment commences. Some find that they have little difficulty with the adjustments to a drug-free, productive life including adaptation to the work world. The majority, however, need vocational rehabilitation services to prepare them with the personal and technical resources to approach competitive employment with the ultimate goal of secure job placement.

Drug treatment programs have then as one of their responsibilities preparing the client for reentry to the community by resolving not only drug problems, but related sociopsychological issues. It is within the community that the final tests of rehabilitation must be countenanced and the results evaluated. A critical test becomes that of employment. In order

103

to achieve the goal of employment, there must be employers and organizations willing to hire those individuals who, having recovered from their drug abuse and related problems, have become suitable candidates for employment. To be successful, the vocational rehabilitation process and the goal of employment require the interaction of vital factors including the individual, the treatment facility, the service providers, and perhaps most significantly the community.

VOCATIONAL REHABILITATION AND CLIENT ADJUSTMENT

Studies conducted within drug treatment programs reflect that vocational achievement is indeed a primary goal in the rehabilitation process for both staff and clients. There is evidence that clients ask for assistance with employment and education with at least the frequency they request other services and in many instances more frequently (Koenigsberg and Royster, 1977). Staff view vocational programming within treatment as being of maximum importance, although the attention paid to this service, in staff assignment and available services, varies considerably (Goldenberg, 1972).

For both groups there is good reason to place this emphasis on the process of vocational rehabilitation. There is evidence to suggest that ex-addicts who are employed do better in treatment in terms of diminished criminality and drug abuse. It is self-evident to all that once employed, ex-addicts cease to be a drain on public support systems and, in fact, become contributors.

However, most would contend that not until the problem of the physical addiction itself has been brought under control can an integrated approach to employment planning be addressed. While involved with drugs, it is difficult for the individual to focus on the demands of the world of work with any real commitment. The goals of treatment therefore, become first a termination of drug use with a view then toward assisting the individual to strengthen and/or develop emotional, physical, social, and vocational resources; with necessary program supports applied to permit planning, integration, problem solving, and, ultimately, a letting go when the client is able to function independently.

The treatment program can become a community in its own right and in such a setting the client is taught to meet designed expectations, to interact with others in a socialized fashion, and to incorporate certain other socially valued behaviors, such as punctuality, cleanliness, and orderliness. The adoption of a sense of responsibility for one's future is inherent in treatment planning. The goal of integration to the community can begin in this simulated community, whether it be a residential facility or an outpatient treatment program.

In that treatment setting, employment to the ex-addict is often seen as a ticket out of poverty, drug abuse, sickness. "If only I had a job" is a plaintive rationale to explain a host of inadequacies in adapting to the prosocial community. For some, that job becomes a means of filling time, the time that had formerly been spent acquiring money for drugs. For many, the job helps to prove a point to family and friends. For all, it can provide the promise of greater success in meeting the demands of the society in which they must live.

Such goals can exist as an incentive to help the individual sustain the momentum of the often difficult rehabilitation process. For those who enter employment, there is not only the prospect of improved financial resources, there is also reason to feel a sense of achievement, and opportunities for new experiences and contacts that can further drive the process of change and growth.

PROBLEMS IN VOCATIONAL REHABILITATION

Many former drug abusers are individuals whose capacities for vocational adjustment appear limited. They are frequently individuals who have had unstable home lives, irregular and poor education, no diplomas, no skill training, negative role models, and limited incentives to change the course of events. Many have worked during their years of addiction, but at jobs which ended because of that addiction or because of incarceration. At the same time, these jobs were often low paying, unskilled, and temporary in nature. While addicted, abusers' thoughts may have been directed more toward money for drugs than for job success and, therefore, work patterns and adjustment were tenuous at best. Recognizing these realities, vocational rehabilitation exists as an integral part of treatment and is designed to help the clients, as individuals, evaluate their employability status, taking into account their vocational and emotional strengths and weaknesses and establishing a plan to maximize employability.

Clearly, to obtain success in terms of treatment generally and vocational rehabilitation specifically, employment opportunities must be available. One can question whether rehabilitation is a failure because the client couldn't find meaningful work, or whether the client couldn't find meaningful work because the treatment was a failure. Without sufficient

employment opportunities it is difficult to assess the impact of treatment
or to planfully improve existing treatment services.

Research efforts in the area of employer attitudes toward former drug
abusers have suggested that initially employers have negative attitudes
toward ex-addicts (Koenigsberg and Royster, 1977). These attitudes
appear to be based upon ignorance, fear of the unknown, stereotyping,
misinformation, and/or simple prejudice. As a result of this, employers in
the main have been resistant to hiring ex-addicts and have included close
scrutiny of drug abuse indicators in their screening procedures (Goldenberg, 1972).

The attitudes of the employment community are understandable on a
number of levels. Why hire a known ex-addict when there are so many
candidates to choose from? Why hire someone who has been unstable and
unreliable in the past? Why risk an "infection" of the existing work force?

Employer restraint and consequent limited availability of employment
opportunities exist despite numerous attempts at public and industrial
education, and the development of some number of corporate incentive
programs. Moreover, they exist despite demonstrated evidence of the
workability of ex-addicts. Research studies have shown that attendance,
punctuality, absenteeism, and overall performance ratings of ex-addicts is
at least equal to those of their nonaddicted counterparts (Yankowitz and
Randell, 1976). Studies also show that their hiring does not increase drug
abuse within organizations (Koenigsberg and Royster, 1977).

The employers who have elected to hire ex-addicts appear to have done
so for differing reasons. For some, that hiring is the expression of their
social consciousness. Thus, providing employment is seen as part of a
larger effort to curtail addiction; or there is the thought that stable
employment may make a real difference in the lives of those individuals an
employer is empowered to aid. For other employers, there is a response to
societal pressure. That pressure may be applied by civic and/or client
advocacy groups, or by the courts (Graham, 1973).

Many of the jobs available to ex-addicts are seen as being at either too
high a level, where few suitable candidates exist; or at too low a level, so as
to create feelings of personal worthlessness or a not unreasonable belief
that "I could get those jobs without help from anyone." Large corporations often have few semiskilled or skilled jobs available. Moreover, these
positions are frequently unionized, and the obstacles this presents often
override whatever limited corporate enthusiasm there is for hiring ex-
addicts. Many of the jobs which have become available are, in fact, in large
organizations, but are of a clerical nature, where the greater part of the

ex-addict population neither has clerical skills nor the background experiences to seek the atmosphere of a clerical operation. Many of the employers who do appear to have available some number of skilled jobs are smaller employers, harder to find, and less willing to consider an ex-addict for employment.

The picture emerges then of few jobs being available and those that are available are seen as being at either too high a level or as too menial. Jobs that do not permit promotions or growth will serve only as a stop-gap, and the individual will be out seeking employment in a short time since the work will be both boring and frustrating.

TO TELL THE TRUTH—YES OR NO

The majority of ex-addicts seeking employment do not reveal their backgrounds to prospective employers. This fact has significance from a personal perspective, as well as from a hiring perspective. It should be recalled that it is found that initial prescreening criteria are often very rigorous and may be used to exclude former addicts and/or ex-offenders. For those who pass the prescreening, there is often a lengthy selection process that includes in-depth medical examinations. If employment is then obtained, there may be detailed and stringent follow-up of the employee's progress.

In examining the more personal elements of the job applicant's decision, a great deal can be learned about the ultimate concerns of the ex-addict when considering entry/reentry to the community and altering his/her life-style. This thinking suggests: a basic skepticism that the community in general can really be accepting; the feeling that employers in particular cannot accept individuals with a history of addiction; the burden created for oneself that the negative label attached to him/her may thereby limit self-acceptance just as it limits community acceptance.

In making the decision to lie about a significant portion of one's life, the individual pays a high price. In some part, he or she must then create a fictional identify simply to maintain the lie. This can create enormous pressure on the job with regard to fear of disclosure and ultimate rejection and discharge, and it creates too an inability to feel comfortable with coworkers and to form new friendships. As a result, the use of those new relationships and activities and their ability to promote further growth and rehabilitation are limited if not destroyed. Feelings and experiences of social isolation may be created, and there will certainly be a generalized inability to relax in the future or to avoid a felt need to be on guard each day.

Those who enter employment and allow the knowledge of their prior addiction to be known often do so because they feel that the employer is going to find out anyway. In some instances such ex-addicts have been unable to obtain jobs by lying and covering the past and have been placed in the position of having to tell the truth themselves or risk having it be told by an advocate agency.

Those who have chosen to reveal their past, may experience—or feel they experience—especially close monitoring of their performance and an expectation that their performance be above that of other comparably employed workers. The pressures to keep up with these demands, whether real or imagined, may become overwhelming. There may indeed be breaches of confidentiality and a substantial part of the staff may know the facts, rather than just the supervisor. This may result in increased feelings of isolation and of difference, and may ultimately lead to the termination of employment.

To be sure, there are those who enter employment without their employers knowing about their prior addiction and who do not feel the burden of "living a lie." These individuals may be employed in a wide variety of occupations and at differing levels. They have been able to achieve a level of self-confidence and/or a distancing of themselves from their situations, such that they can perform in their occupations without forming relationships that could threaten identification and termination. They have arranged their life-styles at work to meet their needs, interact at minimally acceptable levels, and maintain a status quo in other aspects of their lives. Thus, for these persons, the job does not provide relationships that could permit further individual growth.

CURRENT STRUCTURE OF VOCATIONAL REHABILITATION

Vocational rehabilitation or employment services within drug abuse treatment are often seen as support services which address quality of life in the educational and vocational spheres. They offer a broad spectrum of intervention strategies and implementation techniques prescribed to help the individual realize his/her maximum vocational potential.

It is within the sphere of employment counseling, that the client comes to attain a realistic assessment of his/her skills and the work that must be done to upgrade skills and learn new ones; to understand the availability of the labor market; to consider the personal skills needed to engage in job hunting and interviewing; and to learn the art of keeping a job and the capability to face the scrutiny of the business community.

As described above, treatment programs, for the most part, recognize the value of work to the individual and the rehabilitative process. There are frequently differences in regard to the importance placed on it, as well as the degree to which employment services are integrated into the overall process. Even those programs which offer limited employment services suggest to their clients that steps be taken to find a job and make efforts to provide support around the issue.

In treatment programs, vocational rehabilitation becomes the responsibility of one or several of numerous individuals on the service delivery team: a trained vocational rehabilitation counselor; an employment specialist; a treatment program counselor who may or may not have been trained in techniques of vocational counseling; and/or the State Department of Vocational Rehabilitation. The model employed varies in relation to the resources available. However, the following services are the more standard available within the program or accessible through referral to the community: assessment, remedial education, high school diploma preparation, prevocational evaluation, skill training, advanced academic training, work adjustment training, preemployment counseling, job development assistance, job hunting skills, follow-up to employment, and job-upgrading.

Because of the large numbers of clients in treatment and their diversified emotional needs and levels of functioning, it has been extremely difficult to individualize vocational services—and other aspects of treatment—to the extent that clients require. Treatment programs often, at best, make efforts to provide the vocational services that meet the needs of the majority of their clients. Thus, the ability of a program to provide vocational services becomes a function of monetary constraints, staff skills, and the administrative support that exists for those services. Understandably, there has been increasing emphasis on involving appropriate community services rather than relying on a single program to meet all needs.

It is clearly unrealistic to expect that the drug abuse program can and should provide the total rehabilitation program. Since the client is ultimately to return to the community without program affiliation, he/she needs to be able to learn to interact in the social system which exists. The treatment community, in some ways, is a protective network which needs to be withdrawn at an appropriate time in the client's growth and development.

In treatment, the client begins to learn to interact with nonaddicts as counselors, nurses, doctors, vocational rehabilitation counselors, etc. He/she learns appropriate behaviors of dress, speech, punctuality, and communication. With skill in attending to these situations, he/she is ready to test and expand upon such skills outside the program. Can appointments be kept? Can an apartment be sought? Can a problem be resolved without force? Can a job be obtained? Initially, the client needs support in handling these matters, but as he/she becomes more confident and more successful, less support is needed.

Once the client begins to interact with the community, whether that be in employment or recreation, a new social network and new means for coping and succeeding are required. It is in meeting the demands of society that the client begins to test and further develop his/her real capacities. Problems emerge that are not a part of treatment, but are related to succeeding in the "real world."

However, it cannot be left entirely to the ex-addict to make his/her way in testing and refining adaptive skills. A person concerned about a hostile environment is less inclined to take risks. Therefore, the individual will need to be aided and relevant aspects of society so structured that each can come some necessary part of the way to meet the other. The available societal resources must then include not only job opportunities, but also opportunities for recreation and socialization. Work cannot be the only activity in one's life, nor can it meet all life-style needs. With suitable outlets, the pressures of work can then be minimized.

To accomplish effective community integration of the former client, significant movement on the part of the clients, the treatment programs, and the community will be required. The treatment program has the responsibility for preparing the client realistically for employment and for avocational experiences. Thus, the treatment program has responsibility for helping the client develop appropriate behaviors for getting and keeping a job, for considering the value of recreation, for encouraging as broad a scope of community interaction as possible. In addition, the treatment program has the responsibility for educating the community about its clients and about their strengths and needs.

The client has responsibility for acting in accord with newly developed skills and information. The client can be expected to speak up in his/her own behalf in an assertive, not aggressive, fashion. He/she can be expected—with support—to take increasing responsibility for his/her own life.

The community has responsibility for accepting the rehabilitated ex-addict, for making jobs and related resources available without undue or inappropriate demands on that person. The community has the responsibility to communicate an attitude of acceptance rather than an uninformed and unfeeling rejection.

NEW SOLUTIONS

Supported Work

Within the addiction treatment system there have emerged supported work projects, funded through a complex network of federal and state agencies, initiated first by Vera Institute in New York City and now functioning in 14 sites. These projects are centralized manpower-like programs which provide temporary, but actual, salaried jobs to ex-addicts as a means of transition into competitive employment. These transitional jobs allow the person to perform real work tasks and resolve work-related problems before facing an outside employer. Treatment programs are encouraged to refer their chronically unemployed clients to these programs since they are the ones lacking in the skills of learning a job, working with supervisors and coworkers, and developing a career plan. The supported work agency will screen the candidate for the basics of employability, will consider his/her strengths and weaknesses, determine a suitable type of work, and effect a placement. Often jobs are created within industry to meet an individual's needs. In New York City, for example, the Vera Institute Supported Work Project, Wildcat Services, has developed transitional jobs in many divisions of the city's civil service, e.g., in its drafting, maintenance, personnel, social, and library services; as well as jobs in private corporations, and in the utilities. The results of this project to date reveal significant improvement in client skills, positive social behavior, reduced drug abuse, and effective transition into competitive employment (Vera Institute of Justice, 1975).

During the period of employment, the individual is given feedback as to his/her performance and may be assisted with remedial education and/or specialized skill training as an adjunct to work the job. In this fashion, the individual experiences the real demands of work, develops the ability to tolerate a job, learns about his/her capabilities, and develops a reference point for further employment.

Innovations in Public and Private Sector Jobs

As described above, many of the recent advances in job development that have occurred on the addict's behalf have been within larger organizations. In addition to reasons of social consciousness and community pressure cited above, it might also be noted that large corporations have the money and resources for vocational programs that may be pilot in nature and can allow for small-scale hiring, research into the performance of the ex-addict, and demonstration projects intended to show that ex-addicts can, in fact, work in that environment. A controlled study of the performance of ex-addicts in job situations in large corporations making comparison to nonaddicted workers in the same settings demonstrated the high performance potential of carefully selected ex-addicts (Yankowitz and Randell, 1976). Other companies have been willing to use CETA (Comprehensive Employment and Training Act) funds for hiring ex-addicts in a demonstration effort (Bass and Woodward, 1978). Companies have been successfully encouraged to retain on their payrolls ex-addicts who have worked with them through these supported work experiences. State Offices of Vocational Rehabilitation have also established on-the-job training programs to aid as a means of entry for these former clients.

It is evident that jobs must come largely from the private sector since that segment of the economy has far more positions to fill involving a wider variety of job skills. This would seem to suggest that government can and should be a significant model for private industry: developing, testing, and publicizing vocational service models developed. Frequently, the public sector can also offer a system of job security that is far less available within the private sector. Since many ex-addicts experience difficulty in gaining employment, the relief of a secure situation is often welcome as a means of reducing pressure.

Employment Agencies

While many treatment programs have initiated their own job development and placement components, in some communities employment agencies have been established to work exclusively with ex-addicts. Provide Addict Care Today (PACT) in New York City is such an agency. These specialized placement units act as client advocates by paving the way into industry and business. They seek to educate employers about the realities of the ex-addict as a potential employee, counter the myth of addiction as an incurable disease, and demonstrate the employability of the rehabilitated ex-addict. Their primary functions are to selectively place qualified clients in existing and newly developed jobs through a careful prescreening process, which includes a close relationship with treatment programs to assist them in preparing their clients for employment and in referring appropriate clients for jobs available.

Aftercare

By focusing treatment on the primary stages of rehabilitation as is typically the case, we may be guilty of letting go too soon, before the ex-addict is prepared for independent functioning in a changed life-style. For many, the problems just begin when work starts. New pressures emerge. New demands are placed upon individuals and their families. New goals emerge with drives for higher education, promotion, or job change. Many ex-addicts, like many nonaddicts, think that life will be better when they are working. The reality when new problems emerge may be an experience that upsets the individual's equilibrium. The ex-addict may have a few sympathetic and helpful allies and find him/herself with problems without ready solutions. Since the rehabilitation programs do, in fact, allow for such a wide range of growth experiences, to stop short of long-term success is inappropriate and may be counterproductive in that it can result in unnecessary readmissions to treatment. At best it can lead to unwanted shame/embarrassment or simple clumsiness in dealing with a closed chapter of one's life.

The writer had the experience of meeting an ex-addict known to her for many years as a client and worker. She was a fine, respectable, hard-working woman. The meeting occurred quite unexpectedly and in the person's place of employment, previously unknown to the author. The meeting, which should have been truly happy, was shrouded in a sense of secrecy about our former relationship. Despite her trust in me, and I believe she trusts me, she had to remind me to "be cool and say nothing to anyone," or I might jeopardize her job. The legitimate voicing of a pride in her achievements must be foresworn. This person had long since been discharged from treatment. How is she handling her feelings of being different from her coworkers? How is she dealing with her fear of being "found out"? With whom can she share her success? Hopefully, these issues will not lead to any significant difficulty for her. We should consider a means of reducing still further that possibility and making certain that they do not. To do so will mean paying more attention to issues not simply of job finding and placement, but of guided integration into the work force and the life of the community.

REFERENCES

BASS, U. F. and WOODWARD, J. A. (1978) Training, Rehabilitation and Employment for Addicts in Treatment (TREAT). Services Research Report. Washington, DC: U.S. Government Printing Office.

GOLDENBERG, I. I., Employment and Addiction: Perspective on Existing Business and Treatment Practice, Washington, DC: National Technical Information Services, U.S. Department of Labor.

GRAHAM, R. (1973) "Relationship with business and industry" in The State of the Art, Vocational Rehabilitation and the Drug Abuser: Counseling As the Art. Washington, DC: Youth Projects, Inc. and DHEW Social and Rehabilitation Services.

KOENIGSBERG, L. and ROYSTER, E. (1977) Securing Employment for Ex-Drug Abusers: An Overview of Jobs. Washington, DC: Services Research Report, U.S. Government Printing Office.

SELLS, S. B. [ed.] (1974) The Effectiveness of Drug Abuse Treatment. Cambridge, MA: Ballinger.

Vera Institute of Justice (1975) Third Annual Research Report on Supported Employment. New York.

YANKOWITZ, R. B. and RANDELL, J. (1976) "Corporate employment and the Methadone patient." Presented at the National Abuse Conference, New York, March.

PART II

SELF-HELP MODELS FOR CONTINUING CARE

4

SELF-HELP MODELS
Implications for Drug Abuse Programming

TOARU ISHIYAMA

INTRODUCTION

The history, rationale, dynamics and models of services based on the self-help modality will be examined in this chapter, and implications drawn for meeting service needs in the field of drug abuse.

The self-help phenonemon, which has experienced a noticeable acceleration since World War II, and which has continued to pick up speed in the past decade, is not entirely a new kid on the block. Its precursor, the mutual aid movement was known to western civilization as early as the French Revolution, and is still a viable phenomenon in many societies. In a more organized sense, however, the mutual aid approach was epitomized by the Friendly Societies of England which developed during the Industrial Revolution (Katz and Bender, 1976). These societies were designed to aid individuals and groups to cope with the stresses of the significant societal changes wrought by the industrial changes and their economic consequences. These societies developed funds which could be used for the relief and maintenance of members in sickness, old age, and infirmity, much as the more formalized and expanded mutual insurance "societies" do in the modern age.

The development of therapeutically directed self-help groups, however, is of more recent vintage. Viewed from a therapeutic perspective, the grandsire of self-help programs is Alcoholics Anonymous (AA). In what is now considered a landmark event, Bill W., a New York broker and a "hopeless" alcoholic, and Dr. Bob, a surgeon and also an alcoholic, met in Akron, Ohio in May of 1935, and together embarked on a mission to help other alcoholics as well as themselves keep sober. They gathered around them a group of alcoholics and together they struggled with their common problem. Alcoholics Anonymous as an organization was launched in June of 1935, and by 1975, more than 26,000 groups were alive with an unestimable large membership.

The AA movement spawned the self-help, therapeutic communities for drug addicts. The therapeutic community model was essentially the child of Charles Dederich, who broke away from AA because he found AA to be too restricting for him. With some friends from AA, he set up a "free-association" discussion group in 1958. This group attracted and retained an increasing number of drug addicts. The influx of drug addicts culminated in a break with the alcoholic members, and led to Dederich's total involvement with and championship of the addicts. Synanon was thus launched. Synanon has, in turn, become the prototype for the development of a host of therapeutic communities for addicts and ex-offenders, as well as serving as a jumping off point for a number of revisionist movements.

Self-help therapeutic programs have also been developed, not by consumers, but by professionally trained persons.

One of the early, and major, self-help models in the field of mental health was developed by a psychiatrist, Abraham A. Low (1950). This model, Recovery, Inc., is a highly structured program based on the thesis that while mental illness is a physical process and cannot, therefore, be cured by psychological means, the ravages of the illness, the abnormal symptoms, can be controlled through training of the will. Recovery groups are led by a group member, selected on the basis of stability and put through a training regimen. The meeting format is common to and prescribed for every group and provides a comforting structure within which members can interact and focus upon their problems. At latest count, more than 1,000 groups with a membership of between 15,000 and 20,000 are meeting regularly.

The second example of a professionally developed program is the Lodge program, whose chief architect was George Fairweather (1964). The Lodge program is designed for institutionalized chronically mentally ill persons and provides this group with an effective and relevant entry process into the outside society. The main goal is to develop a relatively cohesive and mutually assisting group of patients in the hospital, and then to move the patients, as a group, into a community setting. The group, then, in the best traditions of the mutual aid society, provides a meaningful support system for each group member. Many Lodges also begin small businesses in order to ensure varying degrees of economic independence, again in the tradition of the co-op ventures. While professional help is initially provided, each group moves toward a more independent and self-governing stance.

Self-help groups are now found in an amazingly wide spectrum of human endeavor. The more commonly known groups relate to a range of activities from block clubs and neighborhood associations to welfare rights and ex-offenders organizations, to groups for smokers and compulsive eaters, to groups for the physically and emotionally handicapped. Therapeutic-type groups too are mushrooming.

This ever-expanding self-help approach has had considerable impact on the drug abuse field, first in terms of the aforementioned Synanon type, in terms of Synanon-spawned therapeutic communities, and also in terms of nonresidential treatment and/or aftercare efforts. While Narcotics Anonymous is still the sole national nonresidential self-help organization for the drug-abusing population, there have developed numerous locally based self-help groups for the addict/ex-addict population. These local endeavors are unfortunately not generally reported in established professional or scientific journals. The paucity of reports relating to these local programs can be attributed to two basic realities. First of all, self-helpers are usually not writers nor academicians and are neither interested in nor knowledgable about the formal reporting process. The basic intent of self-help groups is to help and seldom to conceptualize, or to do research, or to report. A second reason is that reports about the self-help programs are usually written by professional observers and researchers who bring in their observational and research tools long after the programs have been established. In effect, programs are reported only after they acquire a certain degree of legitimacy and credibility.

The foregoing is identified simply to point out that any discussion of self-help groups, particularly therapeutically oriented groups, is limited by the information available. It is a fact that not all therapeutic self-help approaches have been identified. Only the well-known and the established form the basis for analysis.

The absence of well-documented, let alone definitive, evaluation or research data add even more to the tentativeness that is being suggested here. As a matter of fact, the Synanon-type therapeutic community programs have actively resisted any research or evaluation ventures. Synanon's point of view is that the evaluation mandate focuses more on form rather than results, that the usual tests of respectability and validity are bureaucratic hang-ups, and that Synanon's business is simply to help addicts. John Maher cryptically asserts that therapeutic communities are in the business of building communities, and not in building replicable techniques. He states, "we didn't build America by stopping cowboys in America and asking them if their lives were stabilized! We just sent an avalanche of them. If you'd gone to Plymouth Rock with your clipboard and pencil a year after the Pilgrims landed and asked them, 'How many of you are leading constructive lives?' what do you think they'd have said?" (Hampden-Turner, 1976).

It is clear that the evaluation process is feared. It is suggested that research probings would harm delicately balanced persons and would ruin the aura of positive expectations so important in the therapeutic process. What is being said here is that the cold, impersonal evaluation methodologies may well destroy or at least negatively affect the necessary evangelistic belief system. It is further argued that standard research methods were developed in static social settings and are not appropriate to a new type of social organization. Finally, the argument is presented that there is no real outcome indicator other than "clean man-days," since there are no other outcomes.

Those self-help programs that are based on anonymity also tend to be inadequately documented, but for a different reason. These programs do not, or will not, maintain membership, process, or other management records. The mandate of anonymity militates against such documentation and against any kind of follow-up evaluation. Furthermore, the fact that self-help groups are self-selecting negates generalizations regarding effectiveness of the helping methodologies to the wider population.

ARGUMENTS FOR SELF-HELP PROGRAMS

The focus of this chapter is to examine the self-help movement as it relates or might relate to treatment and aftercare needs of the drug-abusing population. It is therefore necessary to understand the rationale underlying the upsurge of the self-help method.

What makes the self-help movement a viable one in general, and for the drug abusing population specifically? What does it offer that the professionally directed services cannot provide?

The first most obvious advantage is that of economics. The self-help approach adds a significant manpower resource to the human services system which has been, is, and possibly will be for a long time, experiencing a manpower shortage. While more professionals are being produced, this increase is not keeping up with the population growth, nor with the growing human services needs. The experience of Recovery, Inc. is a case in point. While Low personally supervised Recovery meetings during the early years, a new form of indigenous leadership had to be developed as the movement gained strength and membership. Recovery's leadership training program has been proved successful and has provided the basis for the continuing growth of Recovery. The Recovery experience simply validates the AA movement, which has always relied on indigenous leadership. A second reason for the upsurge in the self-help process can be traced to the consumer movement, which recognizes that the existing institutions have not provided nurturance and social support for the needy, the stigmatized, and the generally excluded groups (Katz and Bender, 1976). This exclusion has to some extent, actually forced these groups to form minisocieties as a reaction to the exclusion and as a defense against the perceived onslaughts of the larger society.

Another related reason is that the professional community is seen as having failed the population with which self-help groups are concerned (Back and Taylor, 1976). AA avers that "almost no recovery from alcoholism has ever been brought about by the world's best professionals, whether medical or professional" (Alcoholics Anonymous, 1953). John Maher of the Delancey Street Foundation speaks to the mistrust of the professional by referring to them as "surplus population" who are part of the problem they are hired to solve (Hampden-Turner, 1976).

Finally, the self-help movement is legitimized by theory/research/ practice which is more aware of the importance and benefits of involving the client or consumer in his/her own learning, relearning, or socialization. The significance of having the client share in the determination of his/her own fate is increasingly recognized and accepted in the human services field.

GENERAL SELF-HELP CHARACTERISTICS

While a literature review suggests a variety of perceptions as to the definition of self-help groups, depending upon the kind of self-help group being looked at, there are some characteristics common to most, if not all, self-help groups. Katz and Bender (1976) have identified a number of what they call underlying motifs. Self-help groups are voluntarily joined and formed by a group of peers who manifest or experience common needs that are not met by the existing social institutions. These groups are generally concerned with providing material as well as emotional assistance to the members of the group, and each member is sensitized to his responsibility and concern for his/her fellow members as the result of consistent, often prescribed face-to-face interactions. The interactions and the fact of group membership are designed to enhance each member's state of personal identity.

Levy (1976) described self-help groups in terms of five characteristics:

(1) Purpose. The purpose of the group is to provide help to each member in dealing with his/her problems and in raising the effectiveness level of each individual's functioning.
(2) Origin and sanction. The origin and sanction for the group existence lies with its members.
(3) Source of help. The primary source of help emanates from the skill and knowledge resources of its members.
(4) Composition. The group consists of those members who share a common core of life experiences and problems.
(5) Control. The control of group processes and destiny is essentially in the grasp of its members.

A recent exploratory conference (1978) on nonresidential self-help organizations and the drug abuse problem sponsored by the National Institute on Drug Abuse identified the following self-help group characteristics:

(1) Self-help organizations (SHOs) are voluntary groups whose origin usually is spontaneous.
(2) SHO members are peers in that they share a common problem/ need/handicap.
(3) SHOs are formed by the members for the purpose of meeting together to deal with/overcome their shared problem/need/handicap and to initiate a desired change (social and/or personal).
(4) SHO members perceive that the needs inherent in their shared problem/need/handicap are not being met by or through the established resources.
(5) An SHO provides help and support through its members' efforts, skills, knowledge, and concern, and without the aid of professionals.
(6) The help and support process involves face-to-face interactions.
(7) The members are responsible for and have control of the group. Parenthetically, it might be added that while SHOs might have

been stimulated or even started by professionals, self-determination and control must become a reality in short time. It should also be pointed out that this chapter will later point out the need to modify the control issue to incorporate the concept of relative and differential degrees of control.

(8) If professionals and government agencies are involved, they function only in a secondary role and at the pleasure of the members.

THE DYNAMICS OF THE SELF-HELP PROCESS

In a brief review of the historical and theoretical background of self-help programs, Glaser (1971) pointed out that the theoretical roots could be traced to a number of sources. Some of these are Alfred Adler's departure from a narrowly focused intrapsychic approach and his recognition of the part social forces played in determining behavior; Lewin's field-theory approach, which emphasized the here and now and influenced the encounter group movement; existential philosophy, which negates the proposition of immutable essences and holds that man is responsible for his essence; and learning theories which postulate that behavior can be shaped via a system of appropriate reinforcement schedules—these are recognized as being some of the major theoretical and intellectual underpinnings of the self-help movement. In addition, the work of Maxwell Jones (1957) in the development of a therapeutic milieu to treat personality disorders provides some of the procedural bases of residential self-help programs. The therapeutic milieu or community concept of Jones assumes that a setting in which all of the participants, staff and patients, could openly and honestly discuss and resolve community issues would provide the basis for an effective therapeutic process. This egalitarian, participative therapeutic community approach provided new and refreshing treatment concepts and made a significant dent in the established hierarchical treatment and social systems in psychiatric settings.

The foregoing theoretical underpinnings provide the backdrop for an analysis of the dynamics of self-help groups. What makes self-help groups effective and useful?

The first reason for the efficacy of the self-help modality relates to the sharing of common life experiences and problems. There is clearly an assumption that because all group members have "been there," they understand, at a basic gut level, each other's problems. There is therefore a high sense of trust and sensitivity among the group members. In addition, the having "been there" reduces the possibility that a group member can "con" another, a possibility that is seen as great between a professional and his client. In the Synanon group therapy experience, the Synanist acts as moderator and, by virtue of his/her own experiences, is able to detect the group member's conscious and unconscious attempts to evade the truth about himself. Self-help group members often see the liberal, non-authoritative professional as someone who can be conned, simply because the professional finds it difficult to be authoritative in dealing with the "victims of society." This difference from the usual professional-client quality has been labeled the aprofessional dimension (Riessman, 1976) and refers to an activist orientation and a greater understanding and identification with consumer/client problems.

A second reason is that the self-help situation permits the individual to participate in and to derive the benefits of the total helping situation both as a receiver and as a giver. Maximum participation in making decisions about group issues; focusing upon the attempt to increase control over issues that affect one personally; and making decisions that count in an accepting situation all should increase one's sense of independence as well as increase one's decision-making ability. Helping others and being important to others defines one's sense of worth. The simple process of helping others provides a social legitimacy to a group of individuals for whom that legitimization may have been lacking. Riessman (1976) refers to this process as the helper-therapy principle. He believes that there are critical and identifiable components of the principle.

(1) By persuading others with respect to a problem, members persuade themselves. By advocating a position or advising on a stance for others, one becomes committed to that position. Antze (1976) refers to this as "a sharing of lessons," and "by advising others, one indoctrinates oneself."

(2) The helping role defines the helper as being less dependent. By playing the relatively independent role as a helper, and reinforced in that role by the group, the member is validated to become less dependent.

(3) The member, by helping others, is afforded the opportunity to observe his "own" problem at a distance. In a sense, this principle is very similar to processes associated with psychodrama.

(4) The helper derives a feeling of social usefulness, of being of value to others. This is an experience which is not available too often to a career client.

(5) The status associated with the helping role provides validation of one's worth.

(6) The helping role provides one with internal support and validity, "if I can help others, I can't be all that helpless."

Another critical aspect of why self-help group works is the development of a support network or system. The program may be a residential one, or it may be one in which members come together on a scheduled basis. Group membership may change, but membership status is determined by each member. S/he may move in and out, but the group support is there when s/he needs it and when s/he chooses to use it.

In addition to the value of the self-help group as a supportive instrument, it also provides a vehicle for defining a different set of values, a different life-style and a milieu which reinforces those changes. In effect the self-help group process not only provides the support for and rewards associated with change, but it also serves to maintain those changes. The group which enabled the individual to make changes becomes the stabilizing reference group. The group provides a sense of community and belongingness and acceptance which is so vital to individuals who have experienced a continuous chain of isolating, rejecting events.

Finally, Antze (1976) points out that self-help groups are fixed communities of belief. Because self-help members are often those who are least likely to benefit from professional therapy, and are in the throes of despair, they are in a state of ready acceptance of a new belief system. As these individuals relate to group members who are sensitive to their needs, and who appear to have resolved their own problems, the persuasive quality of the group advice and admonitions are extremely heightened.

TYPES OF SELF-HELP GROUPS

Levy (1976) has developed a typology of self-help groups in which he identifies four basic types of groups.

The first type is concerned with conduct reorganization or behavioral control. Organizations which are of this type are AA and Synanon, among others.

Groups such as Parents Without Partners and Recovery are aimed at the amelioration of stress by learning how to do something about a stressful situation which cannot be avoided.

The third type of organization is formed for what Levy calls survival purposes. Here the deviant group attempts to help members to maintain self-esteem and to survive in hostile social settings. Gay self-help groups are examples of this type.

There is then a fourth type which is interested in personal growth and self-actualization. T-groups and sensitivity groups typify this category.

Katz and Bender (1976) have developed a similar typology. They list personal growth, developing alternative patterns for living (welfare rights organizations), outcast havens where there is a total involvement in a sheltered environment or subculture, social advocacy groups which attempt to impinge on the larger society to bring about perceived needed changes, and mixed types in which two or more of the basic goals coexist in a group.

A perusal of existing self-help approaches which have relevance for the drug abuse field suggests a schema which nicely orders those programs in terms of several significant variables. The following schema is a refinement of one previously described by Ishiyama (forthcoming).

Self-help programs can be ordered along a service continuum which incorporates the typology of both Levy (1976) and Katz and Bender (1976). Social advocacy groups are socially relevant organizations and provide immeasurable benefits to their members, as well as impacting society, but they will not be included in the following discussion, simply because the focus of the remainder of this chapter will be on those organizations which relate more largely to what Katz and Bender (1976) refer to as reform of self rather than a reform of society. This is not to deny the importance of and the need for reforming society, or the fact that even those organizations which address self-reform are not without interest in reforming society.

The service continuum would include two major group types. The first type is based on growth objectives. Subsumed under the growth objectives are Levy's conduct reorganization as well as those activities and functions which are designed to enhance cognitive, intrapersonal, interpersonal, and coping skills. It is assumed here that drug abusers must first experience changed behaviors, i.e., reduction of drug abuse and criminal activities, before the process of growth can occur.

The second type of groups relevant to the drug-abusing population addresses sustaining objectives. Sustaining objectives relate to activities and functions designed to *maintain* the individual in his/her environment. These maintaining or sustaining activities would include those which help the individual to reduce or make tolerable the stresses that impinge upon the individual, as well as providing an accepting and supportive social system.

The second variable defines activities in terms of movement. Some self-help groups define themselves as simply providing services to individuals in transit. Movement-oriented programs focus on movement from a closed service environment, such as a prison or a hospital, to a more open, less restricting environment. The concern then is to help members make the transition with minimal stress and psychological dislocation.

Finally, the programs can be placed on a residential or nonresidential basis. Residential programs are those where group members reside together, in a location operated by the organization. The residence may be a therapeutic community or a cooperative housing or apartment complex. Nonresidential programs obviously bring together their members to specific settings at specific times, but the residences of the group members are not a common one.

This schema would differentiate five major types of programs: growth and sustaining programs in both residential and nonresidential settings, and a transitional program.

EXAMPLES OF SELF-HELP PROGRAMS

A brief description of the conceptual bases of each of the five types of self-help groups that are deemed relevant to the drug abuse field will be presented in this section. The programs selected as examples are from the fields of drug abuse, mental health, alcoholism, and corrections.

The best known example of a *residential-growth* program is the therapeutic community as evidenced in Synanon and its offshoots, Delancey Street Foundation, Daytop Village, and Phoenix Houses. The therapeutic communities (TCs) have a number of factors in common. TCs developed in response to the needs of drug addicts and subscribe to the belief that addicts need to stop blaming social situations over which they have little control and need to take responsibility for their own actions. Therefore, it is proposed that the members must learn to accept and carry out personal responsibilities and to see themselves as persons who are accountable for their own behaviors. Acting sincere, responsible, and concerned is presumed to result in people becoming sincere, responsible, and concerned.

Being honest is considered an essential requisite to personal growth and to the assumption of a productive life-style not dependent on substance abuse. Techniques were developed to strip the person of the old identity and to build a new one based on an honest assessment of oneself.

Admission into TCs is voluntary but once admitted, the individual enters into a very authoritative and almost prescriptive community structure and participates in highly structured programs which are generally based on confrontation and encounter techniques. In addition to the treatment components, TCs provide a total institutional environment, including participation in the work life of the TC via TC businesses and in TC secured jobs. While all TCs are ostensibly treatment organizations, many TCs have become permanent subcultures from which transition to the larger culture is infrequent. In fact, Synanon and Delancey Street Foundation, for example, no longer allude to a graduation process and expressly hold to the notion that they are prototypes of what the larger culture ought to become.

Residential-Sustaining

The Fairweather Lodge is a good example of a residential-sustaining program. The residential-sustaining program is a relatively permanent residential setting where the members need the structure and support of such relative permanence and where the structure provides supportive interpersonal, vocational, and educational opportunities. While personality changes and improvement in coping skills may occur, they are concomitants and not the expressed goals of the program. The Fairweather Lodge is an aftercare program for chronic schizophrenics. The Lodge consists of members who were brought together in an institution prior to discharge, developed into a relatively cohesive group, and then moved as a group into a community-based residential setting. There is no resident staff and the members are completely responsible for the management of the house. The social system is designed to maximize opportunities for positive social interactions and to learn the practical skills needed to survive in the community. Responsibility for the management of the house is shared by the members via a number of prescribed and identified roles and functions. In addition, like the TCs, many Lodges have started businesses which provide work and income for the members.

Transitional Programs

The transitional model can operate in both residential and nonresidential settings. The example to be presented here encompasses both settings in one program, and is taken from the field of corrections.

Prisoners Personal Act (PPA) is a transitional program founded by an ex-offender for ex-offenders, and has been in existence since 1973. One of the basic assumptions of PPA is that the offender is one who has had to develop grandiose self-perceptions in order to esteem himself and who therefore tries to find the easiest means to legitimize those perceptions. Thus, to reverse the process, aspirations must be made realistic and the person must become responsible and accountable. PPA therefore offers a temporary shelter for parolees who are transitioning from prison to the community. PPA also provides a job placement program, because it considers a job the most critical factor in helping the ex-offender in the community. Furthermore, medical, educational, and social services needs are secured for the ex-offender. The program is distinctly a transitional one in that all services are time-limited and designed to lead to increased independence on the part of the ex-offender.

Nonresidential-Growth

While the best-known self-help group designed to bring about conduct reorganization, behavior changes, and ultimate growth is AA, the example to be presented here is a much lesser known local effort, but one which has direct relevance to the drug-abusing population. FOCAL, Inc., located in Washington, DC, was originated in 1975 by a group of graduates of a therapeutic community. As graduates of a program that had forged a bond between them it was decided to use this relationship to continue to maintain and increase the gains they had achieved in the TC. The group meets once a week for a group session that essentially utilizes a modified form of confrontation techniques more suited to a nonresidential, episodic setting. Outside of the formal meetings, the group meets with the soon-to-be-graduated members of TCs to help them make the transition via a modeling approach. Job referrals are also made for new graduates. This group offers, therefore, transitional support. However, the primary raison d'être is to provide each group member the support and stimulus for continued conduct reorganization and the pursuit of growth and increased self-actualization.

Nonresidential-Sustaining

While Recovery, Inc. embodies many activities which might relate to growth objectives, the basic intent is to help its members recognize the reality of mental illness, and to learn how to reduce the stress and anxieties associated with or resulting from their symptoms of abnormality. Techniques such as "spotting" have been developed to recognize debilitating symptoms, feelings, and sensations and to apply a Recovery concept quickly and appropriately. While recognizing symptoms does not stop the symptoms, the recognition can stop the reaction to the symptoms. The continued use of appropriate techniques is solidified by the mechanism of self-endorsement which simply is the person reinforcing the self whenever s/he uses a Recovery technique.

Each Recovery group meets weekly and follows a highly structured program, focusing on the writings of Low and other Recovery leaders. It is the highly structured and clearly specified procedures which contribute to

the group's ability to handle anxieties and problems. And in this structured and inspirational context, each of the members can hear one another
and can give relevant support and advice.

COMMON SELF-HELP PROCESSES

It is interesting to note that a common theme that permeates many
self-help concepts is the notion that its members are victims of erroneous
explanatory concepts perpetrated either by the victims themselves or by
outside forces. The TCs as well as Prisoners Personal Aid and FOCAL
argue that the members themselves are the victims of false assumptions
and labels. While the members may in fact be victims of an oppressive
environment, the victim abrogates his/her responsibility, and therefore
his/her integrity, when blame is placed on the environment.

Recovery, Inc. and AA aver that the victimization is perpetrated by
society with its erroneous concepts, labels, and practices. Thus, mental
illness and alcoholism are somatic processes and not the results of poor
environments or weak psyches.

All self-help groups do appear to agree that the "pathology" is the
absence of a sense of responsibility and mastery. Therefore, there is a great
emphasis on commitment to responsible behavior and the development of
mastery over one's actions.

The technology to be used in terms of achieving responsibility and
mastery varies. Some utilize positive reinforcement techniques; others rely
on punishment methods. Some attempt to substitute behavior via training;
others attempt to root out bad behavior by assault. Some attempt to
change a whole life-style by forcing acceptable behaviors; others simply
attempt to maintain survival skills. Some use abrasive and aggressive
confronting techniques; others rely more on modeling and supportive
approaches.

In most self-help examples, the organizational structure is an important
component of the group process. Some organizations come from an
authoritative and/or religious frame of reference; others stress secular,
social controls. All subscribe to relatively well-structured, almost prescriptive organizational dynamics.

Cognitive reorganization is espoused and nurtured in many self-help
organizations. New or different value systems are shaped. A different
rationale for problems, for stress, for life in general is offered. Alternative
perceptions and discriminative abilities are encouraged.

As a way of reducing a sense of isolation and uniqueness, most self-help
groups consciously attempt to foster primary-type relationships among

their members. There is a sustained effort to establish the positive kinds of interpersonal relationships that a member has not experienced, either because s/he never had a primary relationship or because the primary interpersonal relationship was an unsatisfactory one.

Finally, there develops a kind of elitism in all of the self-help groups. In their zeal to legitimize their programs, and to explain why the professional society has failed, the need to sell their wares inevitably leads to a kind of cultism. Self-help groups develop an esprit de corps which is enhancing and contributes to the "saving" of its members. There is no zeal to surpass the zeal of the saved.

It should be clear by now that the variety of spontaneously developed self-help forms can be ordered along a rational continuum. Without planning and without communications self-help groups have appeared to meet the wide-ranging needs of the population. The question facing drug abuse services planners and coordinators is whether the spontaneously developed self-help models can be incorporated into the continuum of relevant and necessary programs for the drug abuser. While reviews of self-help organizations point out that most of these organizations were begun by charismatic leadership, it appears that the presence of continued charisma is not necessarily essential to the continuance of the organization. Recovery, Inc., TCs such as Phoenix Houses, and even AA no longer have the counsel of their originators. What maintains these organizations is a belief system, a formal organizational structure, prescribed procedures which, while modifiable, are always clear, and an esprit de corps. It therefore would be logical to assume that a viable self-help group can be started either by a charismatic leader, or through a planning and implementation process carried out by drug services administrators. It matters not so much that the chick is hatched naturally or artificially; it does matter that the nature of the chick is understood and allowed to mature. There is an advantage to the electronically hatched chick. The time, place, and kind of egg to be hatched can be planned and controlled. Natural hatchings must depend on the whims of the hen.

Given the premise that a sufficient variety of relevant self-help models exist, and given that these models can be either naturally developed by charismatic and timely leadership or electronically by planful professionals and administrators, the potential for maximizing the utilization of such models appears enormous.

And if self-help efforts are to be nurtured in a planful way, planners must be sensitive to a number of critical issues generally not considered by spontaneous, indigenously developed self-help groups. The first is to assure a useful degree of linkings. Most self-help efforts, by the very nature of the efforts, are relatively isolated from and in competition with other self-help efforts and with the larger helping systems. Linkages between these systems are weak, if not nonexistent. If the self-help efforts are to take advantage of outside resources and if they are to avoid the isolationism which can breed cultish elitism and an unintegrated, isolated subculture, a major effort must be made to integrate them into the total service system. What needs to be considered is a method of organizing the self-help models so that clients can be afforded a variety of self-help options as well as access to all other components of the helping industry. This may well be easier said than done, the perceptions by self-help groups of the professional and established helping community have been negative. However, the picture is not as dark as it may appear if it is realized that the negative perceptions resulted from the failures of the professional helping system. That system has the enviable opportunity to remedy that situation.

A second critical issue is the development of alternative techniques. The fact that existing self-help programs use highly structured, authoritative methods does not rule out the legitimacy or relevance of other approaches. The existing methods have obviously proven to be relevant to existing self-help populations. Enough observational data exist, however, to indicate that the existing methods are not necessarily relevant to needy populations not now included in self-help group membership. Confrontation methods do not appear to suit members of proud cultures. AA and AA derivative methods do not appear to be attractive to certain socioeconomic, educational, and ethnic-cultural groups. If the self-help modality is to become effective for a larger population, different structures, different group processes, and different techniques may have to be developed. While this need is recognized and some investigatory, developmental programs have been launched, little if any concrete or demonstrably useful progress have been reported.

A third matter of concern is the impact of the inevitable bureaucratization of the self-help process. It is pointed out that the classical pattern of the growth of social groups sees the emergence of a bureaucratic structure as the original charismatic leadership erodes, a general accommodation to societal demands, and a focus on group maintenance, almost for the sake of maintenance. How are the self-help groups to organize efficiently and effectively and endure without losing the vitality and the relevance which now characterize the self-help groups? How is growth to be stimulated and sustained so that the group does not become hackneyed and routine? Perhaps this issue is joined sooner in the noncharismatic leadership modes.

Other critical issues relate to the need to adequately evaluate the efficacy of each of the self-help models and the need to establish a sound fiscal basis and an accountability mandate without diluting the voluntary, mutual aid commitment.

A multitude of critical issues will emerge in any attempt to harness or to reproduce that which was spontaneous, or to organize spontaneous efforts into an integrated or coordinated whole. Spontaneity and organization may well be irreconcilable terms. However difficult the reconciliation may be, success could result in a significantly expanded and relevant service armamentarium. The field of drug abuse services is ready for a concerted effort.

REFERENCES

Aloholics Anonymous (1953) Twelve Steps and Twelve Traditions. New York: Alcoholics Anonymous World Services.

ANTZE, P. (1976) "The role of ideologies in peer psychotherapy organizations: some theoretical considerations and three case histories." Journal of Applied Behavioral Sciences 12 (3): 323-344.

BACK, K. W. and TAYLOR, R. C. (1976) "Self-help groups: tool or symbol?" Journal of Applied Behavioral Sciences 12 (3): 295-309.

FAIRWEATHER, G. W. [ed.] (1964) Social Psychology in Treating Mental Illness: An Experimental Approach. New York: John Wiley.

GLASER, F. B. (1971) "Gaudenzia, Inc.: historical and theoretical background of a self-help addiction treatment program." International Journal of Addiction, 6 (4): 615-626.

HAMPDEN-TURNER, C. (1976) Sane Asylum. San Francisco: San Francisco Books.

ISHIYAMA, T. (forthcoming) "Aftercare: the ex-client as the provider of services."

JONES, M. (1957) "The treatment of personality disorders in a therapeutic community." Psychiatry 20: 211-220.

KATZ, A. H. and BENDER, E. I. (1976) "Self-help groups in western society: history and prospects." Journal of Applied Behavioral Sciences 12 (3): 265-282.

LEVY, L. H. (1976) "Self-help groups: types and psychological processes." Journal of Applied Behavioral Sciences 12 (3): 310-322.

LOW, A. A. (1950) Mental Health Through Will-Training. Boston: Christopher.

RIESSMAN, F. (1976) "How does self-help work?" Social Policy 7 (2): 41-45.

5

SELF-HELP GROUPS SERVING DRUG ABUSERS

Within a broad framework, Katz and Bender (1976) define self-help groups as "voluntary small group structures formed by peers who have come together for mutual assistance in satisfying a common need, overcoming a common handicap or life-style disrupting problem and bringing about desired social and/or personal change." While this definition can be seen as encompassing a multitude of groups, self-help groups can essentially be described in terms of four major issues (Levy, 1976):

Conduct Reorganization. Activities of groups directed at the reorganization of members' conduct would involve efforts at learning to control and/or modify behavior problems which are seen as having a disruptive effect on life functioning. Such groups would include Alcoholics Anonymous (AA), Narcotics Anonymous (NA), and Parents Anonymous (PA).

Coping with Stress. Activities of groups involved in this process would focus on the learning of behaviors designed to ameliorate stress and to cope with a current stressful situation. Such groups are not attempting to restructure behavior as are groups concerned with conduct reorganization, but to allow individuals to develop the capacity to deal with immutable life situations. Some examples of this type of group would be Parents Without Partners, Widow to Widow, and Recovery, Inc.

135

Survival. Groups oriented around survival would be composed of those people labeled as deviant by the mass of society because of different life-styles and values, or of those people who are discriminated against for racial or other reasons. Self-esteem is enhanced through mutual support, consciousness-raising activities, and involvement in political activities aimed at achieving acceptance and/or parity with the majority. Such groups might deal with gay rights, black power, women's consciousness raising, etc.

Human Growth. Groups oriented toward human growth have as their common goal the enhancement and enrichment of lives through psychological or didactic techniques, e.g., gestalt therapy, T groups, sensitivity training, etc. As contrasted with persons drawn to the groups outlined above, members associated with human growth groups typically have no basic problem in common.

The drug abuser is clearly an individual whose behaviors create problems for him/herself and others, i.e., an individual for whom those groups focusing on conduct reorganization would be most appropriate. Consequently, the discussion which follows will focus on the use of self-help groups oriented toward behavioral change for drug-abusing individuals.

BACKGROUND

Self-help groups for drug abusers have been most largely in evidence in the form of residential therapeutic communities, e.g., Synanon, Daytop Village, etc. These therapeutic communities, which usually employ ex-addict staff, provide a total living-in situation within a highly structured framework of "family" and community. Therapeutic communities usually have established focal points:

- A "self-help" therapeutic milieu in which every activity is oriented toward staying "clean" and learning to be a productive member of society. This may include a progression in terms of complexity of work and extent of responsibility assigned first within the therapeutic milieu and later in the outside community. The drug abuser is aided by peers and alumni in reaching the goals of therapy.

- Group sessions which are usually led by an ex-addict and include techniques such as verbal confrontations or encounters. The ex-addict is often seen as both serving as a model for drug abuse residents and as someone who cannot easily be "conned" by the drug abusers' "games."

In this way, residents and staff together form a community that provides both challenge and incentive to effect change, and support and encouragement for the resident seeking to learn and grow. Nonetheless, continued efforts at self-help are typically not available for the former resident exiting into the community and are usually not available for the client exiting from other treatment modalities. In addition, self-help has not been a focus as a primary treatment modality. In this way, the self-help movement in the field of drug abuse has been relegated almost entirely to residential settings. The sister field of alcoholism treatment stands in bold contrast to this limited use of self-help strategies.

ISSUES IN THE FUNCTIONING OF
SELF-HELP ORGANIZATIONS

It would be difficult to overemphasize the importance of Alcoholics Anonymous not only to the field of alcoholism, but to the self-help movement generally. As will be discussed below, it provided the stimulus and the model for the development of Narcotics Anonymous (NA), which remains the single most significant self-help organization for drug abusers. Moreover, it has helped spawn a number of self-help organizations in its image or closely resembling it. Inasmuch as AA forms the basis for a consideration of many self-help groups concerned with conduct reorganization, it will be useful to explore the structure and functioning of that group and those other self-help groups that have developed through a use of its model. Included here will be those groups that make effort to permit individual (or family) change in relation to substance abuse, e.g., AA, NA, Families Anonymous (FA), and Women for Sobriety.

Anonymity. Perhaps the single most important commonality shared by the groups concerned with conduct change is the protection of the individual through anonymity. (Women for Sobriety provides anonymity for those members who desire it, but does not demand it as do other groups.)

In the group, people are typically known by their first name only. No attendance is taken at meetings and no records are kept. People are free to come and go voluntarily. An exchange of phone numbers as part of a buddy system is voluntary (AA, 1972b).

Organizational Leadership. Most self-help groups were started by people who are described by some as charismatic and by others as tireless workers and staunch believers in the cause and who gathered around them a cadre of faithful followers, e.g., Jean Kirkpatrick, Women for Sobriety; Jimmy K., Narcotics Anonymous; Dr. Bob and Bill W., AA. These leaders worked without monetary compensation and have been viewed as an example to their supporters that they can overcome disruptive problems and restructure their lives.

Perhaps in keeping with the towering strength attributed to the initial leadership, these organizations go on to maintain the philosophy of a "fellowship of peers." Typically, there is an attempt to rotate "leadership" positions within both the local group and national organization.

Philosophical Tenets. Most importantly, organizations have developed basic tenets which provide a progressive approach toward behavioral change. These tenets are usually embodied in a stair-step approach such as AA's 12 steps and Women for Sobriety's 13 steps. (It should be noted that although these steps are seen as progressive, individual groups may sometimes skip around in their step discussions.)

In many instances the organization adheres to these tenets with a religious fervor for they reflect the very essence of the group's existence and beliefs. Some of these tenets have spiritual overtones, such as the reliance on a higher power. This higher power can be interpreted by the individual according to his/her own perspective. Other groups (Women for Sobriety and Fellowships Anonymous—to be discussed below) have rejected the spiritual language of these tenets and have incorporated tenets of self-reliance.

Pathways to Help. Pathways into the group usually are through word of mouth, media publicity, group literature, or simply the telephone book.

Most organizations frown upon outreach and solicitation in the community, and believe that the individual will only approach the group upon recognition of his/her need for help. However, groups will accept prospective members even if they come to them under court order, employer, or other agency pressures. Groups recognize that many of their cured members originally attended their first group meeting because they were forced to attend by some outside authority. While this is not seen as positively as voluntary attendance, it is recognized that an individual who has been directed to attend meetings can nonetheless be motivated toward change.

Community Relations. Groups do engage in dispersing information and fostering community understanding of their organization through the media. When invited, group members will talk with schools, churches, and civic groups.

Alcoholics Anonymous adopted a policy of "cooperation but nonaffiliation" with other organizations concerned with alcoholism (AA, 1974).

Essentially this means that while individual AA members may participate in such activities as alcoholism research, or be employed in a medical or psychiatric treatment setting for alcoholism, the organization itself does not engage in these activities, nor does it endorse any causes. In addition, no opinion on outside issues are expressed by the organization, lest its name be drawn into public controversy. This philosophy is part of the 12 traditions of AA, NA, and Families Anonymous. It does, however, recognize that individuals coming to them for help may also be receiving concurrent treatment of another kind. Many metropolitan AA groups have formed an intergroup office which can refer callers to the local AA group in their area. In addition, the intergroup office is often knowledgable about non-AA alcoholism resources in the community and can offer appropriate information and referral to the caller. These intergroups may also have committees whose responsibility it is to keep the public accurately informed about AA and to ensure that local professionals and agencies working with alcoholics know about AA.

Both NA and FA also follow the leadership of AA on the issue of community relations. In the past, NA has been more closed concerning its community relationships, but because of public demand for knowledge, it is becoming more involved in the media and appearances in the community in order to foster greater community understanding of the organization.

Funding. All of the groups are nonprofit, usually run by volunteers and supported through the sale of literature and by member contributions. Contributions from outside organizations are not accepted. The 12 traditions of AA, NA, and FA are most emphatic in their statement that the organization "should never endorse, finance, or lend its name to any related facility or outside enterprise lest problems of money, property and prestige divert it from its primary purpose."

Types of Meetings. Women for Sobriety meetings are always closed. AA, FA, and NA often hold both open and closed meetings. Both open and closed meetings are similar in the discussion of tenets, guest speakers, members' discussions of their experiences, etc. However, members often feel more free in their discussion during a closed membership meeting than one that is open to the public.

Because of the anonymity of the groups, there are no official membership records etc., so that the honor system is in force for attendance in open/closed meetings. If it is suspected that someone from the general public is in attendance at a closed meeting, that person will be requested to leave.

Organizational Structure. AA and NA have each developed an organizational structure consisting of local, area (regional), and national levels. AA and NA have a national office to handle inquiries and to serve as informational clearinghouses. Women for Sobriety conducts national seminars for field representatives who wish to start local groups, but has no formalized organizational structure. The organizational structure of AA and NA provides a means of easy access for communication and coordination between local groups. The most active members on the local level usually become representatives on a regional or national level. Regional representatives may be instrumental in organizing and lending support to fledgling groups, or in initiating an area phone listing where information can be obtained concerning local group meetings. National level representatives may review and/or make changes in the literature or review the organization's steps and their traditions.

More details will be presented below on various aspects of the individual self-help groups. Some groups not mentioned in the previous discussion will also be examined. The discussion should be reviewed with an eye toward the relevance of the organizational model explored for drug abuse.

Alcoholics Anonymous

As has been described, Alcoholics Anonymous is the grandmother model upon which many non residential self-help groups are organized. There are over 30,000 local AA groups in 92 countries, consisting of approximately 1 million members. Each group is autonomous except in matters affecting other AA groups or the AA fellowship as a whole. It is interesting to note that only about 1,300 of these groups are in hospitals, and an additional 1,300 are in correctional institutions (AA, 1966). Groups are run by short-term steering committees to avoid permanent leadership or dominance. The basic tenets of AA can be found in its 12 steps. In accepting the 12 steps, the individual first recognizes the power that alcoholism has in controlling his/her life. Reliance on alcoholism is transferred to reliance on a power greater than the individual. This higher power is interpreted within the individual's own personal concept.

Research designed to evaluate and/or understand the effectiveness of AA has been limited and at times has been simply self-serving. Two reports worthy of note are those of Leach (1973) and Madsen (1974). Leach (1973) reports on four studies of AA conducted in New York, London, Finland, and the United States/Canada. These four studies consisted of self-report questionnaires from 12,946 AA members. They were not scientifically controlled studies, nor did they involve pre/post measures. Self-reported abstinence was the only measurement of effectiveness. Large numbers of AA members, moreover, also reported concurrent treatment in addition to AA. Therefore, it cannot be concluded that AA was solely responsible for the recoveries found in the studies.

The studies report that many alcoholics began to maintain unbroken sobriety in AA after an initial period of AA membership marked by relapses. In the largest of the four studies, which was conducted in the United States/Canada and involved 11,355 subject, 38% of the AA members are reported as having been abstinent less than one year and 35% reported themselves as abstinent from one-five years. The numbers of people who have tried AA once and left are unknown. Although the above studies are self-serving and subject to bias, the claims of success can rival many treatment programs.

Madsen (1974) did an ethnographic investigation of AA in California using participant observation procedures and making extensive use of questionnaires, biographies, and taped interviews. He concluded that "in comparison with other therapies, the AA success rate is really miraculous."

Narcotics Anonymous

This first, and still major, self-help group for the support of drug abusers had its origins in Alcoholics Anonymous. NA is a nonprofit organization which was formed in 1953 by a group of drug abusers who felt that the AA fellowship did not offer a program of recovery from drug addiction. AA's concern with drugs has traditionally been limited. It has viewed alcohol as the major issue for individuals abusing both drugs and alcohol and has been generally loath to take on the problem of drug abuse unless a problem of alcohol use was also established.

NA's goal has been that of drug abstinence. Like AA, NA does not speak of cures, but of recovery. The organization is wedded to the AA model and has incorporated the identical 12 steps of AA as its philosophical base. These 12 steps are described as spiritual, not religious, and provide the support necessary to permit the individual to remain abstinent. These 12 steps are as follows:

(1) We admitted that we were powerless over our addiction, that our lives had become unmanageable.
(2) We came to believe that a power greater than ourselves could restore us to sanity.
(3) We made a decision to turn our will and our lives over to the care of God as we understood Him.

(4) We made a searching and fearless moral inventory of ourselves.

(5) We admitted to God, to ourselves, and to another human being the exact nature of our wrongs.

(6) We were entirely ready to have God remove all these defects of character.

(7) We humbly asked Him to remove our shortcomings.

(8) We made a list of all persons we had harmed, and became willing to make amends to them all.

(9) We made direct amends to such people wherever possible, except when to do so would injure them or others.

(10) We continued to take personal inventory, and when we were wrong promptly admitted it.

(11) We sought through prayer and meditation to improve our conscious contact with God, as We understood Him, praying only for knowledge of His will for us, and the power to carry that out.

(12) Having had a spiritual awakening as a result of those steps, we tried to carry this message to addicts and to practice these principles in all our affairs. [NA, 1976b]

In addition to the 12 steps, and again in accord with the AA structure, there are 12 traditions which are used. The 12 steps and 12 traditions must be solemnly adhered to by NA members. The traditions are as follows:

(1) Our common welfare should come first; personal recovery depends on NA unity.

(2) For our Group purpose there is but one ultimate authority—a loving God as He may express himself in our Group conscience, our leaders are but trusted servants, they do not govern.

(3) The only requirement for membership is a desire to stop using.

(4) Each Group should be autonomous, except in matters affecting other Groups, or NA as a whole.

(5) Each Group has but one primary purpose—to carry the message to the addict who still suffers.

(6) An NA Group ought never endorse, finance, or lend the NA name to any related facility or outside enterprise, lest problems of money, property, or prestige divert us from our primary purpose.

(7) Every NA Group ought to be fully self-supporting, declining outside contributions.

(8) Narcotics Anonymous should remain forever nonprofessional, but our Service Centers may employ special workers.

(9) NA as such ought never be organized; but we may create service boards or committees directly responsible to those they serve.

(10) NA has no opinion on outside issues; hence the NA name ought never be drawn into public controversy.

(11) Our public relations policy is based on attraction rather than promotion; we need always maintain personal anonymity at the level of press, radio, and films.

(12) Anonymity is the spiritual foundation of all our Traditions, ever reminding us to place principles before personalities. [NA, 1976b]

Today, Narcotics Anonymous consists of over 700 affiliated groups throughout the U.S. and abroad. To be considered an NA Group, the organization must meet regularly at a specified place and time, follow the 12 steps and traditions, and be duly registered with the World Service Office of NA, located in Sun Valley, California.

As stated previously, because of its anonymity there are no statistics on NA members. It is suggested that there is no single predominating drug among persons coming to NA. NA claims that the type of drug used is irrelevant—whether pills or heroin one's life is being controlled by drugs and the fight for abstinence is therefore the same. Moreover, NA warns against the substitution of alcohol for other substances (Narcotics Anonymous, 1976b). While it has been suggested that membership in self-help groups generally tend to achieve a uniformity of significant background characteristics, e.g., sex, race, age, socioeconomic status, etc., reports of drug abusers in the NA literature range from street addict to housewife, and reflect a wide variety of backgrounds and experiences.

The NA program is viewed as following a 24-hour plan such that all effort is expended on remaining drug-free for 24 hours and thereby getting through life one day at a time. Experienced members are portrayed as models for new members and act as "buddies" to new members to help prevent relapse into drug use. It is the NA meetings, however, that are viewed as integral to the individual group member's recovery (NA, 1976d).

Each active NA Group (NA, 1976a) has a steering committee consisting of a secretary, treasurer, and a general service representative (GSR). These people are elected by the NA membership in the spirit of "trusted servants," to attend to the business of NA. They are expected to serve for one year. NA literature suggests that problems have arisen when unqualified people or people without a history of sobriety have been elected (NA, 1976a). The group secretary has primary responsibility for planning meetings. Groups are maintained by member donations. The treasurer is responsible for handling legitimate expenses incurred by the group, e.g., refreshments, supplies, rent (where applicable), etc. The general service representative is a vital link between the local NA and other groups. As shown below, the NA member is tied to a national program in a loosely maintained, but precise, complex of relationships. The representative serves on an (geographic) area service committee which, in turn, sends representatives to a regional service committee. Both committees oversee NA concerns in their respective areas or regions.

Organizational Structure of NA

Member
Group
Area Service Committee
Regional Service Committee
World Service Office—World Service Board
World Service Conference

Like AA, NA states "once an addict, always an addict" (NA, 1976c). The individual is unable to use drugs normally and must resist temptation to ever use drugs again.

NA has also reported that even those who relapse show marked gains from their efforts to achieve abstinence. These individuals are viewed as having dropped many of the behaviors supportive of drug abuse that characterized them in the past. In this sense, the NA experience is described as analogous to climbing up a tower, one step at a time before reaching the top. One may slip down a few stairs without necessarily reaching the bottom and having to start all over again. The NA influence can remain and a relapse need not mean all has been lost. Indeed, the relapse and resulting dissatisfaction with oneself may provide an impetus to seek larger personal change. In this sense, even relapse can be seen as instrumental to recovery (NA, 1976c).

Fellowships Anonymous

Self-help groups have been viewed as having limited appeal for minority group members (National Institute on Drug Abuse, 1978). The idea of speaking up in a group, a majority of whose members share a significantly different cultural background and set of experiences, and surrendering oneself to a higher power (as in NA's 12 steps) can be seen as a reaffirmation of the powerlessness and separateness which many minority group members may feel. Although NA has claimed that the 12 steps can apply to anyone regardless of religion, and that the "higher power" may be whatever an individual deems appropriate, the image of NA as a quasi-religious organization persists in many quarters. Fellowships Anonymous, a pilot project for heroin addicts in the Detroit ghetto area has taken the principles of self-help and incorporated the format of the AA/NA structure, but has largely rejected the spiritual/religious language of the 12 steps. They have substituted a humanistic statement and positive social values incorporated into eight steps with each step representing a higher level of achievement in the effort to achieve abstinence (Detroit Self-Help Group Research Project, 1978). These eight steps are as follows:

(1) We admit that drug addiction, in taking over our lives, kept us from achieving purpose, dignity and meaning in living.
(2) We accept the need for receiving stable lives of purpose, dignity, and value to ourselves and others.
(3) We know that the purposes of our fellowship are not achieved if we become dependent upon alcohol or other drugs which make our lives unmanageable.
(4) We do not recognize any environmental problem as a valid reason for continued drug use now or in the future.
(5) We affirm that within ourselves as individuals and as a group there are sources of strength sufficient to change our lives.
(6) We aim for lives that are not simply drug free but are full of meaning and value because of purposeful living on behalf of our brothers and sisters.
(7) We know of a peace of mind which drugs cannot provide which is based on overcoming defects in character, attaining a clear conscience, and achieving strong positive relationships with others.
(8) Out of gratitude for achieving stability, dignity and meaning in our lives, we seek to share our new experience with others who are drug dependent.

Thus, while NA's steps emphasize the need of the individual to give him/herself over to a higher power and accept the strength available through that power; the Fellowship's steps emphasize strengths that are within oneself and one's group, place a particular emphasis on one's responsibility to the immediate community and reject any effort to find fault for one's addiction in environmental factors.

The organization currently has six-eight groups with a membership of 50-100 persons. Two ex-addict paraprofessionals have responsibility for developing and helping to maintain the groups. They do not, however, participate in group discussions.

Women for Sobriety

Much as Fellowships Anonymous was formed to meet the special needs of minority group members, Women for Sobriety was formed largely because some women felt that their needs were not being adequately met by AA (although many members of this group have retained their AA membership). The organization was started in 1975 by Jean Kirkpatrick, a recovered alcoholic. There are now 250 groups across the nation. This self-help group helps alcoholic women rebuild their self-concept and self-esteem focusing on "self-power" rather than on any higher spiritual power. The member must rid herself of "negative emotion," create new ideas about herself and her world, and act rather than react. The Group has 13 steps to aid in the development of self-esteem and the building of positive social networks. These 13 steps are:

(1) I have a drinking problem that once had me.
(2) Negative emotions destroy only myself.
(3) Happiness is a habit I will develop.
(4) Problems bother me only to the degree I permit them to.
(5) I am what I think.
(6) Life can be ordinary or it can be great.
(7) Love can change the course of my world.
(8) The fundamental object of life is emotional and spiritual growth.
(9) The past is gone forever.
(10) All love given returns twofold.
(11) Enthusiasm is my daily exercise.
(12) I am a competent woman and have much to give others.
(13) I am responsible for myself and my sisters. [Kirkpatrick, no date]

Women are encouraged to read these statements upon arising in the morning and retiring at night. They are to take one particular statement and use it consciously all day. Before going to sleep, they are to review the day's activities and to put their feelings down in a notebook.

Groups are composed of eight to ten women with conversations in the round in which an experienced leader, coleader, and secretary-treasurer who are group members share leadership responsibility. The leader must have at least two years of sobriety and is often the woman who started the group. The secretary-treasurer is selected by the group. Topics consist of the 13 steps, loneliness, the handling of aggression, family relationships, jobs, etc. Nutrition and meditation are also emphasized. As an organization, Women for Sobriety is not based upon anonymity among its members, but provides anonymity for those who wish it. It is a voluntary, self-supporting organization. This group will admit women who are having problems with alcohol and polydrug abuse, but is not geared toward women whose sole problem is drugs. Its model, however, appears appropriate for drug-abusing women.

Families Anonymous

As the name implies, the focus of Families Anonymous is on the family of the individual showing a behavior problem. It is the family that must learn to cope with the problem; it is the family that may be inadvertently contributing to the problem. This group, too, is modeled after AA and has adapted its 12 steps and traditions. While the group originally focused only on the families of drug abusers, it now includes parents whose children manifest other behavior problems, e.g., runaways, delinquents, etc. The thrust of the program is to shift emphasis from the "problem" person toward the *self,* with emphasis placed on the development of personal coping and problem solving techniques and an abandonment of guilt feelings and anxiety.

The group helps the family to realize that it cannot control the drug abuser's behavior and that the drug abuser must take responsibility for his/her actions. The sharing of experiences within the group help to lift the burden of guilt and aid family members to cope with the situation in which they find themselves. Each person is viewed as being responsible for his/her own actions and reactions to the drug abuser, and how their behaviors may serve to aggravate the situation. In extreme cases, the group has given support to families who find it necessary to "kick" the drug abuser out of the house in order to regain family equilibrium. At regularly scheduled meetings there may be discussion around specific themes and/or use of guest speakers, as well as the sharing of experiences in an atmosphere of group warmth and support. FA follows the same 12 steps and 12 traditions as NA and AA. There are over 100 Families Anonymous chapters across the nation. The organization has a World Service Office similar to AA and NA, but does not have a regional structure. Like NA and AA, each chapter is self-supporting through the sale of literature and member donations (Families Anonymous, 1975).

Parents Anonymous

Although this is a self-help group for parents who abuse their children, it will be briefly considered here because of the manner in which it makes use of professional staff. In the effort to integrate the work of group members with that of professional helpers, Parents Anonymous differs markedly from the self-help groups discussed above. In Parents Anonymous, the professional acts as a group sponsor who guides, but does not lead, the group. This may have particular relevance for work with drug abusers, many of whom may benefit from the input of a professional in the facilitation of group activity, the encouragement of verbalization, and discouragement of disruptive behavior within the group.

Parents Anonymous also differs from other groups in that it does not follow a structured ideology, i.e., a use of steps or their equivalent. Group meetings are focused on the goal of stopping child abuse.

There are over 800 Parents Anonymous chapters across the nation with a membership that is largely white, female, and drawn from welfare or low-income families. Unlike the other organizations, PA is not financed by member contributions. Major support is based on grant monies received from the National Center on Child Abuse and Neglect, HEW (NIDA, 1978).

SELF-HELP ISSUES

In the exploration of the various self-help models and their applicability for drug abusers, several issues arise which require consideration. These issues are (1) the types of drug abusers for whom these different models may be appropriate, (2) self-help and its relationship to the treatment cycle, (3) funding, and (4) level of professional involvement.

Which Model for Whom?

The heroin addict, the adult multidrug user and the youthful multidrug user share the commonality of drug abuse. However, one may question whether that similarity alone is sufficient to their working effectively with each other. At one extreme it would appear that the male or even female street addict would have little in common with the middle class housewife who abuses polydrugs. Youthful multidrug abusers may share little or nothing with either the street addict or the housewife. Does self-help appeal to all such groups? Could all benefit from attendance at the same meeting?

Most of the self-help groups take a "generic" approach in their ideology stating that their group has appeal for anyone desiring help with the focused problem for which the self-help group was organized. Nonetheless, NA groups recognize that persons involved in drug abuse cannot always be united as peers on this basis alone (NIDA, 1978). Both AA and NA believe that life-style groups, rather than type of drug used, is an important rallying point. Although NA reportedly has had good experiences with a diversified group, it has reported that people with similar life-styles tend to draw together. Groups based on demographics such as socioeconomic status and sex may also be more congenial. Whatever the group, the basic NA format and philosophy remain the same.

In regard to self-help groups for youthful multidrug abusers, the facilitative activity of a professional or an adult may be crucial. However, the professional must act as group facilitator only, lest the group become distrustful of the "expert" who attempts to dictate to group members. The isolation felt by many adolescents, the tendency for adolescents to congregate in groups, and the ability of adolescents to be influenced by peers appear to indicate that self-help groups geared to specific needs of the youthful multidrug abuser may have particular merit. Adolescents may be more largely influenced by the examples of peers who have stopped taking drugs than by the examples of adults.

Self-Help and the Treatment Cycle

The question arises as to the point in the treatment cycle at which a self-help group may be most effective and the role to be assumed by the self-help group. The self-help initiative may occur at any of several points, with each of several objectives:

(1) prevention (prior to taking drugs, or while drug-taking is still in the experimental stages);
(2) primary treatment (change would be mediated through the self-help group only);
(3) support for ongoing treatment (self-help would supplement treatment in a formal drug abuse program);
(4) aftercare services (self-help would be initiated only after the formal treatment program has been completed); or
(5) some combination of all or any of the above.

Most of the groups that were discussed in this chapter see themselves as providing the primary treatment. In fact, many make claims of attaining success through the self-help group after previous treatment failure.

Nonetheless, for the youthful experimenter, or for the trouble-prone youth, self-help as prevention/early intervention may be highly appropriate. In the case of multiple drug use, self-help groups may be an appropriate form of primary treatment for those who may not wish an association with a treatment program or need its network of support and counseling. However, a heroin addict may have needs, e.g., detoxification, vocational rehabilitation, medical care, education, etc., that preclude the use of self-help in isolation. In this case, self-help may be more appropriate as part of a complex of ongoing treatment (NIDA, 1978). In this regard, the methadone client may pose a special concern. That client cannot immediately achieve, and may not wish to achieve, a goal of abstinence. Consequently, he or she cannot ally with abstinent group members and may require a separate self-help group structure.

The need for self-help groups to undertake the task of aftercare appears to many a crucial element in the treatment process for drug addiction. The use of self-help groups as alumni associations to permit the development of prosocial friendships and negotiation of the nonaddict community may help prevent client recidivism. Self-help groups as a form of aftercare support may prove to be the most important "last step" in the treatment cycle. For those clients leaving the protective environment of the therapeutic community, reentry is clearly an essential part of the treatment cycle. Since residential treatment clients live in a relatively artificial environment, it may be helpful for clients who are approaching graduation to attend self-help meetings off site. This may allow an easy adaptation to a new community structure upon exiting from the therapeutic community. For those leaving methadone maintenance or outpatient drug-free programs, community reentry is not as pronounced an event. It is at program completion, however, that community resources must be surfaced and coordinated on behalf of the ex-drug abuser to give support to a drug-free adjustment. The self-help group can provide a new base of friendship and support for the former addict who remains in virtually the same environment which helped to stimulate and/or support his/her drug-abusing behavior.

Self-help groups may be of particular importance for prevention or primary treatment in rural communities that have little or no prevention/treatment dollars. Self-help groups may also supplement the ongoing treatment services offered by these and other programs suffering from resources inadequate to their task. Similarly, there is opportunity for self-help groups to provide an important aftercare resource which might otherwise be unavailable.

In summary, self-help groups are viable at any point in the "treatment cycle." Their appropriateness at a particular phase in the cycle depends on the individual's need and the community's resources.

Levels of Professional Involvement

Widely differing roles can be assumed by professionals vis-à-vis self-help groups. Professionals can aid in the development of self-help groups; and/or or facilitate group discussions; and/or consult to groups regarding problems the groups are having in functioning, or problems an individual group member is having where those problems are seen as beyond the group's interest or expertise. The aprofessional dimension espoused by Gartner and Riessman (1977) helps to distinguish self-help groups from traditional professionally led therapeutic groups. The concept of true peer support, sharing, and group reinforcement rather than professional guidance/direction are seen as the foundations upon which the self-help group is shaped. Indeed, most self-help groups (AA, NA, FA, Women for Sobriety) accept professionals as group members only if they have a problem. In NA, as well as AA, it is the older members, not professional therapists, who are the pillars of the group. It is they who will support and facilitate the group process.

The AA approach is that of complementarity between community professionals and the AA organization in providing needed services to the alcoholic (AA, 1972a). AA is anxious to acquaint professionals with its program and maintain open communication. It recognizes the need for additional services which are offered by the community, that are not available in AA, such as detoxification, medication, psychological and/or legal counseling, research, etc. AA recognizes that many of its members are treated concurrently by professionals and many active members first attended AA on the recommendation of a professional.

Parents Anonymous views the professional as a "back-up" person who may support and facilitate the group process, if needed, but will not act as a therapist with the group. Prior study suggests that professionals often remain available to individual members of self-help groups although those professionals never become invested in the workings of the group.

In spite of the aprofessional emphasis, professionals have played a variety of roles in relation to self-help organizations. They have aided in the initiation of groups (Low, 1950; Ch'ien, 1977), have helped to facilitate groups and provided consultation to self-help groups and members. It is important that the professional who seeks to affiliate with the self-help group in any capacity maintain an appropriate respect for the integrity of that organization such that he or she does not compromise its peer relatedness. Thus, the professional involved in efforts to initiate a self-help group will likely have to taper off his/her association with that group over time and/or allow the group to develop its own cadre of leaders. The professional who remains as facilitator or consultant will have to take care that his/her role remains properly limited and that any such assistance does not become a thinly disguised variant of group therapy.

Funding for Self-Help

Another issue that must be addressed is the source of operating expenses for work by self-help groups. To what extent, if at all, should government support be sought; to what extent should private donations be utilized? As with the issue of professional support, the major concern is with program integrity. Who pays the piper can call the tune. The program which seeks to guard its autonomy may feel obliged to obtain the funding that carries with it the least entanglements. Little wonder that most self-help organizations attempt to be self-supporting, making use of dues collections, literature sales, and donations to cover the relatively small costs associated with organizational maintenance. Where possible, volunteers staff central offices.

Narcotics Anonymous, AA, and FA state that every group should be fully self-supporting, declining outside contributions. Also, they stress that a group should never endorse, finance, or lend its name to any related facility or outside enterprise lest problems of money, property, or prestige divert the group from its primary purpose. These groups adhere strictly to this policy.

More atypically, Parents Anonymous has obtained its support through federal grant dollars. These monies have lent impetus to the rapid growth of that organization. When the grant ends, however, Parents Anonymous will find itself in the same position as other self-help organizations in search of funds. Consequently, it is currently seeking foundation support.

Other self-help groups, such as SmokeEnders and Weight Watchers, charge a fee for participation in the group and have maintained themselves on that basis. That course of action will likely remain open only to those few self-help organizations developed to meet the needs of comparatively affluent persons who share a relatively large-scale, nondisabling behavior problem.

At a self-help conference (NIDA, 1978), indication was given of the ways in which it was felt the government could assist self-help groups for drug abusers. These were as follows:

(1) Endorsement of self-help groups;
(2) reducing stigma of drug abuse;
(3) information dissemination, i.e., developing national self-help direc-
    tory, coordination of conference for information exchanges, etc.;
(4) technical assistance in developing "how to" packages for groups,
    training for self-help group leaders, funding of community-based
    organizers who could provide technical assistance to groups; and
(5) research on characteristics of self-help groups, group processes, and
    pathways into groups, etc.

It appears that while direct funding by governmental sources is generally rejected, government is seen as having a role in facilitating the
establishment of self-help groups.

In conclusion, the need to support self-help approaches alone or in
conjunction with traditional interventions can be important to drug abuse
clients and those staff involved in developing and implementing effective
treatment plans. The phenomenon of self-help is well established, its
ultimate significance for the field of drug abuse will unfold in the years to
come.

SELF-HELP GROUPS

Narcotics Anonymous
World Service Office
P.O. Box 622
Sun Valley, California 91352

Parents Anonymous
2810 Artesia Boulevard
Redonda Beach, California 90278

Families Anonymous
P.O. Box 344
Torrence, California 90501

Women for Sobriety, Inc.
Box 618
Quakertown, Pennsylvania 18951

Alcoholics Anonymous
Box 459
Grand Central Station
New York, New York 10017

Fellowships Anonymous
Detroit Health Department
1151 Taylor Street
Detroit, Michigan 48202

REFERENCES

Alcoholics Anonymous (1966) Alcoholics Anonymous in Your Community. New
    York: Alcoholics Anonymous World Service.

――― (1972a) If You Are a Professional AA Wants to Work with You. New York: Alcoholics Anonymous World Services, Inc., 1972.

――― (1972b) Understanding Anonymity. New York: Alcoholics Anonymous World Services.

――― (1974) How A.A. Members Cooperate with Other Community Efforts to Help Alcoholics. New York: Alcoholics Anonymous World Services.

――― (1975) A Community Resource for Coping with a National Health Problem. New York: Alcoholics Anonymous World Services.   ⟂

CH'IEN, J.M.N. (1977) "Voluntary treatment for drug abuse in Hong Kong." Addictive Diseases: An International Journal 3(1): 99-104.

Detroit Self-Help Group Research Project (1978) Unpublished.

Families Anonymous (1975) Group Handbook. Torrance, CA.

GARTNER, A. and RIESSMAN, F. (1977) Self-Help in Human Services. San Francisco: Jossey-Bass.

KATZ, A. H. and BENDER, E. I. [eds.] (1976) The Strength in Us. New York: New Viewpoints.

KIRKPATRICK, J. (no date) The Program Booklet. Quakertown, PA: Women for Sobriety, Inc.

LEACH, B. (1973) "Does Alcoholics Anonymous really work?" in P. G. Bourne and R. Fox (eds.) Alcoholism: Progress in Research and Treatment. New York: Academic Press.

LEVY, L. H. (1976) "Self-help groups: types and psychological processes." Journal of Applied Behavioral Science: Special Issue/Self-Help Groups 12(3): 310-322.

LOW, A. (1950) Mental Health Through Will-Training. Boston: Christopher.

MADSEN, W. (1974) The American Alcoholic. Springfield, IL: Charles C. Thomas.

Narcotics Anonymous (1976a) The Group. Sun Valley, CA: World Service Office.

――― (1976b) Sun Valley, CA: Narcotics Anonymous World Service Office.

――― (1976c) Recovery and Relapse. Sun Valley, CA: Narcotics Anonymous World Service Office.

――― (1976d) We Made a Decision. Sun Valley, CA: Narcotics Anonymous World Service Office.

National Institute on Drug Abuse, Services Research Report (1978) "Nonresidential self-help organizations and the drug abuse problem: an exploratory conference, 1978." (ADM) 78-452, July.

RIESSMAN, F. (1976) "How does self-help work." Social Policy. September-October: 41-45.

6

ALUMNI ASSOCIATIONS OF HONG KONG

JAMES M. N. CH'IEN

Drug addiction in Hong Kong is a serious and long-standing problem. Its origins go back to the Opium War with China (1840-1842), as a result of which Hong Kong was ceded to Britain. For the next 100 years, the sale of opium was legalized under an official monopoly, which was first leased out and then operated directly by the government after 1913. After the first international opium conference in Shanghai in 1909, Hong Kong's laws were revised to prohibit the export of opium, and all "divans" (small huts where opium was smoked) were ordered closed. Smoking on private premises, however, continued to be permitted. Following World War II, all legalized sale of opium was abolished. Since then, the Dangerous Drugs Ordinance (1946) has prohibited the use, manufacture, or possession of opium and its derivatives in Hong Kong without a license. Illicit trafficking is also strictly prohibited by law; however, by virtue of Hong Kong's free port status and its geopolitical situation, such trafficking can hardly be stopped. Moreover, among the many refugees who came to Hong Kong in the late 1940s and early 1950s to escape China's Civil War, were many opium smokers who switched to heroin after arrival for reasons of economy as well as convenience.[1]

As the population grew from 600,000 at the end of World War II to nearly 3,000,000 in the 1950s and as rapid industrialization took place following the Korean War (1950-1953), the spread of opiate addiction among manual laborers, industrial workers and unemployed youth aroused public alarm. During 1958, out of a total of 18,410 persons sent to prisons, 11,863 (11,471 men and 392 women forming together 64.4% of the prison population) were found to be narcotic dependents. Of these 7,544 (63.6%) took heroin in various ways, 4,271 (36%) smoked opium, and 48 (0.4%) injected morphine.[2] By extrapolation from prison figures and the quantity of narcotics seized, the official estimate in 1959 of the total number of narcotic dependents in Hong Kong was 150,000 to 180,000 persons.[3] Ironically, there was no organized treatment program for drug addicts until late 1958 when the H. M. Prison Tai Lam with a 700 bed capacity was converted to a treatment center for addicted male prisoners. In 1960, a pilot center with 60 beds for voluntary male patients was opened in the Castle Peak Mental Hospital in the New Territories and within a year its waiting list for admissions built up to over 3,000 men.

THE SOCIETY FOR THE AID AND REHABILITATION OF NARCOTIC ADDICTS

In view of the pressing demand of facilities for voluntary treatment, a group of community leaders, notably the Hon. Dr. Sir Albert Rodrigues and Mr. Brook Bernacchi, Q.C., formed a committee in 1960 to plan for such a program and incorporated the Society for the Aid and Rehabilitation of Drug Addicts (SARDA) in 1961 to begin fund raising to build a treatment center. The island of Shek Kwu Chau at the south west corner of Hong Kong waters was rented from the government at $1.00 per year, and construction work began shortly after financial support was secured. Special legislation, which provided protective custody for up to 180 days for voluntary patients under treatment was enacted. When the Shek Kwu Chau Rehabilitation Center (SKC) was opened in mid-1963 with a 250 bed capacity, its operation was originally linked with the pilot center of the Castle Peak Hospital (CPH), where voluntary patients were sent to be detoxified and from which they were transferred to the island center for continued rehabilitation. The total length of consecutive stay at the two centers for every patient was uniformly set at six months. Aftercare facilities consisted initially of a borrowed desk and phone used as a makeshift office and staffed by the author alone.

Folding beds were used for weekly nalline test to ascertain the drug-free status of the rehabilitees returning from SKC to live in the urban area.[4] In September 1965, SARDA set up its own social center in town to conduct both preadmission registration and follow-up and aftercare services. In

November of that year, SARDA absorbed the CPH detoxification service and formed a complete program of treatment-rehabilitation-aftercare for voluntary patients in Hong Kong. Since every voluntary patient had to go through the same procedure, this early program with a 3-1/2 year time span was described by a foreign observer as the "sausage machine."[5]

ELABORATION OF THE TREATMENT MODEL

During 1967-1968, SARDA secured additional capital grants from the Hong Kong Lottery Fund and expanded the SKC capacity from 250 to 500 beds to meet the growing demand. A separate Women's Treatment Center (WTC) with 30 beds was also opened in December 1968 in Wanchai, Hong Kong, which was known as the "Suzie Wong District" and is full of bars and dance halls. In order to reduce aftercare caseloads to more manageable levels than the 100 cases per worker which were arbitrarily set for SARDA in 1963, more trained social workers were recruited to render family-oriented case work and group counseling. As more male patients were coming from the mainland side of the Hong Kong harbor (i.e., Kowloon and New Territories), and more public housing estates were being developed there rather than on the supersaturated island of Hong Kong, efforts were made to decentralize social and clinical services and serve clients in residential areas where prevalence of narcotic addiction appeared high. By the end of 1971, a regionalized intake and aftercare service structure was completed, which represented a bold experiment in social administration.[6]

Another innovative program launched in January 1970 was the preadmission methadone stabilization scheme (PAM), which was, in fact, a low-dosage short-term maintenance effort to reduce the high attrition rate of applicants for treatment between time of registration and actual admission into institutional care. In the first year of the scheme, only ten participants out of 253 dropped out during the waiting period while the overall attrition rate was 18%.[7] This scheme was introduced when there was still strong opposition in Hong Kong toward methadone maintenance. That opposition did not subside until 1975 when the government's medical department established its own methadone clinics in different parts of Hong Kong and Kowloon.

THE REHABILITATION PROCESS DEVELOPED

The process of rehabilitation is shown in the flow chart (see Figure 6.1). Although drug-free rehabilitation through institutional treatment is

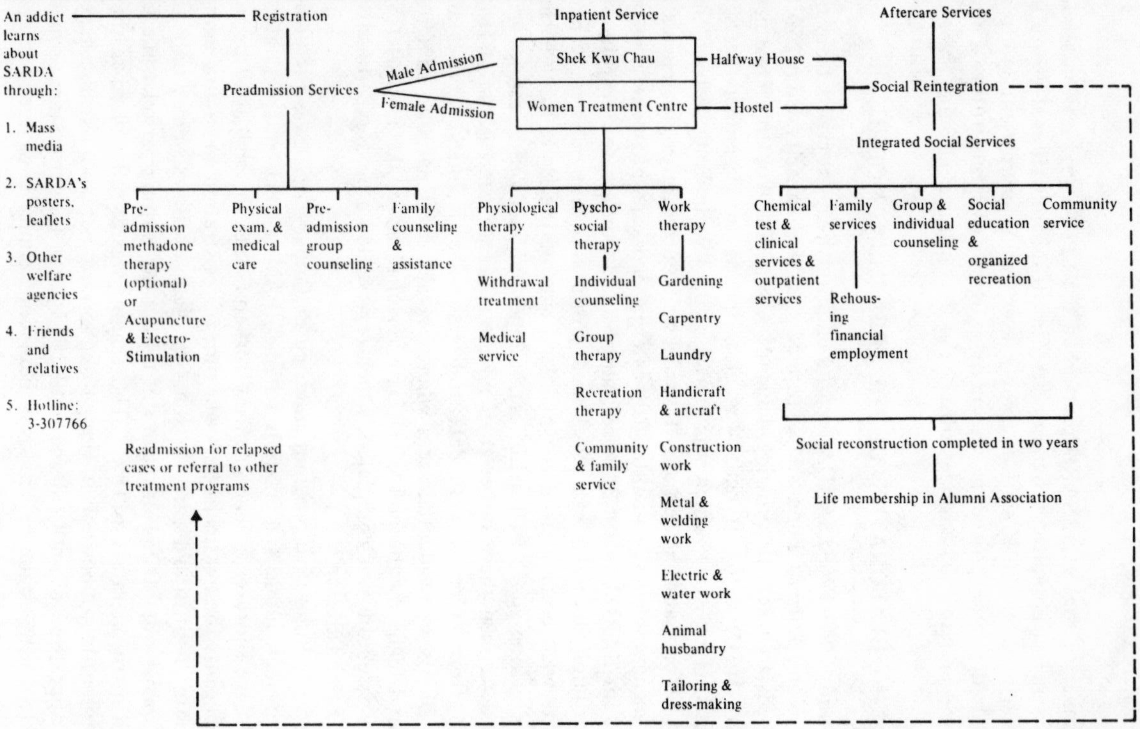

An addict learns about SARDA through:
1. Mass media
2. SARDA's posters, leaflets
3. Other welfare agencies
4. Friends and relatives
5. Hotline: 3-307766

Registration

Preadmission Services
- Family counseling & assistance
- Pre-admission group counseling
- Physical exam. & medical care
- Pre-admission methadone therapy (optional) or Acupuncture & Electro-Stimulation

Male Admission / Female Admission

Inpatient Service
- Shek Kwu Chau
- Women Treatment Centre

Physiological therapy
- Withdrawal treatment
- Medical service

Psycho-social therapy
- Individual counseling
- Group therapy
- Recreation therapy
- Community & family service

Work therapy
- Gardening
- Carpentry
- Laundry
- Handicraft & artcraft
- Construction work
- Metal & welding work
- Electric & water work
- Animal husbandry
- Tailoring & dress-making

Aftercare Services

Halfway House — Hostel

Social Reintegration

Integrated Social Services
- Chemical test & clinical services & outpatient services
- Family services: Rehousing financial employment
- Group & individual counseling
- Social education & organized recreation
- Community service

Social reconstruction completed in two years

Life membership in Alumni Association

Readmission for relapsed cases or referral to other treatment programs

FIGURE 6.1: Treatment and Rehabilitation Process

the major goal of SARDA's programs, flexibility in outpatient treatment and variable inpatient length of stay was adopted after 1972. Of the several hundred ambulatory cases stabilized on PAM each year, only 2-3% achieved complete detoxification without the need for institutional treatment as confirmed by a series of negative urine tests.

The great majority of PAM participants as well as those who do not opt for the scheme, enter institutional programs for inpatient detoxification which usually take one-two weeks. Therapeutic communities are organized for those who are motivated for fuller rehabilitation after detoxification. On the island of SKC, a detoxified patient is invited to join any one of eighteen houses each of which has a group living, working, and recreational unit with its own dormitory, tea house, workshop, vegetable garden, and animal farm. The new resident earns his acceptance by the house-group through helpfulness in the dorm and diligence in work while the senior residents give him encouragement and advice. Confrontation techniques and attack therapy as practiced in American therapeutic communities are seldomly applied because traditional Chinese culture advocates harmony and cooperation.

Each house bears the title of a cultural value, such as "Humanity," "Righteousness," "Fortitude," "Wisdom," etc., and leaders are usually ex-addicts who have gone through the program and successfully completed the aftercare period without evidence of relapse. These former clients are trained to serve as group leaders and trade instructors, and work under the supervision of a senior professional staff member. The staff leaders are assisted by elected representatives for each house, whose responsibilities progress from simple inspection of cleaning to storekeeping and disciplinary activities. The senior representative is treated as a partner of the house leader in managing the group's affairs. Intergroup competition in cleanliness, work production, arts, and sports is encouraged, and fair play as well as honesty are promoted. Interhouse meetings, participated in by both senior representatives and staff are conducted each Monday to plan for the weekly programs.

Each Tuesday evening there is a graduation ceremony to bid farewell to those completing the full course of rehabilitation which runs from 20 to 25 weeks. The ceremony is always followed by entertainment programs with musicals or skits performed by different houses.

ROLE OF THE ALUMNI ASSOCIATION

After leaving the center every Wednesday morning the new dischargees are welcome by their respective aftercare workers at the head office of the

Alumni Association (AA) of SARDA. The AA is a self-help and mutual support organization composed of and managed by ex-addicts. Those who have problems of accommodation or difficulties in family relationship may be temporarily placed in any one of five hostels/halfway houses run by the AA or other affiliated organizations. Decentralized aftercare is provided at five area offices with social casework, group work, and community services rendered flexibly by teams of professional workers and volunteers. The overall objective is to reintegrate the aftercare client into the community as a drug-free, crime-free, and productive member. Supporting goals are to enhance family reconciliation, vocational training or placement, severance from secret society or other antisocial connections, prompt readmission to treatment or referral to another agency for those relapsing to drug abuse, and to provide wholesome fellowship through the district chapters of the Alumni Association. There are five such chapters for men and one for women, each having 200-300 members. Those who can maintain themselves drug-free and crime-free for six months are accepted by the chapter as associate members and those who can lead productive lives for two years in the community can qualify for full membership. Badges bearing the insignia of AA in different colors to signify different number of years of continued abstinence from narcotics are worn proudly by its members. Since the establishment of the association in 1968, its membership has grown from a dozen or so founding members to more than 1,300 dues-paying members in ten years, making it the largest ex-addict organization outside the United States.[8]

SELF-EVALUATION OF THE AA PROGRAM

Recently a random sample of 100 new members of the AA and 100 Shek Kwu Chau graduates who chose not to join AA were studied and compared. After two years of follow-up, 57% of the AA group was abstaining from narcotic drugs voluntarily compared to 9% of the non-AA group (see Table 6.1).

Statistically significant differences were also confirmed in crime-free status, family relationship, and voluntary service to the community, all in favor of the AA members. While unemployment was lower in the AA group, the difference was not statistically significant probably because of the generally full employment conditions in Hong Kong in recent years. Of course the self-selection of AA membership creates some obvious bias in that the members would have been better motivated to start with, but without the closely knit social support system in the local community it is

TABLE 6.1: Follow-up Status at Time of Closing of Cases, 1976–1978

	AA		Non-AA	
Drug-free	57	(57.0%)	9	(9.0%)
Recovered after relapse	23	(23.0%)	22	(22.0%)
Readdicted and other status, e.g., imprisoned, under repeated treatment, etc.	17	(17.0%)	54	(54.0%)
Lost contact	3	(3.0%)	15	(15.0%)
Total	100	(100%)	100	(100%)

extremely doubtful that even the best motivated discharges could have succeeded as well.

PREVENTION AND COMMUNITY ACTION THROUGH THE ALUMNI ASSOCIATION

By the end of September 1978, 19,358 male cases (including 6,913 readmissions) and 816 female cases (including 320 readmissions) had been treated by SARDA. As a result of financial restraints imposed since the energy crisis of 1975 in Hong Kong, SARDA's aftercare period was reduced from three years to two years. However, with the timely and growing support of the Alumni Association there was provided the voluntary manpower to help with all aftercare activities to provide peer role-models for group counseling. Consequently, the abstinence rate of all follow-up cases has been maintained at an average of 25% at the end of each course of treatment and social rehabilitation. The association continues to extend constructive fellowship and a positive group influence which are essential to replacing the negative influence and identification with triad societies and/or street gangs. Therefore, the AA is playing a very important role in tertiary prevention, i.e., in reducing relapses.

AA members also form community action teams to reach into ghetto areas like the "Walled City" of Kowloon and other urban centers of crime and delinquency to help SARDA with case finding and crisis intervention, thereby contributing to secondary prevention. At the primary level, AA's Lion Dance Troup, variety show teams, Chinese music and pop bands, drama group, and social education group have been active since 1972 in supporting the annual drug abuse prevention campaigns organized by the Hong Kong government in various districts of Hong Kong, Kowloon, and the New Territories.

COMMUNITY ATTITUDES AND FUTURE CHALLENGE

Fifteen years ago the community of Hong Kong viewed drug addiction as a physical-moral problem. Community attitudes toward treated addicts were largely one of nonacceptance. In order to overcome the unemployment problem of SARDA's clients, the author encouraged those clients to form small business cooperatives to render cleaning and sanitation services, provide street numbering plates, carpentry work, interior decoration, etc. Some of these projects flourished after a few years of struggling and some stopped due to mismanagement, but all helped to demonstrate to the community that ex-addicts could work as well as nonaddicts.

One of the goals of the decentralized aftercare program was to mobilize treated addicts to allow them to offer voluntary services to local communities, such as building small parks, cleaning playgrounds, and supporting district campaigns against narcotic pollution and crime. Gradually, the community learned to accept rehabilitated persons as friends and neighbors and to trust and even acclaim AA members.

In 1975, the Lions International, District 303 in Hong Kong began to sponsor an employment guidance scheme to help to place SARDA's aftercare clients in meaningful jobs. Nearly a thousand treated addicts have benefited in the past three years from this joint program which is staffed by ex-addicts who have completed university educations. The improved community attitudes further stimulate AA members to do more for the community which accepts them and this unique phenomenon has been termed "reciprocal altruism."[9]

In spite of all the progress made in Hong Kong, there is recent evidence that the long-standing problem of narcotic addiction is slowly but surely diversifying into polydrug abuse including the misuse of opiate substitutes such as methadone, codeine, and pethidine, as well as nonopiate drugs such as barbiturates, tranquilizers and alcohol.[10] SARDA is working closely with the Drug Abuse Committee of the Hong Kong Council of Social Service in studying the shifting patterns of abuse and in designing new programs to meet the changing needs. SARDA is examining plans to restructure its small women's treatment center to better serve the increasing number of young bar girls, entertainers cum hostesses, and street walkers who frequently abuse a wide range of synthetic drugs in contrast to the older generation's "simple" addiction to opium or heroin smoking. The problem of drug abuse in the 1980s will almost certainly involve a more complex quality even if the quantitative burden is reduced. The challenge to SARDA and to aftercare will be to adapt the technology already developed to meet this situation.

NOTES

1. C. O. Lee, "History & Medical Aspects of Drug Addiction," in *Proceedings of the 4th Pan Pacific Rehab. Conference, Hong Kong September 1-7, 1968,* Hong Kong Joint Council for the Physically and Mentally Disabled, 1969, p. 178.

2. Hong Kong Government, *The Problem of Narcotic Drugs in Hong Kong,* paper presented to the Legislative Council, November 11, 1959, p. 3.

3. Ibid.

4. SARDA First Working Report 1963-1964, Hong Kong, 1964.

5. Michael Whisson, *Under the Rug,* Hong Kong Council of Social Service, 1965.

6. SARDA, Annual Reports, 1969, 1970, and 1971.

7. SARDA, Annual Report, 1970, pp. 61-62.

8. The Alumni Association of SARDA, Tenth Anniversary Report, 1977. The Narcotics Anonymous in America may have a larger membership, but its chapters are rather loosely organized and not active in community affairs as is the AA of Hong Kong.

9. James M.N. Ch'ien, "The socio-biological approach in drug abuse treatment and prevention," presented at the IVth World Congress of Psychiatry, Drug Abuse Section, Honolulu, September 1977.

10. James M.N. Ch'ien, "Applying public health concepts in drug abuse programme planning," presented at the Biennial Meeting of Drug Abuse Committee, Hong Kong Council of Social Service, November 4, 1978. More than 50% of women admitted in 1977 and 1978 by SARDA for heroin addiction treatment were actually polydrug abusers; proportionately speaking fewer men abuse synthetic drugs but many are found to be abusing alcohol and codeine (often condensed cough syrup) following detoxification from heroin.

PART III

MODELS FOR CONTINUING CARE
USING COMMUNITY ORGANIZATIONS

7

THE USE OF VOLUNTEERS IN DRUG
ABUSE AFTERCARE

As clients exit from formal treatment programs, it appears that community support systems often become necessary to their successful integration into the community. Various treatment programs may have their own follow-up and aftercare procedures, such as self-help (alumni) groups and halfway houses. In large part, however, the development of a more complex network of community support is necessary to meet the goal of successful reintegration. The issue to be explored in this chapter will be the degree to which that task can usefully be addressed by the voluntary sector of the community. As will be discussed, the role of the voluntary sector is important not only because of limited resources available elsewhere, but also because of its own special attributes.

While volunteer movements in other human service areas, e.g., mental health, corrections, etc., have become integral to aftercare planning in those areas, there has been only limited study of volunteer utilization in the field of drug abuse treatment. Specific areas of concern to this chapter will be (1) the identification of that which is currently known about the extent of volunteer utilization in drug abuse programs, (2) the examination of the varying roles that volunteers might assume in aftercare settings, (3) discussion of the diverse organizational settings from which volunteers

167

are recruited, and (4) exploration of advantages and disadvantages of using volunteers under different conditions. To provide a suitable framework for discussing volunteers in drug programs, selected examples from the mental health and corrections literature as regards aftercare will be presented.

Who Are Volunteers?

The term volunteer is typically defined in terms of economic and motivational factors. A volunteer is most commonly seen as someone who provides services at no charge to others, and who provides those services out of a desire to make a personal contribution. For most purposes, this definition appears sufficient. The federal agency ACTION, which has the responsibility of coordinating all federal volunteer efforts, also defines volunteers in terms of an absence of renumeration although stipends may be paid to volunteers as a means of providing some baseline standard of living. The money is not viewed as a payment for services, but as a necessary mechanism to enable a variety of people to participate in volunteer activities. For the purposes of this chapter, volunteers will then be defined as people who offer to provide any of a wide range of services, without any apparent renumeration, e.g., money, college credits, aid to a relative; but from a felt need or desire to provide a service to an organization and/or to the people served by that organization.

Volunteer Utilization in Drug Abuse
Treatment Programs: A Perspective

The National Institute on Drug Abuse (NIDA) annually surveys volunteer utilization. Findings from that survey (1977) indicated that 9% of staff members in federally funded programs (N=385) and 23% of staff in nonfederally funded programs (N=1,329) were categorized as volunteers. These figures drop considerably when consideration is given to actual hours worked by volunteers as compared to paid staff. Thus, 3% of all hours worked within federally funded programs can be considered as volunteer hours.

The largest differences occur in terms of those staff positions that can be seen as most significantly invested in the counseling process. Thus, 20% of social workers involved in nonfederally funded programs are volunteers compared to only 5% of those in federally funded programs; and 36% of those persons categorized as counselors in nonfederally funded programs are considered volunteers compared to only 12% of the counselors in federally funded programs. Nonetheless, as can be seen in Table 7.1,

TABLE 7.1: Staffing for Drug Abuse Treatment Units

Staffing Categories	Staff in Federally Funded Programs (N=385)		Staff in Nonfederally Funded Programs (N=1329)	
	Paid	Volunteer	Paid	Volunteer
Physicians	139	10	512	59
Psychiatrists	161	6	422	42
Psychologists	191	14	549	67
Social workers (M.S.W.)	312	18	751	192
Nurses	448	5	1,657	64
Lawyers	6	8	51	47
Counselors[a]	1,418	186	4,338	2,450
Vocational specialists	90	12	181	33
Administrative staff	820	21	2,779	163
Other	525	117	1,338	642
	4,110	397	12,578	3,759

a. Other than those classified above.

persons working as volunteers are distributed over a variety of staffing categories.

In addition to staffing categories, it is also possible to determine the extent of volunteer participation by geographic region and by program modality (see Table 7.2).

As can be seen from Table 7.2, methadone programs use volunteers least, whereas therapeutic communities use them the most. There is also variability by region, such that treatment programs in the West—exclusive of methadone maintenance—are most likely to make use of volunteer workers. Although these data provide some general descriptive background, they do not indicate the extent to which volunteers are used in aftercare programs as compared to other service components.

TABLE 7.2: Volunteers in Drug Programs by Region and Modality

	Methadone Maintenance	(N)	Drug-Free	(N)	Therapeutic Communities	(N)
Northeast	6.3%	(9)	29.4%	(151)	30.3%	(30)
North central	50.0	(13)	25.0	(79)	33.0%	(21)
South	19.0	(5)	20.0	(87)	39.0	(25)
West	16.0	(11)	36.0	(156)	58.0	(57)
Total	15.0	(38)	28.0	(192)	41.0	(36)

AFTERCARE SERVICES FOR DRUG ABUSERS

Activities which can be considered necessary to the former client's community adjustment may vary by program modality and within program modality. In programs where "transitions" are not considered to be important either philosophically or programmatically, reentry needs and support services may be largely overlooked. Therapeutic communities, on the other hand, with their emphasis on "graduation" and community reentry, would appear to have a particular investment in aftercare programming. Methadone maintenance programs may be expected to vary in their commitment to providing clients with the range of services necessary to permit his/her retention in the community. Where heroin addiction is viewed as a chronic relapsing disorder, as it is in many methadone programs, greater emphasis may be placed on ensuring clients' ability to return to treatment (Sells, 1977) than on aftercare functions. Finally, it must be recognized that not all programs have the resources necessary to provide the community assistance desired.

Clients too, are likely to show wide variability in their needs regarding community adjustment. Clients with family problems, with poor employment histories, with legal entanglements, with prolonged criminal justice histories, etc., may all suffer larger adjustment problems than peers with more normative community living situations.

It is a premise of this chapter that the volunteers and volunteer organizations have considerable and unique qualifications to help address many of these posttreatment needs and problems. Other, and related, human service areas have already provided evidence that volunteers can be effectively and creatively used in aftercare programs. Selected literature will be presented to describe processes and outcomes in two of these areas.

VOLUNTEERS IN MENTAL HEALTH AND CORRECTIONS AFTERCARE SETTINGS

Mental Health Settings

There has been developed a considerable literature examining aftercare activities in mental health settings, with particular emphasis on follow-up care by nonprofessional workers. In fact, much of the community psychiatry and community mental health movement is premised on the use of noninstitutional and nonprofessional people (cf., Caplan, 1964, 1974; Baker and Schulberg, 1967, 1969). Volunteers have undertaken roles involving the provision of case aide services, education and recreation programs, varying aspects of care for chronically ill patients, child care, and crisis intervention.

A study of aftercare involving volunteers in a family service agency for patients released from a mental hospital (Fisher et al., 1973) describes, in part, the benefits that could accrue to the volunteer:

> An interesting and gratifying development in staffing occurred early in the project, when a 76 year old man, Mr. W., himself a former patient in a mental hospital, volunteered his full-time services to the Aftercare Project. The staff was quick to recognize his strengths, vitality, and experiences and to match these with some of the needs of the aftercare program. His services were welcomed and he became a full-time volunteer staff member in 1969, a role he held throughout the project. He worked as an assistant to each staff member and was supervised by the project director. At times his supervision was replaced by counseling about his own problems of living. However, at no time in over 2 years did those problems interfere with the performance of his job. He was most effective in taking clients to clinics, to apply for food stamps or public assistance, to job interviews, to recreational activities, and so on. His identification with the Aftercare Project clearly was therapeutic for him. He no longer saw himself as an isolated, retired, former patient. He was an active, employed mental health worker. As he gained self-confidence, he became more aggressive in helping clients obtain their rights. For example, he refused to remain passive when clients' applications for obtaining public assistance or food stamps were needlessly delayed. He became a model for identification for many of the clients—a caring, concerned father for some; a gentle, good natured grandfather for others. Most of the clients knew he had been a former patient himself. When the agency offered aftercare to geriatric clients in the second year of the demonstration project, it was Mr. W., who took charge of a daycare center program for geriatric clients, with members of the staff acting as consultants.

Obviously, of larger significance is the impact of volunteers' efforts on program clients. Numerous studies have suggested the effectiveness of volunteers in providing services to clients in institutional programs. A study by Katkin et al. (1975) has particular significance for aftercare programming making use of volunteer workers. In that study, involving a comparison of two aftercare programs, volunteer therapists in one program were assigned tasks insuring that former mental hospital inpatients took their medication, observing former clients for evidence of decompensation, helping ex-clients find jobs and housing, and providing that supportive counseling seen as warranted. In a two-year follow-up period, it was found that 24 of the 36 former clients treated by volunteers were able to remain in the community compared to 14 of the 34 former clients not served by volunteers.

Nonetheless, not all studies exploring the use of volunteers have yielded positive findings. A study initiated in 1966 in three VA hospitals, attempting to determine effectiveness of volunteers in aftercare services, found no difference in performance between 89 mental patients assigned "anchormen" (volunteers) and 82 patients without volunteers (Watson et al., 1975).

Correctional Settings

Volunteers in corrections aftercare may be used following institutionalization, e.g., in parole and outright release; or in instances of a partial deinstitutionalization, e.g., in halfway houses and work release settings. Former correctional clients may be expected to have problems of reintegration into the community similar to those of former mental patients. Similarly, there are numerous reports of the use of volunteers to provide services to probationers in one-to-one relationships with an emphasis on the volunteer as model (cf., Leenhouts, 1970; Lonergan, 1971; Morris, 1970; Goddard and Jacobsen, 1967; Hennepin County Court, 1973; Schwartz, 1971; Scheier, 1970; Edelen, 1971.)

A National Center for Voluntary Action publication, *Volunteers Assisting the Offender in Prison and in the Community* (1974), presents a series of program descriptions summarizing correctional models utilizing volunteer assistance both in prison and in the community. The programs described present a variety of role potentials for volunteers. Among those most largely emphasized are providing aid to clients' families both in prison and in the community, assisting in educational and/or vocational training programs, sponsoring inmates for community release, advocacy on behalf of jail and prison reform, offering child care services during reformatory visiting hours, and developing neighborhood-based alternatives to incarceration.

Organizational Variations in the Use of Volunteers

There are numerous variation potentials in the organizational control and utilization of volunteers. Organizational arrangements involving volunteers appear to be of three major types. The first type involves a maximum of program control. In this model, recruitment and orientation of volunteers occur at the individual program level. Under this arrangement, each agency develops and initiates its own mechanisms for recruiting, orienting, training, and utilizing volunteers. Agencies of any size can develop such procedures with the nature of those efforts being related to available resources and program interest. Nonetheless, larger agencies with their greater command of resources may find themselves in a stronger position to develop volunteer auxiliaries where desired. The volunteer auxiliary is an organizational arm that can directly supplement the activities of a larger organization. Hospitals, nursing homes, and other institutions often receive a variety of support services from volunteer auxiliaries that are directly attached to them. Voluntary auxiliaries have been used to initiate and sponsor social events, create and implement fund-raising projects, develop community awareness for the goals, objectives, and programs of their host organization, and provide a variety of other activities. Paid agency staff are required to coordinate the volunteer components. Programs of this type retain significant control over the types of volunteers recruited and the functions that volunteers would provide.

A second organizational model admits of somewhat lessened agency control over volunteer recruitment and functioning. In this structure, an agency other than the program for which the volunteer will eventually work is responsible for selected aspects of volunteer activities. That second agency may be national, state, or local. The major national effort in this regard is found in ACTION. ACTION was established in 1971 as an independent federal agency, embracing the several federal volunteer programs organized in the 1960s. The ACTION program works through a series of smaller programs, which can be combined or used separately to meet community needs. ACTION programs may be used by community agencies seeking volunteer support in either of two ways. They may:

(1) provide individual volunteers or volunteer support directly to an ongoing project or agency, e.g., Volunteers in Service to America (VISTA), ACTION Cooperative Volunteers (ACV), and University Year for Action (UYA); or

(2) award grants to communities to initiate or expand whole volunteer projects, e.g., UYA, Foster Grandparent Program (FGP), Retiree Senior Volunteer Program (RSVP), and Senior Companion Program (SCP).

Although most ACTION volunteers ultimately become involved in local program activity, ACTION still retains considerable control (particularly through the mechanism of grant awards) over program selection for volunteers and the purposes for which volunteers will be used. Currently, 36 states maintain ACTION-sponsored Volunteer Coordination Services, offices which have responsibility for coordinating a significant portion of the range of volunteer services carried out within the state.

The ACTION program provides drug abuse treatment agencies with a variety of options for the development of volunteer programs. Where effort is made to recruit mothers into treatment, the Senior Companion Program may be used to provide volunteers to organize day-care enrichment programs for the children of the addicted mothers. The Retired Senior Volunteer Program (RSVP) could provide opportunities for persons over 60 years of age to develop and maintain a guide to community employment for ex-addicts in need of vocational assistance and guidance. Volunteers from the National Student Volunteer Program (NSVP) could also be recruited. NSVP encourages and assists the development and improvement of local, independent college and high school student volunteer programs across the country through the provision of technical assistance materials, training, and on-site consultation. Its older recruits might be used in companionship counseling with clients exiting drug treatment programs.

In the private sector, there are a number of types of organizations that have provided and/or have the potential to provide volunteer pools for different aftercare services. Civic/fraternal/service organizations, religious institutions, and business organizations, for example, have the capabilities and manpower to provide different services for drug abusers, and, in some instances, have taken the initiative to do so. Compared to ACTION, these programs can *themselves* utilize volunteer pools rather than only serving a "broker" function, i.e., providing others with volunteers. Thus, the Kiwanis International, through the work of its membership, initiated a major campaign in support of drug abuse prevention and education in 1969 called Operation Drug Alert, and has continued efforts to affiliate clubs to continue and expand that effort (Shue, 1978). At one point, Kiwanis International also had a program to enable Vietnam veterans with drug problems to seek out club members for help in the solving of various problems. Other service organizations, e.g., Jaycees and B'nai Brith, have also been involved in providing drug abuse prevention and other intervention services.

Religious institutions have had long and extensive involvement in numerous facets of drug abuse prevention and treatment. Different religious groups have themselves funded various treatment programs which have included both professional, nonprofessional, and volunteer roles.

Included here are such programs as Teen Challenge, supported by the Pentecostal Church; the Breakthrough House, a residential and outpatient treatment facility for women maintained by the Urban Ministries, Board of Missions of the Methodist Church of Atlanta, Georgia (whose staff consists of four full-time and five part-time volunteers); the Catholic Service Bureau of the Archdiocese of Miami, Florida, which maintains four drug abuse treatment programs initiated since August 1970. The extent to which churches and synagogues have acted to initiate volunteer activities in relation to drug abuse services is simply unknown. Given the service aspects of religious institutions and their obvious concern with prosocial functioning in the community, these settings would seem to offer a significant resource for volunteers, particularly to allow former clients to adapt to the "straight" community.

Colleges and universities represent another significant body of organizations that can work with drug abuse agencies to generate a pool of volunteers. The school, like the church, may be expected to maintain some control over its volunteers. The involvement of students, to be considered truly voluntary, given the author's earlier definition, must not be services offered for either reimbursement or college credit. Students have been cited in numerous studies as providing services in mental hospitals (cf., Brown and Ishiyama, 1968; Reinherz, 1963, 1969). One example of a student volunteer project involving drug abuse services was a community action program (The Cincinnati Experience) in which students attempted to stimulate a responsiveness to social issues and problems on the part of both grassroots community groups and established community institutions (National Clearinghouse for Drug Abuse Information, 1973). Additionally, students became involved in methadone maintenance programs in a variety of volunteer capacities.

A third organizational structure for understanding the control and utilization of volunteers would be the private nonprofit organization that acts as a clearinghouse for volunteer services. This organization would retain near total control over its volunteer workers, making them available to community agencies only at the organization's discretion. Examples would be the Visiting Nurses Association or the American Red Cross, whose small cadre of staff depend on large numbers of volunteers for the work of the organization, and whose mission embraces, but is not relegated to, the development and training of volunteers. This agency would not be connected with any specific drug abuse treatment program, but would be in a position to provide volunteer services. A drug abuse program whose clients receive services from such an organization would depend entirely upon the policies and practices of that organization. Control of the volunteers would thus be maximal for the service organization and minimal for the drug abuse program. Such a structure remains a theoretical one for the drug abuse field.

ROLES FOR VOLUNTEERS

Volunteers, depending on background and experiences, may be used to perform roles identical to those of paid staff members. Typically, however, service and other organizations will want to restrict certain key roles and tasks only to those persons from whom it can exact a full-time commitment (often problematic for a volunteer) and from whom it can make further demands not only in terms of degree of commitment as regards time, but in terms of the way in which tasks will be carried out. Paid employees, more dependably than volunteers, can be expected to serve an organization. The volunteer's greater freedom to act can be both a challenge and advantage to the organization and its clients. As will be discussed below, that freedom admits of volunteers taking roles different from those of paid staff.

Counseling Roles

Counseling has been shown to be a major role for volunteers in drug abuse treatment programs (National Institute on Drug Abuse, 1978). Counseling may be defined decidedly differently by paid and unpaid workers. The worker whose payment is associated with his/her reporting to an agency and office setting for defined periods of the day may legitimately perceive counseling as a role to be performed primarily or exclusively in that agency or office setting. The counselee is regarded as a client; indeed the counselee is the organization's client. As such, the counselee is expected to come to the agency to receive its services. Admittedly, most volunteer counselors will accept this same view of theirs and the counselee's roles. However, consider the other roles more largely available to the volunteer than the paid employee. The volunteer, lacking the paid employee's contractual obligation to the counselee through the organization, can meet with the drug abuser in the client's home, at his/her job, in the home of a family member, in the volunteer's home, or in whatever community setting is appropriate to a discussion, investigation, and resolution of the counselee's concerns. Even more pointedly, the volunteer, in any setting, need not play a traditional counselor role as must the paid worker wedded to a job description or having a need to demonstrate the satisfactory performance of a narrow range of job functions in order to obtain promotion. The volunteer is free to act as counselor, as advisor, as friend, as aide in negotiating with the straight community. For the paid worker, the individual who comes to see him/her is a recipient of services, is someone to whom or for whom things are done. Peer relationships are not available in this structure.

The Volunteer as Organizational Support

As may be apparent, there are a variety of volunteer services which would be conducted under the close direction of paid staff. These activities would be truly support services to staff engaged in providing aid of clients. These support services could include driving clients from their homes to interviews, arranging for agency picnics, typing reports, etc. These and many other roles may be indispensable in permitting the implementation of an aftercare program. Given the time, resources, and personal constraints operative in many settings, the use of volunteers may be absolutely essential to constructing and maintaining an aftercare program.

As has been noted above, much of the volunteer's work in the area of aftercare involves effort with families and community members significant to the exiting client. Thus, the volunteer as organizational support, may—under staff direction—act to locate community services for which the family is eligible, to provide supportive counseling to spouses/friends and children, etc. In this way, the volunteer can facilitate and soften the reintegration of the former client into his/her family and permit both former client and family to adopt somewhat differing roles toward each other. Both intrapersonal and environmental problems may be more easily addressed and resolved.

Volunteers may also undertake a variety of agency administrative tasks under staff supervision. Volunteers can be called upon to examine and interpret legislation, regulations, and guidelines, write reports, assess community needs, write grants, speak to community groups, aid in evaluation, etc. Volunteers may provide coordination of drug abuse treatment activities with the activities of other relevant agencies in the community. Included here may be aftercare services and their coordination with other program activities. It might be noted that these activities, unlike many of the volunteer activities to be described, are designed to enhance the functioning of the agency without promoting institutional change or a development of new roles and tasks.

The Volunteer as Ombudsman

Another role that may be assumed by the volunteer in relating to the drug abuser is that of ombudsman. This role allows the volunteer to serve as an enabler to the agency's drug abuse client. The volunteer, in this instance, would serve as a resource to the client to negotiate different action systems, e.g., probation and parole, employment, and social services. Thus, the volunteer can help to provide some "cushioning" for the client in the community. This may be done on a one-to-one basis involving negotiation on an individual client's behalf with an individual employer, or this function may be performed through use of a group, e.g., a body of volunteers who together form an employment clearinghouse for agency X and attempt to implement an employment program with the National Alliance of Businessmen or other relevant group. Clearly, such an employment program could serve the needs of clients exiting from a number of treatment settings.

The ombudsman could help facilitate needed supports for the client (job interviews, food stamps, out-of-town probation passes) and might also serve to allow the client to develop his/her own capacities and skills for negotiating different community systems. As drug abuse clients are attempting to integrate themselves fully into the community after being involved in intensive treatment experiences, the acquisition of these skills may be crucial to their drug-free adjustment to the community. It can be reasoned that clients who are not aided to develop skills necessary to the negotiation of community systems are likely to be good candidates for recidivism. The ombudsman role can be assumed by volunteers derived from the variety of organizational contexts discussed earlier—in-house volunteers, volunteers from a defined volunteer organization, or volunteers associated with a private community agency.

The Volunteer as Advocate

Advocacy responsibilities are in many ways similar to those associated with the ombudsman role. Difference may be largely one of degree with greater active support provided for clients by the volunteer as advocate than as ombudsman. The volunteer may become the *sponsor* for the client. He/she may appear at a court hearing for the client. He/she may speak in the client's defense regarding a posting of bond. If a client were denied various social service or medical benefits, the volunteers could go to the appropriate office with the client and provide additional visibility for the client in demanding his/her rights. Typically, activity in assuming this role must be carefully coordinated between the drug abuse treatment agency, the volunteer, and the client.

Advocacy need not be limited to individual clients or former clients. As has been noted above, volunteers have acted to promote reform of existing social institutions and the initiation of new service delivery systems.

Paid Workers and Volunteer Interaction

Depending on the policy of the agency, there are various structures in which paid staff members and volunteers may work together. There can be an assignment of certain volunteers directly to paid staff members or to certain units directed by paid staff members. A second approach would involve locating volunteers in a unit that receives guidance and direction from a director of volunteers, who administratively would report to the agency director. A third approach would permit differences between volunteers and paid staff to be blurred; both would be given similar duties and reporting requirements and both would be responsible to paid supervisory staff. The way in which volunteers are used in agencies will determine the types of administrative structures to be utilized. It is unclear to what extent drug abuse treatment programs make known to clients the presence and/or functions of volunteers. Volunteers are generally in a better position to leave an agency at any time with minimal personal ramifications. Volunteers do not depend upon the program for financial purposes. They are unlikely to receive an evaluation that would affect their future job placement. Their real commitment and accountability are essentially based upon a *personal* understanding with other agency personnel, clients, and other volunteers.

ADVANTAGES AND DISADVANTAGES OF VOLUNTEERS IN AFTERCARE

Advantages

Given limitations in agency human and financial resources, volunteers may be employed to undertake important community support roles that agency staff may be unable to provide. Volunteers serving in drug abuse aftercare programs would appear capable of fulfilling certain functions similar to those provided by paid staff as well as certain special, unique functions. Where volunteers have training and experiences similar to that of paid staff, volunteers can and do perform a variety of nontraditional, frequently "nonprofessional" and/or advocacy functions that would not always be feasible for paid staff or sought by them. Volunteers may provide for program continuity while being less likely to feel constrained by considerations about time and place. In aftercare programming, particularly, this relative flexibility can be a considerable advantage. Moreover, under certain circumstances, the relationship of volunteers to clients may approach that of mutuality.

In this way volunteers may help to obviate labeling problems that clients may feel when interacting strictly with agency staff. Volunteers, when coming from the client's community, may also be more aware of community resources than staff members could be and thus have an advantage in helping ex-clients negotiate various community action systems. In addition to individual advocacy and ombudsman functions presented earlier, it will be recalled that volunteers can act as a body to advocate institutional reform. A voluntary auxiliary or other organization may negotiate as a pressure group to effect change in other community service systems and/or in the way in which those systems relate to each other.

Disadvantages

While there are clear advantages of using volunteers in treatment aftercare programs, there are undeniable disadvantages. The status of volunteer can create problems for both the individual so designated and the organization in which he or she is placed. For the volunteer, there is the clear danger that his or her role and actions will not be taken as seriously as will those of the paid employee. We live and work in a society that lays a heavy emphasis on payment for services rendered. "You get what you pay for" is for many an article of faith. The volunteer's contribution may be suspect, not by virtue of any deficiency in his or her performance, but simply because that which costs nothing may be less valued. Indeed, the volunteer may value his or her own work less for this same reason.

The use of volunteers can create other kinds of problems for the treatment program. Inclusion of any or large numbers of staff volunteers does not allow an administrator the luxury of being guaranteed a stable work force. Not only may the volunteer feel a greater freedom to leave the program, he or she may feel a greater freedom to depart from the organization's regulations and traditions. Sanctions that can be used against paid employees are likely to have little salience for the volunteer.

Similarly, volunteers are not faced with the same accountability to clients that paid staff members have. Since agencies and paid staff require some type of credentialing and have certain obligations and responsibilities to clients, there are known responsibilities implied. Thus, it becomes important for administrators to investigate professional and legal accountability of volunteers for clients. Finally, volunteers may also pose a threat to paid staff. Both in terms of volunteers' expertise and in terms of the financial resources available to the host agency, the volunteer may be seen as a rival for paid workers' jobs.

CONCLUSIONS

A variety of human service areas have made use of volunteers with different backgrounds to fulfill a series of needed functions. Aftercare would seem to offer many of the same opportunities for volunteer work. Volunteers may play traditional service delivery roles, may aid paid staff in performing those roles or—most intriguing of all—may play unique roles as representatives of the local community capable of dealing with a variety of support systems in helping former clients reintegrate themselves into the community. It is in the community that the effects of treatment will be tested, hopefully reinforced and built upon. In this context, it is the thoughtful and effective administrator who will be able to take advantage of the volunteer's "special" talents in performing both traditional and atypical roles within the program. Administrators should develop a knowledge of volunteer resources so that they will be able to recruit and to employ volunteers effectively.

REFERENCES

BAKER, F. and SCHULBERG, H. C. (1967) "The development of a community mental health ideology scale." Community Mental Health Journal 3: 216-225.
——— (1969) "Community mental health ideology, dogmatism, and political-economic conservatism." Community Mental Health Journal, 5(6): 433-436.
BROWN, B. S. and ISHIYAMA, T. (1968) "Some reflections on the role of the student in the mental hospital." Community Mental Health Journal 10(1): 33-40.
CAPLAN, G. (1964) Principles of Preventive Psychiatry. New York: Basic Books.
——— (1974) Support Systems and Community Mental Health: Lectures on Concept Development. New York: Behavioral Publications.
EDELEN, R. J. (1971) "Volunteer courts: a child's helping hand." Fulton, MO: Missouri Thirteenth Judicial Circuit.
FISHER, T., NACKMAN, N. S., and ASHUTOSH, B. (1973) "Aftercare services in a family agency." Social Casework 54 (March): 131-141.

GODDARD, J. and JACOBSEN, G. (1967) "Volunteer services in a juvenile court." Crime and Delinquency 13: 337-343.

Hennepin County Court (1973) One to One: The Volunteer Probation Officer Program 22. Courthouse, Minneapolis.

KATKIN, S., JIMMERMAN, V., ROSENTHAL, J., and GINSBURG, M. (1975) "Using volunteer therapists to reduce hospital readmissions." Hospital and Community Psychiatry 26 (March): 151-153.

LEENHOUTS, K. (1970) "Royal Oak's experience with professionals and volunteers in probation." Federal Probation (December).

LONERGAN, B. (1971) "The professional-volunteer partnership working in corrections." Volunteer Administration.

MORRIS, J. A. (1970) First Offender: A Volunteer Program for Youth in Trouble with the Law. New York: Funk and Wagnalls.

National Clearinghouse for Drug Abuse Information (1973) Voluntary Action in Drug Abuse Prevention Programs. Report Series 5, No. 2 (December).

National Institute on Drug Abuse (1978) Data from the National Drug Abuse Treatment Utilization Survey (Executive Report, April 1977). Statistical Series F, No. 3 (January).

National Center for Voluntary Action (1974) Volunteers Assisting the Offender in Prison and in the Community (Portfolio No. 18). Washington, DC: Author.

REINHERZ, H. (1963) "College student volunteers as case aides in a state hospital for children." American Journal of Orthopsychiatry 33: 544-546.

——— (1969) "The therapeutic use of student volunteers," in B. G. Guerney (ed.) Psytherapeutic Agents: New Roles for Nonprofessionals, Parents and Teachers. New York: Krieger.

SCHEIER, I. (1970) "The professional and the volunteer in probation: perspectives on an emerging relationship." Federal Probation (June): 12-18.

SCHWARTZ, I. M. (1971) "Volunteers and professionals: a team in the correctional process." Federal Probation 35 (September): 46-50.

SELLS, S. B. (1977) "DARP followup evaluation research findings: a summary report." Unpublished paper.

SHUE, P. (1978) Director of Communications Services, Kiwanis International, Chicago, Illinois. Personal Communication, August 24.

WATSON, C. G., FULTON, J. R., and GUREL, L. (1975) "Project anchor: a study of an unsuccessful volunteer program to help former patients." Hospital and Community Psychiatry 26 (March): 146-151.

8

COMPANIONSHIP THERAPY
IN THE TREATMENT OF DRUG DEPENDENCY

KENNETH WOLF
DOUGLAS M. KERR

INTRODUCTION

It is commonly recognized that recidivism is one of the most serious, persistent, and difficult problems in the treatment of heroin abuse. It is also widely acknowledged that the problem of recidivism is closely tied to the problem of integrating the client into nondrug-using segments of his or her own community. This process of integration involves a wide range of community settings, social networks, and changes in coping behavior on the part of the client. Unfortunately, clinical success in integrating clients into the community is often limited to certain areas: stabilizing clients physiologically, enrolling them in educational and vocational programs, and securing job placement.

In other areas, however, traditional treatment programs have often appeared to be unable to exert a much needed degree of therapeutic impact. These areas include (a) training the client in new, nondrug-related leisure time activities, (b) integrating the client into nonheroin-using social networks, and (c) helping the client develop nondrug-related coping behaviors for responding to stress.

183

The present chapter discusses the use of companionship therapy interventions in addressing these latter three areas of therapeutic impact. An outline of this type of companionship program is presented, and is illustrated by data from a pilot study of companionship therapy with clients in two drug treatment clinics in Detroit. The chapter begins with a description of companionship therapy, its previous applications, and its typical areas of therapeutic impact, on the one hand, and a discussion of characteristics common among the pilot clinic clients on the other hand. The rationale for the current intervention is derived from this discussion. A brief description of a pilot study conducted by the authors is followed by a discussion of the programmatic aspects of using companionship therapy in substance abuse treatment. These programmatic considerations are divided into three areas: client variables, variables relating to volunteer companions, and the relationship between companionship programs and counseling services conducted in drug treatment clinics. A final section discusses preliminary conclusions drawn from the pilot study data.

CHARACTERISTICS OF COMPANIONSHIP THERAPY

Conceptually, companionship therapy interventions involve face-to-face contacts between two or more individuals, one or more of whom is typically defined by outside programmers as a "companion," while other participants are defined as clients. The companion and client have customarily had no contact prior to their introduction through the companionship intervention. Perhaps the most widely recognized example among companionship therapy programs is the Big Brothers of America.

Companionship therapy participants engage in recreational or leisure time activities, such as going to a restaurant, playing table or athletic games, going to a concert, or taking a walk. Activities may be chosen by either the companion or the client. However, client determination of activities is a general goal of the therapeutic process, since activities are also chosen to maximize the client's enjoyment of the companionship encounters. Choosing activities may also facilitate the development of some clients' decision-making skills. Further, because they are designed to emphasize client enjoyment, companionship therapy activities are ordinarily chosen with comparative spontaneity—commonly not more than two weeks in advance, and often not until the beginning of the companionship session itself.

Companions are supposed to encourage as warm, trusting, and egalitarian a relationship as possible between themselves and the clients. In this sense they are to act like companions or friends rather than "therapists"—they are not to attempt to act distant, or to engage in detached observation or interpretation of the clients' behavior. Regardless of how troubled the clients may appear, the companions are to elicit discussion about the clients' problems only to the extent that the clients appear genuinely interested in having such discussions. A lack of interest in such discussions does not indicate inappropriate behavior or "resistance" on the part of the clients. During these discussions, if any occurs, the companions are to be as personally and emotionally involved, and as self-disclosing, as is appropriate within a definition of the relationship as a companionship rather than as conventional psychotherapy.

It is appropriate to refer to the agent of therapeutic impact in this intervention as a "companionship therapist." For the sake of clarity, however, the term "therapist" will be applied only to counselors working at the methadone clinics participating in the study described below. Individuals working with clients in companionship dyads will be labeled "companions" or "volunteers."

PREVIOUS APPLICATIONS OF COMPANIONSHIP THERAPY

Although in a number of studies (cited below) companionship therapy has demonstrated varying degrees of clinical effectiveness, there are few published companionship therapy investigations relevant to the current chapter's focus upon adult, community-based former heroin addicts. For the most part, the companionship therapy literature has focused upon two mental health populations which provide a poor basis for generalization to the ex-addict client.

The first of these is the population of adult, institutionalized mental health clients (Beck et al., 1963, 1965; Bergman and Doland, 1974; Buckey et al., 1970; Greenblatt and Kantor, 1962; Holzberg et al., 1966; Kantor, 1957; Poser, 1966; Rappaport et al., 1971; Umbarger et al., 1962; Verinis, 1970).

The almost exclusive attention to hospitalized individuals, among adult clients, creates a lacuna for even the mental health-oriented reader of the companionship therapy literature. Only a few studies (Kerr, 1978a, 1978b, 1978c; Kerr et al., 1978a, 1978b; Ledvinka and Denner, 1972) have addressed the important area of companionship therapy as aftercare for former mental hospital clients living in the community. And, by extension, this paucity of community-based studies provides little basis for generalizing to adult, community-based methadone or drug-free clients.

Those community-based studies which do exist tend to evaluate companionship therapy with children and adolescents exhibiting manifest or incipient mental health problems (Belz et al., 1967; Cowen et al., 1975; Goodman, 1972; Mitchell, 1966a, 1966b; Patterson & Patterson, 1967; Stoffer, 1968; Stollak, 1969; Vander Kolk, 1973). These community-based studies of younger clients provide no clear basis for generalizing to clients of the present intervention—ex-addicts 18 to 40 years of age.

Studies of volunteer services to prisoners and probationers are also only marginally relevant to the present intervention. First, as Berger et al. (1975) have observed, "There have been quite a few less-than-rigorous studies" of the effects of volunteer programs on probationers of juvenile courts (see reviews by Cook and Scioli, 1975; and Shelley, 1971). The same might be said of similar studies with adult populations. For example, in a program described by Hogges and Hogges (1976), prisoners nearing release were paired with community volunteers who offered friendship and practical assistance with housing, employment, and supportive services. Most male clients' criminal charges involved drug abuse or alcoholism. Rearrest statistics were reported to be favorable, but no statistics for comparison groups (particularly other clients surviving the same professional prescreening given treatment clients) were reported.

Brockman (1975) reported anecdotal positive results in a program pairing community volunteers with probationers.

Barr (1971) described a program in which single volunteers were paired with incarcerated or discharged prisoners, or with parolees. These relationships focused upon either practical assistance to the client (sometimes lasting only one or two sessions), or developing an ongoing friendship. Pairs of volunteers were sometimes assigned to prisoners' families. No conclusions about client recidivism or community adjustment as a result of program participation were drawn.

Somewhat more rigorous studies also exist. Ku et al. (1975) found that high-risk misdemeanor probationers assigned to "volunteer counselors" had significantly fewer new offenses, as well as less serious offenses, as compared to similar subjects who proceeded through regular probation programming. Some volunteers engaged in "primary counseling" and "direct supervision" of clients, while others occupied a "suitable adult model" or "friend companion" role.

Berger et al. (1975) discussed an undated study by Beier and Zantra. When examining clients' interests, friendships, employment, arrest records, and other indicators of community adjustment, Beier and Zantra found no significant differences between adult misdemeanants who were randomly assigned to either volunteer workers or to probation officers. Berger et al. quoted Beier and Zantra's conclusion that "the volunteer probation program is designed for the 'willing and able' probationer, and ordinarily does not reach the more rebellious individuals and those unable to help themselves" (pp. II-1—II-2).

Berger et al. (1975) randomly assigned juvenile probationers to one or more of three types of volunteer services (p. IV-1), or to a control group. One of these services—the role of the "Volunteer Probation Officer"—appears to have functioned as a companionship therapy intervention. "Each of the three kinds of programs," the authors concluded, "seemed to increase delinquency by one or another criterion" (p. VII-2). Interestingly, unlike the demographic characteristics of the clients, "there were almost no blacks or lower class volunteers" (p. VII-3).

Two further problems arise when we attempt to generalize from these latter studies to the present intervention. First, the comparability of prisoners and probationers on the one hand, and substance abusers on the other, is unclear—even when we acknowledge the frequent existence of criminal behaviors among drug users. Second, most of these studies involved a "counselor/friend" volunteer role which was defined at the outset to include a continuous focus upon problem solving and counseling activities. Such roles differ from companionship therapy's emphasis upon leisure time activities. While there are no studies directly comparing the counselor/friend role to the companionship role, clients' perceptions of these two roles may be significantly different. The counselor/friend role may carry with it a hierarchical expectation of the volunteer as a helper and the client as needing help. The companion role may more readily allow the clients to perceive themselves as coequal participants in friendships based upon leisure activities—even if the volunteers occasionally help the clients with practical matters. Thus, it is difficult to generalize to the present companionship intervention from other programs which utilize a counselor/friend volunteer role. Similarly, it is difficult to generalize from studies whose analyses combine the clients of volunteer counselors with the clients of volunteer companions.

Finally, apart from program descriptions of exploratory work on the present project (Wolf and Panyard, 1974a, 1974b), there are no published outcome studies of companionship therapy with former heroin addicts.

In the absence of a truly relevant literature, formulation of the present program's rationale stemmed less from published antecedents than from a consideration of companionship therapy's areas of potential therapeutic impact on the one hand, and the common characteristics of pilot study clients on the other.

AREAS OF THERAPEUTIC IMPACT
WITH COMPANIONSHIP THERAPY

Companionship therapy can be viewed as having therapeutic impact in three general areas. Limiting the discussion to studies of adult clients, therapeutic gains might be expected, first, in the clients' cognitive or attitudinal functioning—as measured by relevant self-report psychological tests (Buckey et al., 1970; Greenblatt and Kantor, 1962; Holzberg et al., 1966; Kantor, 1957; Poser, 1966).

Second, therapeutic gains might be expected in the clients' overt behavior, as measured by observers' ratings (Bergman and Doland, 1974; Kerr, 1978a; Kerr et al., 1978b; Umbarger et al., 1962; Verinis, 1970), ratings of client behavior during standardized interviews (Beck et al., 1965), or hospital release statistics (Beck et al., 1963). It should be noted that increasing the clients' self-initiated leisure time activity is a reasonable goal for this recreationally based intervention (Kerr, 1978a, 1978b). This point will be elaborated later in the discussion.

A third area of therapeutic change is equally important although frequently neglected. Client might be expected to integrate themselves into new social networks—or to reintegrate themselves into earlier social networks—which are similar to those of the volunteer. This process might be seen as occuring in two general ways. First, the volunteers might be viewed as providing models of social behavior which the clients can emulate when dealing with social situations by themselves. This conceptualization is perhaps more properly categorized as part of the changes in behavior and emotions (self-confidence, depression, etc.) discussed above.

However, there is a second possibility which sufficiently discriminates companionship therapy from most other techniques as to warrant its separate discussion here. Specifically, because companionship therapy can evolve toward the establishment of a friendship between the participants, it is possible for the companions to include the clients in some of their own friendships by introducing the clients to their own friends. If additional relationships independent of the volunteers arise between these new individuals and the clients, the latter can become integrated into a social network first represented by their companions.

That this possibility is only rarely discussed is probably attributable to the two populations with which the companionship therapy literature has predominantly been concerned. Because hospitalized adults commonly have serious deficits in basic social skills, dealing with these problems inside the companionship itself ordinarily supersedes consideration of the clients' integration into the companions' own larger social networks.

In the case of mildly disturbed children and adolescents, the clinical goal is routinely to enhance the child's functioning within his or her current social networks—e.g., school, family, clubs, or friendship groups. Because the volunteer and the members of his or her social network are ordinarily appreciably older than the child or adolescent, integration into this network could often amount to establishing a surrogate family for the client. Although such surrogate families are sometimes discussed as positive interventions arising spontaneously among nonprofessional community support systems, the goals of companionship therapy are ordinarily less ambitious than the supplanting of the younger client's family with the volunteer's own network. However, the companionship may be used to reduce a child's "extreme dependency" upon his or her own family (Perlmutter and Durham, 1965).

For the methadone or drug-free clients, however, integration into a volunteer companion's social network is a plausible and desirable outcome. These clients are approximately the same age as their volunteers, and unlike some institutionalized individuals, they would rarely exhibit extreme psychopathological symptoms. Even if assimilation into the volunteers' network is not fully realized, the clients will have an opportunity to observe and imitate the volunteers' social behavior with their friends. Clients may appreciate the recognition and approval implicit in being introduced to them, and they will probably be well received by the companions' "straight" associates. All of these factors may encourage the clients to believe in their ability to become integrated into a nondrug-using social network on their own.

RECIDIVISM AND COMMON CHARACTERISTICS OF THE METHADONE TREATMENT CLIENTS

The treatment rationale for the companionship intervention was based upon three problems common among clients in the pilot clinics. The first of these was clients' frequent lack of nondrug-related leisure time skills. Some clients may have lacked these skills prior to becoming addicted.

Other may have lost their leisure time skills during the course of their addiction, since the process of obtaining money, buying drugs, and administering them three or four times each day functioned as a full-time job seven days a week.

Ironically, this lack of leisure time skills could become a major impetus toward recidivism because of the nature of methadone treatment itself. After the clients were stabilized on methadone, their time was no longer absorbed by the "full-time job" of addiction. At this point, however, they were frequently unready to return to school or to find employment. Thus, during this period in methadone treatment the clients were faced with enormous amounts of what was often reported to be extremely boring free time. Minor pastimes such as television failed to provide any meaningful activity. In the absence of adequate nondrug-related leisure time skills, heroin abuse (or similarly, alcohol abuse—see Preble and Miller, 1977) could emerge as one of the most familiar and rewarding diversions available to the clients. In these cases recidivism resulted from the clients' boredom—a boredom which might have been avoided if the clients could have engaged in meaningful nondrug-related leisure time activities.

A second impetus toward recidivism stemmed from some clients' alienation from the nondrug-using community, including family and friends who they had lied to or stolen from in the course of supporting their addiction. Because of this alienation, clients ordinarily found no models and few rewards for remaining drug-free while associating with practicing addicts. On the contrary, active peer pressure for the clients to return to heroin abuse was often reported by clients and clinic personnel. It was not surprising, then, that some clients did return to heroin use in response to these pressures.

A third impetus toward recidivism concerned some clients' lack of nondrug-related strategies for coping with stress. Formal clinic counseling routinely attempted to address this lack, but the difficulties in teaching effective nondrug-related coping techniques were frequently considerable. Even the beginnings of adequate coping techniques were sometimes missing from the clients' behavioral repertoire. The clients' presence in treatment could not be assumed to reflect adequate coping strategies, since many clients entered treatment in response to coercion by family, employers, or criminal justice authorities (Panyard et al., forthcoming). Thus, some clients were ambivalent toward treatment, or were unable to actively participate in rehabilitation efforts (Panyard et al., 1973). If clinic treatment could not overcome these odds while attempting to teach new coping skills, clients might return to heroin use when confronted with stressful life situations.

TREATMENT RATIONALE OF THE CURRENT INTERVENTION

In 1956 Raskin et al. recommended two aftercare interventions in the treatment of heroin addiction which have only recently received widespread considered. One of these was the use of "group activity programs of formerly addicted persons organized in much the same manner as Alcoholics Anonymous" (p. 17). The second recommendation was the use of an intervention which the authors likened to the Big Brothers of America—a companionship therapy intervention. For the client in this intervention, "The sincere and conscientious interest of a fellow human being would be his, someone to help him gain a self-sufficiency and not breed a helpless dependency" (p. 17).

Although prompted by Raskin et al.'s suggestion, the present companionship program has evolved a more specific treatment rationale based upon the conceptualization of client recidivism discussed above. First, it was believed that companionship therapy might effectively address the substance abuse clients' need for nondrug-related leisure time skills. It has already been noted that companionship therapy might be expected to influence the clients' overt behavior, particularly the leisure time activity level (Kerr, 1978a, 1978b). In the present context, the companionship might be viewed as step by step, experiential instructions in leisure time activities available to the clients in their own communities. In this connection it is particularly advantageous that companionship therapy is a leisure activity-based intervention, and that the activities are spontaneously chosen so as to maximize the client's enjoyment of the experience.

Second, it was believed that companionship therapy might be able to address the former addict's need to become resocialized into nondrug-using social circles in the community. A central factor here would be companionship therapy's impact upon the client's emotional state through the establishment of a relatively warm, trusting, nonexploitative relationship between the companion and client. This might provide the client with a safe environment in which to reduce his or her anxiety and sense of alienation from "straight" people. Further, it might provide an environment in which learning to get along with a "straight" companion is rewarding, and in which these lessons might be obtained through both operant rewards and a process of identification and modeling. In this connection it is particularly advantageous that companionship therapy can—as discussed above—facilitate the client's integration into a specific social network of which the companion is already a member. It was believed that the companion might eventually introduce his or her own friends to the client, and that the client might become integrated into this social network. In any event, the client might be able to generalize lessons learned in relating the volunteer to other "straight" social circles which he or she might ultimately approach on his or her own.

Finally, it was believed that companionship therapy might assist the clients in learning nondrug-related techniques for dealing with stress. At both the emotional and behavioral levels, the companionship might promote the clients' sense of competence and independence rather than dependence and longing for chemically induced escape. Meeting the volunteer companion would itself be a source of stress. The clients' persistence and assertiveness in continuing the companionship would hopefully be rewarded by the establishment of relatively close and meaningful relationships. Further, the clients would be able to witness the volunteers' techniques for dealing with stress in the companionship, as well as learning from the volunteers' descriptions of how they handle difficulties in their own lives. With regard to promoting the clients' sense of independence and self-sufficiency, it is advantageous that the activities in companionship therapy are basically unpredictable, and that the clients must participate in the presumably rewarding process of deciding and planning the activities of companionship sessions.

THE PILOT STUDY

Pilot work in an ongoing demonstration project forms the basis for the following section's discussion of programmatic issues in the use of companionship therapy with substance abuse clients. Development of this project has extended over several years. Early exploratory work (Wolf and Panyard, 1974a, 1974b) led to an application for funding (Wolf et al., 1976). After funds were obtained for a demonstration grant from the National Institute on Drug Abuse, research began on the pilot phase of the study (Kerr et al., 1978a; Wadleigh et al., 1978; Wadleigh and Rencher, 1978; Wolf, Kerr, and Mills, 1978; Wolf, Kerr, Rencher, and Wadleigh, 1978). Two Detroit methadone clinics agreed to cooperative work on the project, and companionship therapy services were offered to clients screened by counselors in both clinics. Clients and volunteers were matched in one-to-one dyads. Matching was based upon the participants' community of residence, race, and sex. A lesser attempt was also made to match the client and volunteer on the bases of age and leisure time interests. Companionship dyads were scheduled to meet once a week for at least three hours over a six month period. It is this program structure which serves as the basis for the present discussion of companionship therapy in substance abuse treatment.

As of this writing the pilot study is drawing to a close, a summative evaluation design has been developed (Kerr, Mills, and Wolf, 1978; Kerr et al., 1978b), and random assignment of treatment and control clients from additional clinics has marked the beginning of the project's summative evaluation phase. Although a variety of significant findings stemmed from the pilot study, space limitations confine the present chapter to those results which are most illustrative of the concept and basic operation of the intervention. A more thorough discussion of the pilot study data is presented elsewhere (Kerr, Mills, and Wadleigh, 1978).

CLIENT VARIABLES

Not all drug treatment clients would be considered appropriate for a companionship intervention. As discussed above, such programs would be seen as addressing problems of recidivism emerging in the later phases of drug treatment. Accordingly, clients just beginning treatment—e.g., clients undergoing initial methadone stabilization—would not be referred to a companionship program. Similarly, in its current conceptualization, companionship treatment is not seen as addressing problems of psychosis among drug treatment clients. Thus, the few clients who show psychotic symptoms—even if these symptoms are subsequently masked by methadone dosage—would not be referred for companionships. For obvious reasons, clients who are judged to represent a potential danger to a community volunteer would also be excluded.

In the pilot study, clinic counselors were asked to refer clients who conformed to these three screening criteria, and who were seen in therapy at least once a week. Given the large number of clients who could be expected to fit these generally unrestrictive criteria, it is not surprising that referred clients did not appear to be a group composed solely of individuals who were doing well and probably had the least need for the intervention. Some referred clients were still using heroin or other drugs not medically prescribed. Counselors appeared to screen out most consistent heroin users, but to refer clients who were still using heroin periodically—often in response to stressful life situations. In addition, some clients were in poor health due to past drug usage and other causes. Many were severely withdrawn and lacking in social skills.

On the other hand, some clients who were doing relatively well were also referred. A few clients who had progressed to drug-free status (who were not using heroin and had successfully finished methadone detoxification) were suggested for companionship treatment as part of their continued therapy at the methadone clinics.

A second screening—which was imposed by clients themselves—appeared to eliminate many individuals at two extremes of the group of 117 clients who were offered companionship services. On the one hand, many clients declining offers of service appeared to be among the least successful in clinical treatment. They were more often reported by their counselors to be consistent heroin users, and to be avoiding participation in clinical therapy and employment or educational opportunities. Many clients declining offers of companionship therapy service appeared to be among the most successful in clinic treatment. These clients often seemed to be more self-confident and were more frequently reported to be employed or in school, and to have social relationships with nonaddict friends.

Thus, the sample of clients accepting offers of companionship services appeared to fall between two extremes of client well-being and little progress in clinical treatment. While clients accepting offers of service often appeared to be motivated to take advantage of their clinical therapy and employment or educational opportunities, they still exhibited a genuine need for a range of rehabilitative programs. They primarily had practicing addicts as friends, they tended to lack many basic social skills, and they were occasionally unemployed and/or out of school.

At the first pilot clinic—which had a predominantly white clientele—39% of the treatment population was referred for companionship services by their counselors, while the corresponding figure for the second pilot clinic with a predominantly black population was 50%. At the first pilot clinic 29% of referred clients accepted offers of companionship services; these clients constituted 11% of the clinic's population. At the second clinic 24% of referred clients accepted service; these clients constituted 12% of the clinic's population. Thus, of the combined total of the two clinics' populations, 44% were referred for companionship services. Of the combined total of clients referred, 26% accepted offers of service. This meant that of the combined total of the two clinics' populations, 11% survived the screenings imposed by counselors and self-selection.

Two general questions remain, however, as to whether these clients agreed to participate in companionship dyads for appropriate reasons. First, there is the concern that clients will attempt to take advantage of volunteers. It is important to consider whether any harm befalls volunteers as a consequence of their association with ex-addicts. The simplest answer to this question is that no crimes, attempted crimes, or any similar incidents occurred in the pilot study or among treatment dyads in the final sample to date. A broader answer would note two factors which may have contributed to this absence of threats to volunteers.

The first of these concerns client characteristics. Clients accepting offers of companionship treatment generally appeared to be oriented toward conventional or socially acceptable behavior, rather than feloneous or antisocial behavior. This orientation may have been characteristic of clients in general. However, it seemed more probable that this prosocial orientation was related to the screenings imposed by clinic counselors and/or client self-selection. Counselors appeared to be well informed about their clients' recent behavior, and this probably contributed to their accuracy in judging client dangerousness. Any biases in their judgment appeared to favor a conservative labeling of false positives rather than the production of false negatives. Further, clients' willingness to associate with a "straight" companion may have stemmed from a broader prosocial orientation among these individuals.

A second factor concerns volunteers' characteristics as these were influenced by self-selection, screening, and preservice training. An analysis of volunteer self-selection was difficult because of the lack of comparative data concerning persons who were exposed to recruitment messages—e.g., through mass media appeals—but who failed to volunteer. Even face-to-face recruitment presentations—e.g., in college classrooms—provided relatively anonymous contact with the audiences involved. Still, it was possible to note that persons who volunteered usually appeared to be relatively sophisticated and to have good judgment. Perhaps this lack of naivete might be expected of individuals who would volunteer for one-to-one relationships with persons from a "deviant subculture." In any case, volunteer screening—described more fully in the next section—may also have eliminated individuals whose poor judgment would have encouraged client antisocial behavior.

The preservice training of volunteers—also described more fully in the next section—appeared to be another influence in this area. Because they often knew little about substance abusers, volunteers usually seemed to pay close attention to the content of training. During training, a distinction was drawn between "active addicts" and "methadone- or drug-free clients" in treatment at a substance abuse clinic. Trainees were told that companionship clients seemed to be among the safest clients in treatment at the participating methadone clinics. It was also stressed, however, that certain precautions should nevertheless be exercised: e.g., "do not lend money to the client, do not take the client to your hone until you have gotten to know each other well," etc. Such instructions appeared to be successful in making volunteers cautious and aware of the "games" addicts sometimes play, without also making them fearful or inhibited.

A second general question about clients' involvement in companionships concerns the strength of their motivation to participate actively. Clients from the pilot clinics often resisted the scheduling of initial and subsequent companionship sessions. Some clients appeared to be afraid of being rejected by their "straight" companions, while others appeared to be afraid of intimacy generally. One client seemed to try to hide her problems, and saw her volunteer only when she was doing well and not feeling depressed—which happened infrequently. Other clients were found to "play games" when avoiding companionship sessions. One client, for example, joked about listening on an extension telephone during several conversations in which his sister told a member of the companionship program staff that he was not at home. It should be noted, however, that some volunteers also failed to appear punctually for initial companionship sessions. In general, these problems of client and volunteer participation did not appear insoluble—unfortunately, space limitations preclude a discussion of remedies for the difficulties currently under study.

VOLUNTEER VARIABLES

Volunteer companions might be recruited for drug treatment programs through a variety of channels. Mass media recruitment would include advertisements—ordinarily free public service announcements—on radio and television, or paid advertisements in mass circulation and college newspapers. It would also involve appeals made through columnists' articles and appearances on community-oriented radio and television public service programs. Recruitment in colleges would include face-to-face classroom presentations and posting of announcements. Recruitment in community-based (noncollegiate) formal organizations would include face-to-face presentations or the posting of announcements in churches, unions, businesses, block clubs, fraternal organizations, other volunteer recruitment agencies, governmental bodies, cooperatives, housing councils, and other organizations.

Predictably, volunteer recruitment proved to be a difficult aspect of the pilot study. Out of the 219 individuals initially contacting the companionship program during its first 11 months of volunteer recruitment, only 30% (ignoring nine persons screened out by program staff—63/210) continued through the initial phases involving a screening interview and a preservice training session. Thus, the first difficulty in recruiting volunteers was the large number of individuals who eliminated themselves from participation prior to becoming ready for assignment to a client.

Moreover, difficulties in volunteer recruitment varied by type of recruitment channel. Because space limitations preclude a detailed discussion of the data (see Kerr, Mills, and Wadleigh, 1978), only the most basic conclusions in this area are summarized here. First, with regard to mass media, radio and newspaper appeals were far more productive than televised appeals. This was partially true because free radio and newspaper publicity was easier to obtain than free televised publicity. Moreover, in obtaining volunteers capable of assignment to a client, radio, newspaper, and college recruitment channels were superior to recruitment through television or community-based formal organizations. Thus, although obtaining community volunteers for a drug treatment companionship therapy program can be difficult, this problem may be reduced by an emphasis upon radio, newspapers, and colleges as principal volunteer sources.

A further issue concerns the screening and training mechanisms which might be used to help assure volunteers' appropriateness for, and effectiveness in, the companion's role. As discussed above, during the first 11 months of volunteer recruitment, 219 individuals contacted the companionship program, 63 continued through the screening interview and preservice training, and nine persons were screened out by program staff. Most of the characteristics which led project staff to screen out a volunteer may be grouped under four headings. First, a volunteer was eliminated if he or she was judged to be severely neurotic or psychotic. One psychotic individual and four severely neurotic individuals volunteered as companions during the pilot study. Second, a volunteer was eliminated if he or she viewed heroin addicts as "exotic" persons, and manifested a morbid or supercilious curiosity about them (the "tourist" volunteer). Notwithstanding project staff's concern about such individuals, no volunteer of this type contacted the project. Third, volunteers were eliminated if they wanted to perform a variant of formal verbal or behavioristic psychotherapy, rather than acting as a friend or companion. One individual was eliminated for this reason, and many volunteers contacting the project screened themselves out when they first heard the "friendship" versus "therapist" expectations of the companion's role. Fourth, volunteers were not retained if they exhibited condescending or pitying attitudes toward substance abuse clients. Two volunteers were eliminated for this reason.

In addition, one volunteer was screened out after two companionship sessions because the client did not feel comfortable with him—the client disliked the disorganized atmosphere of the volunteer's home—and because the volunteer "misplaced" two expensive concert tickets provided by the project.

In general, problems in volunteers' actual performance as companions usually emerged during the first two weekly companionship sessions. Thus, it became a policy to have additional trained volunteers ready as replacements when new dyads were initiated.

Minor problems in volunteers' performance were dealt with in monthly group supervisory meetings required of volunteers who were assigned clients. These meetings also provided an opportunity for volunteers to ask additional questions of project staff, to share their successes and anxieties, and to give each other support and advice.

There were three principal opportunities for project staff to assess and screen out volunteers. The first of these was the volunteer's initial telephone contact with the project, the second was a one-to-one screening interview conducted with all volunteers, while the third was an eight-hour training session conducted before the volunteer was assigned to a client. This training session was composed of (a) an initial exercise designed to permit group members and staff to get to know and feel comfortable with each other; (b) a didactic presentation concerning the major drug groups, as well as the physical, social, and psychological aspects of heroin addiction; (c) a didactic presentation in basic empathy skills; (d) exercises in which triads of volunteers and project staff alternated in playing the roles of methadone client, volunteer, and observer; and (e) didactic discussions stressing the rationale and limitations of the companionship intervention. Successful ex-heroin addicts participating in the training programs offered a description of the addict life-style, and conducted question and answer sessions with volunteers. The initial exercises, role play, and volunteers' comments during the didactic presentations all provided opportunities for project staff to learn volunteers' preconceptions about heroin addicts, and to observe volunteers' interactions in social situations.

THE COMPANIONSHIP PROGRAM'S RELATIONSHIP TO CLINIC-BASED COUNSELING

As discussed above, client resistance to scheduling and attending companionship sessions was observed during the pilot study. This fact focuses attention upon the clinic counselor, who is in a uniquely important position to facilitate the client's participation in a companionship program. The counselor is perhaps the only person who can address the client's resistance to the companionship at an emotional level. Companionship staff and the volunteer typically do not know the client well enough at the outset to discuss the emotional content of the client's resistance. Their remedies to client resistance are largely structural, e.g., having the first companionship session at the clinic so that the client is familiar and comfortable with the setting, or instructing the volunteer to schedule the day, time, and place of each future session with the client before the end of any current session. The clinic counselor, on the other hand, can often discuss the client's fears openly while being empathic and supportive, or can challenge the client to overcome a resistance which is familiar to both parties from their past therapeutic work together.

Given the clinic counselors' significance to the operation of a companionship program for ex-addicts, it is important to consider the opinions these staff members have toward such an intervention. During the pilot study, counselors were enthusiastic about the companionship program's approach to aspects of client recidivism with which they were personally familiar from clinical experience. Counselors occasionally sought some assurance, however, that the volunteer would not compromise their own therapy with the client. This assurance was provided by emphasizing that volunteers were screened, trained, and supervised to act as friends and companions rather than as "therapists."

Rather than creating an obstacle to formal therapeutic work with clients, there was some evidence that a companionship could provide useful therapeutic material for the clinic-based therapy. Counselors could draw parallels between maladaptive behaviors which clients used with their volunteers, and similar behaviors they used in other situations. Moreover, counselors could draw parallels between the constructive behaviors they suggested for dealing with the volunteers, and the need for similar behaviors in other settings. When such suggestions worked well in the companionship, the counselor could point to the possibility of success in other contexts. The counselor could also label, interpret, and assist the client in identifying those of his or her emotions which underlay many of the maladaptive responses toward the volunteer (and, by extension, toward others). Through these means, counselors could have considerable influence upon the therapeutic impact of the companionships, even though they typically had contact only with the client and not with the volunteer. In fact, case study analysis suggested that positive client outcome was associated with the counselor's discussing the progress of the companionship with the client. This point will be elaborated below.

PRELIMINARY CONCLUSIONS

Five preliminary conclusions about companionship therapy in drug treatment are drawn from pilot work on the present project. These pertain to (a) clinical outcomes among substance abuse clients, (b) clinical outcomes among volunteers, and (c) outcomes at the community systems level.

Clinical Outcomes Among Substance Abuse Clients

(1) *Companionship therapy may be clinically effective in reducing recidivism among substance abuse clients.*

This conclusion is drawn tentatively because only case study data unaided by comparison to control subjects are available as of this writing, and because difficulties in maintaining volunteers' and clients' scheduling of regular companionship sessions (discussed above) limited the number of dyads which continued for longer periods of time. The clinical success observed appeared to be related to (a) the frequency of face-to-face companionship sessions (frequent volunteer-client telephone conversations appeared to be an inadequate substitute for face-to-face meetings); (b) the volunteer's assertiveness in overcoming client resistance to scheduling regular face-to-face meetings; (c) the personality of the client (very dependent clients may have aided the companionship process by becoming dependent upon the volunteer in early phases of the relationship); and (d) the clinic counselor's use of events in the companionship as material for the client's formal therapy. The last of these factors—the counselor's use of the companionship—suggests a conceptualization of this intervention which is discussed below.

(2) *Companionship therapy may be optimally conceptualized as an ancillary treatment in relation to the clinic counselor's formal verbal therapy with the ex-addict.*

In the mental health literature, companionship therapy has typically been viewed as a separate intervention intended to have an independent impact upon the client. In the pilot study there were some respects in which companionship therapy appeared to have such an independent impact—as when a client's self-image seemed to change from "addict client" to "coequal friend" with the volunteer.

However, even in the mental health literature it has not always been clear that companionship therapy is best utilized as an independent treatment. Kerr's (1978a, 1978b) study of former mental hospital clients, for example, recommended that companionship therapy be viewed as ancillary to formal skill-focused therapy for that population. Similarly, during the present pilot study it often appeared that the client's more important insights and attempts at new behaviors in the companionship resulted from the clinic counselor's formal therapeutic work. The companionship appeared to function as a diagnostic tool, and as a relatively sheltered proving ground for the therapist's suggestions to the client. In essence, the companionship resembled an applied laboratory which paralleled and augmented the clinic therapist's verbal intervention. It is in this sense that the companionship appeared to function in an ancillary relationship to the clinic-based treatment.

It is worth noting that when the companionship is viewed as ancillary to clinic-based treatment, a client's failure to accept an offer of companionship services may not be a negative outcome. Counselors sometimes used their clients' negative or defensive feelings toward the companionship as a source of important material in their formal therapeutic work with these individuals. Similarly, discussing a client's refusal to meet with his or her volunteer—after accepting an offer of service—may also be profitable for the counselor-client interaction. When the companionship is viewed as an ancillary treatment, the most negative outcome (aside from any conceivable iatrogenic effect) may be a combination of the client's failure to accept or reliably participate in the companionship, coupled with the clinic counselor's failure to use the client's behavior profitably as material in the formal clinic-based therapy.

Clinical Outcomes Among Volunteers

(3) *The companionship therapists' activities in working with methadone clients may be appropriate as an intervention for the volunteers themselves.*

The possible use of companionship therapy as a therapeutic intervention for the companionship volunteer has only infrequently received
attention. Kerr (1978a, 1978b) recommended that this possibility be
considered when establishing companionship therapy programs with
former mental hospital clients, while Cowen et al. (1968) utilized retired
persons as companions for troubled grade school children in order to
realize "the possibility of considerable 'therapeutic' help for the 'helper' "
(p. 901). "Tuned out" high school students have also been used effectively
with troubled grade school children (Clarfield and McMillan, 1973;
McMillan, 1973; McWilliams and Finkel, 1973).

In the present intervention, two general approaches might be used in
making the companionship experience therapeutic for the volunteer. First,
program staff might consider intentionally recruiting volunteers from
within certain target populations. For example, if the methadone clients
are recent war veterans, programmers might consider other veterans who
have not been heroin users for use as companionship therapists. These
companions, if they are only mildly disturbed, might be aided in coming
to terms with their own war experiences by discussing those of the
ex-addict (cf., Caplan, 1974: 16).

A second approach would focus on volunteer reaction to client behavior regardless of the population from which the volunteer was recruited. In
this instance volunteers can be seen as learning about themselves and
modifying their behaviors in association with their routine participation in
the companionship.

Two aspects of the companionship process were seen to provide the
basis for such change. Both involved an apparently "negative" attitude
toward the volunteer. First, clients often resisted the scheduling of regular
companionship sessions. Second, clients frequently dominated companionship conversations, often by talking about themselves. When volunteers
tried to remedy this problem by purposefully talking about their own
experiences, clients commonly appeared not to listen, or else interrupted
with another topic.

A few volunteers appeared to view these client behaviors as personal
rejections, rather than seeing them as the result of either the client's fear
of the companionship, or the client's frequent pattern of self-absorbtion
and narcissism. To this extent, these few individuals appeared to rely
excessively upon the clients' behavior—rather than their self-esteem—in
judging their self-worth. Other volunteers, although they were frustrated
by such client behaviors, did not appear to feel personally rejected or hurt.

That learning how to react to the client's resistance and self-absorbtion could prove a positive opportunity for the volunteer is illustrated by a companion's description of his reaction to this situation:

> I learned more not to lean on another person's acceptance of me. At first it was kind of like that: like "When am I going to hear from you about me." But then I saw it was an opportunity just to accept myself—something I could use in other relationships.

Administrators may wish to be sensitive to this issue of volunteers' dependence and self-esteem, and to deal with it directly in training and supervision. Two purposes would be served in doing so. First, it would afford the volunteer a supportive setting in which to do limited therapeutic work for his or her own personal growth. Thus, the clinical focus would broaden from a principal concern with the client to an additional concern with the volunteer's feelings and behavior both inside and outside the companionship. Assuming this responsibility as a programmatic goal would require that experienced therapists be involved in volunteer supervision. The supervisory/therapeutic task would require eliciting the volunteer's expression of feelings while also limiting the depth of the material under discussion.

A second purpose would be enhancing the volunteer's therapeutic effectiveness as a companion for the client. This might occur in two ways. First, if the volunteer ceases to view client resistance to the companionship as a personal rejection, he or she may become more assertive in trying to schedule regular companionship sessions with the client. Such assertiveness is often essential in showing the reluctant client that he or she is accepted by the volunteer, and that actually participating in the companionship can be nonthreatening and enjoyable. Second, it may make the volunteer more self-assured in telling the client what his or her reactions are to the client's behavior. It is an axiom in conventional verbal therapy that the client can sometimes profit from being told the reactions he or she engenders either in the therapist, or—in group therapy—in other clients. It is no less likely that the substance abuse client could benefit from plainly stated and well-meaning explanations of the volunteer's reactions to the client. That the client's resistance to scheduling and attending companionship meetings ocasionally "bothers" or "hurts the volunteer's feelings" is but one possible example.

Outcomes at the Community Systems Level

(4) *Companionship therapy programs for substance abuse clients can be used as a means of conducting community education programs about substance abuse.*

Several authors have suggested that companionship therapy programs for mental health clients can be used to educate volunteers and their associates in the community concerning the nature of mental illness, and to counteract negative stereotypes about the mental health client (Bergman and Doland, 1974; Cowen et al., 1966; Greenblatt and Kantor, 1962; Holzberg, 1963; Holzberg and Gewirtz, 1963; Holzberg and Knapp, 1975; Iguchi and Johnson, 1966; Kantor, 1957; Kerr, 1978a, 1978b; Kulik et al., 1969; Linden and Stollak, 1969; Umbarger et al., 1962; Vander Kolk, 1973; Zax and Cowen, 1967). In a similar fashion, companionship volunteers' client contacts, the content of volunteer training, and the content of speeches made during volunteer recruitment can all represent opportunities which program administrators may use to educate the community about drug dependence.

In this context, the difficulties in volunteer recruitment discussed above may also be associated with certain secondary benefits. It was found that extensive volunteer recruitment within formal organizations such as churches, unions, and business hierarchies yielded few volunteers. Nevertheless, members of these organizations often appeared to learn a great deal about heroin abuse and treatment during these recruitment appeals. Such an appeal necessarily contained a discussion of the methadone or drug-free treatment client as distinct from the active addict, and an explanation of the ex-addict's characteristics as these related to the rationale for companionship therapy. This closer look at the former addict and the social forces acting upon him, as well as the structure, goals, and procedures of community-based treatment clinics, frequently appeared to counter listeners' more severely pejorative stereotypes in this area. Audience comments commonly shifted from an initial focus upon addicts' criminal behaviors toward questions about treatment success, clients' medical problems, and the similarity of drug clients to alcohol clients with whom some audience members could more easily identify.

(5) *Companionship therapy programs for methadone clients can be used to build community support for drug treatment in general, and for a local drug treatment agency in particular.*

As discussed above, an exploratory project preceded application for funding of the present study (Wolf and Panyard, 1974a, 1974b). Volunteer recruitment during this exploratory work showed the potential such efforts can have for increasing a community's support for drug treatment in general, and for a local drug treatment agency in particular.

Specifically, companionship staff, working out of a local methadone clinic, approached a regional community council composed of block club representatives in an effort to recruit volunteers. The council responded enthusiastically. They reported that the drug clinic and other related agencies had approached them in the past only when something was being forced upon their community, or when such officials needed their support for a drug treatment issue. They expressed feelings of powerlessness against such officials because their wishes were not often respected.

The companionship program, on the other hand, was viewed as an innovative approach to the "drug problem" in which the community group could effectively participate. The community council felt that by publicizing the companionship program to its members, and by assisting in the recruitment of companionship volunteers who would help other community members—i.e., the drug abuse patient—it was performing the kind of community service which justified its own existence. The council wrote a letter endorsing the companionship program, complimented the clinic on including and working with the community in its drug treatment efforts, and advertised for volunteers in its newsletter. In general, the council appeared to develop a new respect for and understanding about the treatment efforts of the clinic. At the same time, a more cooperative and reciprocal relationship between the two agencies developed.

SUMMARY

The present chapter discussed the use of companionship therapy to address certain apparent causes of recidivism among drug treatment clients. Companionship therapy's characteristics, previous applications, and typical areas of therapeutic impact were described. These were related to the needs of clients in methadone clinics participating in a pilot study of this intervention. It was argued that companionship therapy could assist clients in (a) learning nondrug-related leisure time skills, (b) becoming integrated into nondrug-using social circles, and (c) learning nondrug-related techniques for coping with stress. The pilot study was described briefly.

Programmatic considerations in operating such an intervention included client screening; the characteristics of clients who would accept offers of companionship services; the differential effectiveness of recruiting companionship volunteers through various channels; volunteer screening, training, and supervision; and the relationship between a companionship program and the verbal therapy offered by drug clinic counselors.

Further discussion noted the factors potentially associated with the intervention's impact upon both client and volunteer, as well as the use of companionship for community education and organization concerning substance abuse issues.

REFERENCES

BARR, H. (1971) Volunteers in Prison After-Care. London: Allen & Unwin.

BECK, J. C., KANTOR, D., and GELINEAU, V. A. (1963) "Follow-up study of chronic psychotic patients "treated" by college case-aide volunteers." American Journal of Psychiatry 120: 269-271.

––– (1965) "Impact of undergraduate volunteers on the social behavior of chronic psychotic patients." International Journal of Social Psychiatry 12: 96-104.

BELZ, J. F., DREHMEL, V. W., and SIVERTSEN, A. D. (1967) "Volunteer: the community's participant in treatment of schizophrenic children in a day care program." American Journal of Orthopsychiatry 37: 221-222.

BERGER, R. J., CROWLEY, J. E., GOLD, M., GRAY J., and ARNOLD, M. S. (1975) Experiment in a Juvenile Court: A Study of a Program of Volunteers Working with Juvenile Probationers. Ann Arbor: Institute for Social Research, University of Michigan.

BERGMAN, J. S. and DOLAND, D. J. (1974) "The effectiveness of college students as therapeutic agents with chronic hospitalized patients." American Journal of Orthopsychiatry 44: 92-101.

BROCKMAN, W. (1975) "Experiences of volunteer counselors with juvenile offenders." Presented at the American Personnel and Guidance Association National Convention, New York City, March.

BUCKEY, H. M., MUENCH, G. A., and SJOBERG, B. M. (1970) "Effects of a college student visitation program on a group of chronic schizophrenics." Journal of Abnormal Psychology 75: 242-244.

CAPLAN, G. (1974) Support Systems and Community Mental Health: Lectures on Concept Development. New York: Behavioral Publications.

CLARFIELD, S. P. and McMILLAN, R. C. (1973) "High school students in a human service practicum." American Journal of Community Psychology 1: 212-218.

COOK, T. J. and SCIOLOI, F. P., Jr. (1975) The Effectiveness of Volunteer Programs in the Area of Courts and Corrections. Washington, DC: National Science Foundation.

COWEN, E. L., LEIBOWITZ, G., and LEIBOWITZ, E. (1968) "The utilization of retired people as mental health aides in the schools." American Journal of Orthopsychiatry 38: 900-910.

COWEN, E. L., TROST, M. A., LORION, R. P., DORR, D., IZZO, L. D., and ISAACSON, R. V. New Ways in School Mental Health. New York: Human Sciences Press.

COWEN, E. L., ZAX, M., and LAIRD, J. D. (1966) "A college student volunteer program in the elementary school setting." Community Mental Health Journal 2: 319-328.

GOODMAN, G. (1972) Companionship Therapy. San Francisco: Jossey-Bass.

GREENBLATT, M. and KANTOR, D. (1962) "Student volunteer movement and the manpower shortage." American Journal of Psychiatry 118: 809-814.

HOGGES, R. and HOGGES, L. (1976) An Exploratory Study of Transition, Inc. School of Health and Social Services, Florida International University, Taiami Trail, Miami, Florida, April.

HOLZBERG, J. D. (1963) "The companion program: implementing the manpower recommendations of the Joint Commission on Mental Illness and Health." American Psychologist 18: 224-226.

——— and GEWIRTZ, H. A. (1963) "A method of altering attitudes towards mental illness." Psychiatric Quarterly Supplement 37: 56-61.

HOLZBERG, J. D. and KNAPP, R. H. (1975) "The social interaction of college students and chronically ill patients." American Journal of Orthopsychiatry 35: 487-492.

——— and TURNER, J. L. (1966) "Companionship with the mentally ill: effects of the personalities of college student volunteers." Psychiatry 29: 395-405.

IGUCHI, M. T. and JOHNSON, R. C. (1966) "Attitudes of students associated with participation in a mental-hospital volunteer program." Journal of Social Psychology 68: 107-111.

KANTOR, D. (1957) "The use of college students as "case aids" in a social service department of a state hospital: an experiment in undergraduate social work education," in M. Greenblatt, D. J. Levinson, and R. H. Williams (eds.) The Patient and the Mental Hospital. New York: Free Press.

KERR, D. M. (1978a) "An evaluation of paraprofessional volunteers as companionship therapists for aftercare boarding home clients." Presented at the meeting of the International Association of Psycho-Social Rehabilitation Services, Miami, November.

——— (1978b) Nonprofessional Companionship Therapy as Aftercare for Former Mental Hospital Clients Living in the Community: A Report to the Community Mental Health Center and the State Department of Mental Health. Ann Arbor: Washtenaw County Mental Health Center.

——— (1978c) Nonprofessional Companionship Therapy with Former Mental Hospital Clients Residing in Aftercare Boarding Homes (Ph.D. dissertation, University of Michigan). Ann Arbor: Washtenaw County Community Mental Health Center.

———, MILLS, K., and WADLEIGH, P. (1978) "Preliminary results of the use of companionship therapy in the treatment of substance abuse clients." Presented at the meeting of the Alcohol and Drug Problems Association of North America, Seattle, September.

KERR, D. M., MILLS, K., and WOLF, K. (1978) "Differential advantages of group versus within subjects designs in a summative evaluation of companionship therapy intervention for substance abuse clients." Presented at the meeting of the Alcohol and Drug Problems Association of North America, Seattle, September.

KERR, D. M., WOLF, K., and MILLS, K. (1978a) "A companionship program with the heroin abusing patient." Presented at the meeting of the Michigan Alcohol and Addiction Association, Jackson, Michigan, May.

——— (1978b) "Research issues in companionship therapy with the drug dependent client." Presented at the meeting of the Michigan Alcohol and Addiction Association, Jackson, Michigan, May.

KERR, D. M., WOOD, S., TESKE, Y., and PINES, C. D. (1978a) Nonprofessional Companionship Therapy with Former Mental Hospital Clients Residing in After-

care Boarding Homes. Ann Arbor: Washtenaw County Mental Health Center.
——— (1978b) Nonprofessional Companionship Therapy with Homebound Former Mental Hospital Clients Residing in Aftercare Boarding Homes. Ann Arbor: Washtenaw County Community Mental Health Center.
KU, K., MOORE, R., and GRIFFITHS, K. (1975) An Exemplary Project: The Volunteer Probation Counselor Program, Lincoln, Nebraska. Washington, DC: National Institute of Law Enforcement and Criminal Justice, U.S. Government Printing Office.
KULIK, J. A., MARTIN, R. A., and SCHEIBE, K. E. (1969) "Effects of mental hospital volunteer work on students' conceptions of mental illness." Journal of Clinical Psychology 25: 326-329.
LEDVINKA, J. and DENNER, B. (1972) "The limits of success." Mental Hygiene 56: 30-35.
LINDEN, J. I. and STOLLAK, G. E. (1969) "The training of undergraduates in play techniques." Journal of Clinical Psychology 25: 213-218.
McMILLAN, R. C. (1973) "Attitudinal and behavior changes in tuned out high school students as a function of participation in a human service program as mental health aides in an elementary school. Ph.D. dissertation, University of Rochester.
McWILLIAMS, S. A. and FINKEL, N. J. (1973) "High school students as mental health aides in the elementary school setting." Journal of Consulting and Clinical Psychology 40: 39-42.
Mitchell, W. E. (1966a) "Amicatherapy: theoretical perspectives and an example of practice." Community Mental Health Journal 2: 307-314.
——— (1966b) "The use of college student volunteers in the outpatient treatment of troubled children," in H. R. Juessy (ed.) Mental Health with Limited Resources. New York: Grune & Stratton.
PANYARD, C., WOLF, K., and DREACHSLIN, J. (forthcoming) "Source of referral as an indicator of motivational factors in treatment outcome with drug dependent clients." International Journal of Addictions.
PANYARD, C., WOLF, K., SNOWDEN, L., and SALL, J. (1973) "Personality characteristics common to patients in drug treatment centers in Detroit." Presented at the International Meeting on Alcohol and Other Drugs, San Juan, Puerto Rico, November.
PATTERSON, N. B. and PATTERSON, T. W. (1967) "A companion therapy program." Community Mental Health Journal 3: 133-136.
PERLMUTTER, F. and DURHAM, D. (1965) "Using teen-agers to supplement casework service." Social Work 10: 41-48.
POSER, E. G. (1966) "The effect of therapists' training on group therapeutic outcome." Journal of Consulting Psychology 30: 283-289.
PREBLE, E. and MILLER, T. (1977) "Methadone, wine, and welfare." in R. S. Weppner (ed.) Street Ethnography: Selected Studies of Crime and Drug Use in Natural Settings. Beverly Hills, Sage Publications.
RAPPAPORT, J., CHINSKY, J. M., and COWEN, E. L. (1971) Innovations in Helping Chronic Patients: College Students in a Mental Institution. New York: Academic Press.
RASKIN, H. A., PETTY, T. A., and WARREN, M. (1956) "A suggested approach to the problem of narcotic addiction." Presented at the Annual Meeting of the

American Psychiatric Association, May.

SHELLEY, E.L.V. (1971) An Overview of Evaluation Research and Surveys of Volunteers in the Justice System. Boulder, CO: National Center on Volunteerism.

STOFFER, D. L. (1968) "Investigation of therapeutic success as a function of genuineness, nonpossessive warmth, empathic understanding, and dogmatism in the helping person." Proceedings of the 76th Annual Convention of the American Psychological Association 3: 619-620.

STOLLAK, G. (1969) "The experimental effects of training college students as play therapists," in B. G. Guerney, Jr. (ed.) Psycholtherapeutic Agents: New Roles for Nonprofessionals, Parents, and Teachers. New York: Holt, Rinehart & Winston.

UMBARGER, C. C., DALSIMER, J. S., MORRISON, A. P., and BREGGIN, P. R. (1962) College Students in a Mental Hospital. New York: Grune & Stratton.

VANDER KOLK, C. J. (1973) "Paraprofessionals as psychotherapeutic agents with moderatedly disturbed children." Psychology in the Schools 10: 238-242.

VERINIS, J. S. (1970) "Therapeutic effectiveness of untrained volunteers with chronic patients." Journal of Consulting and Clinical Psychology 34: 154-155.

WADLEIGH, P., MILLS, K., RENCHER, D., and CRAWLEY, C. (1978) "Recruiting clients to be recipients of companionship therapy." Presented at the meeting of the Alcohol and Drug Problems Association of North America, Seattle, September.

WADLEIGH, P. and RENCHER, D. (1978) "Issues in recruiting volunteers as companions for substance abuse patients." Presented at the meeting of the Alcohol and Drug Problems Association of North America, Seattle, September.

WOLF, K., KERR, D. M., and MILLS, K. (1978) "The use of companionship therapy in the treatment of the drug-dependent individual." Presented at the meeting of the Alcohol and Drug Problems Association of North America, Seattle, September.

WOLF, K., KERR, D. M., RENCHER, D., and WADLEIGH, P. (1978) "Goals and cautions in implementing companionship therapy programs in community settings." Presented at the meeting of the Alcohol and Drug Problems Association of North America, Seattle, September.

WOLF, K. and PANYARD, C. (1974a) "A triadic model for community treatment of drug dependence." Criminal Justice Digest 2: 6-9.

——— (1974b) "Indigenous companions: a community intervention strategy for the treatment of drug dependency." Presented at the National Drug Abuse Conference, Chicago, March.

——— and RASKIN, H. (1976) "Indigenous companions: a community intervention strategy for the treatment of heroin and reduction of recidivism." Grant application submitted to the National Institute on Drug Abuse, March.

ZAX, M. and COWEN, E. L. (1967) "Early identification and prevention of emotional disturbance in a public school," in E.L. Cowen, E.S. Gardner, and M. Zax (eds.) Emergent Approaches to Mental Health Problems. New York: Appleton-Century-Crofts.

PART IV

HUMAN RESOURCE ORGANIZATIONS
IN CONTINUING CARE

9

HEROINISM AND HUMAN SERVICES
Toward a Social-Psychological Model
of Addict Aftercare

MICHAEL J. MINOR
STEPHEN M. PITTEL

INTRODUCTION

For more than 40 years—since the opening of the first federal narcotics hospitals in 1935 and 1938—heroin addicts have frustrated the best efforts of treatment programs designed to cure them of their self-inflicted dependence on heroin. Statistics vary from time to time and from one treatment modality to the next, but the cumulative evidence suggests that most heroin addicts do not seek treatment voluntarily, and that those who are treated tend to return to the use of heroin within a year or so, if not within the first few hours or days.

These disquieting facts cannot be explained away as a failure of medical knowledge or technology; even the most seriously addicted individuals can be relieved of their immediate need for heroin in a month or less of detoxification treatment (Newman, 1979). The problem appears to rest on

AUTHORS' NOTE: Work on this chapter was supported by a grant from the Services Research Branch of the National Institute on Drug Abuse (#H81-DA-01901). We thank Barry Brown, Bernice Van Dort, and Laurie Hill for their many useful suggestions.

the failure of existing treatment modalities in their approach to the addict's underlying "heroinism"—his compelling attachment to a way of life based in the world of drugs. First, it seems that addicts have not been offered services worthwhile enough to attract them to treatment voluntarily, and second, those who do come forth are disappointed because they leave treatment unaddicted, yet still unprepared to succeed in a world whose ways they do not know.

In response to these failures and disappointments there have been recent attempts in the drug abuse field to provide a wide range of human services beyond those usually available in the traditional course of treatment. In contrast to primary treatment services which focus on the addict's use of heroin, per se, these services are referred to as ancillary or supportive services when they are provided by drug treatment programs, or as aftercare or reentry services when they are provided under other auspices. To date, the emphasis of these services has been on vocational needs (Ward, 1973), but attention has focused also on such diverse needs as family therapy (Stanton et al., 1978), housing and legal assistance (Dorus et al., 1977), support group involvement (Brown and Ashery, 1979), and social skills training (Wacker and Hawkins, 1978).

Elsewhere (Pittel, 1974, 1975, 1976, 1978, 1979; Pittel and Foster, 1976; Pittel et al., 1979; Freudenberger and Pittel, 1979) we discuss some fundamental issues in establishing an effective human services model for (former) heroin addicts and other disadvantaged groups with severe psychosocial needs. Many of these issues fall under the rubrics of: reconsideration of the life circumstances of heroin addicts, clarification of treatment strategies and goals, recognition of the barriers and gaps in community service systems, and acknowledgement of the demands of adapting to a life-style without drug addiction.

In calling for reconsideration of the addict's life circumstances we argue first, that in many significant aspects, the addict's psychosocial needs are no different from those of persons in other disadvantaged groups. Second, we argue that activity level and coping skills are distributed across addicts much the same as they are across nonaddict groups. Third, the key differences between addicts and nonaddicts are in the context of activity and in the situational demands rather than in the overall goals (to survive and live well). Fourth, we maintain that the use of heroin is a symptom, not the cause of the addict's plight, although, of course, secondary symptoms such as some health problems are direct results of using heroin. A fifth point is that there are definite opportunities for financial and psychological rewards in the lives of heroin addicts, albeit such opportunities are usually infrequent and short-term.[1]

In the second set of issues, clarification of treatment strategies and goals, we underscore the central role of assessment in determining the appropriateness of various interventions and therapies. Comprehensive assessment, the cornerstone of any effective service delivery model, should include measures and evaluation of vocational and prevocational skills, psychological competencies, networks and support systems, and needs in other service domains (such as housing and transportation), as well as indicators of drug and alcohol abuse, employment status, and criminal justice status. We also argue that not only should treatment strategies provide a wide range of human services in the beginning of primary treatment instead of at some point during or near the end of treatment, but also that they should be based on supportive relationships between addicts and providers (in most instances counselors) instead of on supervisory relationships. Our final comment here is about the utility of standard treatment goals. In our opinion, the widely accepted tripartite model of treatment success (drug abstinence, gainful employment, and freedom from criminality) has two major drawbacks. The first is that most drug treatment programs are not adequately funded or properly designed to help clients with psychosocial needs; thus, indicators of psychosocial status (such as criminal justice status and employment status) are inappropriate measures for the evaluation of treatment program effectiveness. Second, this tripartite model is restrictive and biased as an overall composite of a well-functioning person in our society.

In discussing the third set of issues, which pertain to the barriers and gaps in community service systems for former heroin addicts, we examine the paucity of integration and continuity in service delivery. Agencies within single communities are often competing for the same funds, and thus there are disincentives for coordinating long-term care and developing effective referral systems. Consequently, there has been minimal appreciation for the concept of an assessment-based brokerage system whereby clients can be sent to appropriate service delivery settings through the matching of their needs profile with agency characteristics. We also note the pervasive discrimination against former addicts within particular agencies which suggests the need for an advocacy service that will help clients maneuver through bureaucratic mazes laden with the obstacles of prejudice and purposive inefficiency.

The final set of issues focuses on the demands of adapting to a life-style without drug addiction. In these discussions we argue that former addicts are most vulnerable during the first few months after they have given up heroin, and also that the shock of (re)socialization into the nondrug world is as severe as would be the plight of a middle-class person attempting to adapt to the role of a "righteous dope fiend." Another point is that the subtle demands of a nonaddict life-style, which are often trivialized, are nevertheless exceedingly important obstacles to addicts; for example, those pre-vocational social skills necessary for getting a job (Friedman, 1978). Finally, we argue that the most appropriate indicator of a well-functioning former addict (or for that matter, any person) is not the quality of "problem-freeness," but instead the ability to garner the resources of the nondrug world to cope effectively with problems. Thus, long-term success in adaptation to a nonaddict life-style is dependent on the adoption, transference, and (re)learning of psychosocial competencies (coping skills), and not the mere amelioration of drug-specific problems.

In this chapter we extend our analysis of the themes summarized above to focus on their relevance for aftercare policy and program design. Our purpose is to discuss some aspects of a social-psychological model of addict aftercare that might catalyze and give direction to a growing trend toward an integrated human services approach to narcotic treatment and rehabilitation (Bourne, 1974; Domestic Council Drug Abuse Task Force, 1975; Dupont, 1978). We first discuss three issues which have been implicit in our conceptual orientation toward developing an effective aftercare model but have received minimal explicit attention by us and other investigators in this area. These three issues, which reach to the heart of public policy regarding the treatment and rehabilitation of heroin addicts and other socially stigmatized and disadvantaged groups, are: the distinction between exiting and reentering; the definition of reentry goals in terms of indicators of well-functioning; and the importance of social networks. After examining these issues, we turn to a recurrent theme in our previous writings: the role of assessment. In this fourth section we review some key conceptual and practical aspects of assessment in aftercare and discuss the assessment implications of the three issues presented in the preceding sections. The final section of this chapter consists of a discussion of the policy implications of the concepts examined here and also some suggestions for directions of future aftercare research.

EXITING AND REENTERING

Careful delineation of an aftercare model suggests a differentiation between services designed to break the addict's dependence on heroin (and his other ties to the illicit world of drugs), and those designed to help him form attachments to conventional society. In other words, it is necessary to underscore the distinction between exiting or disengagement from the world of drugs, and entering or reentering a world in which drug use has no place.[2] Exiting is the treatment goal, whereas reentry may be seen as the goal of aftercare. Thus, we argue that exiting is but the penultimate stage in an addict career; the final stage is reached when the former addict has achieved a meaningful stage in "straight" society, which he is unwilling to jeopardize by becoming involved again in past misdeeds.[3]

This crucial point is probably understood (at least implicitly) by tender-minded observers of the drug abuse field who believe that freedom from drug dependence paves the way for the former addict to improve his lot. The tender-minded view addiction as a social tragedy, and they regard the addict as a hapless victim of circumstance who has turned to drugs to escape from a bleak reality. They believe that the use of heroin further condemns the addict to a life of misery and despair from which he cannot extricate himself. They want the addict to give up his use of drugs so that he might enjoy a better and more fulfilling life. For them, the right to treatment and rehabilitation services cannot be denied, and goals are cast in terms of human dignity.

On the other hand, this point is usually missed entirely by tough-minded observers of the drug abuse field, who are concerned primarily with the social costs of narcotic addiction. They view the heroin addict as a willful villain whose behavior must be changed for the public good. They insist that the addict must give up his use of illicit drugs, that he must refrain from other criminality, and that he must find employment to keep him off the public dole. For them, there is no other bottom line to justify the cost of drug abuse treatment and rehabilitation programs.

While it is more common to focus on the differences between tender-minded and tough-minded stances toward drug abuse, the fact remains that both usually rest their argument on the assumption that the addict's plight results mainly from his use of drugs. Thus, advocates of both positions believe that the most important goal of treatment is to free the addict from his dependence on heroin. Those with a tender-minded disposition believe that freedom from drug dependence will make it possible for the former addict to deal constructively with the harsh conditions of his life and to find success instead of mere relief. The tough-minded believe that once the former addict is drug-free, he will no longer be forced to engage in crime to support an expensive habit and no longer be prevented from gainful employment by debilitating drug effects.

But if successful disengagement from addiction and criminality rests on the achievement of meaningful ties to conventional society, it is clear that neither tender- nor tough-minded aims are served until this goal is reached. Thus, in our opinion, subscription to one or the other ideological stance toward drug abuse does not obviate the importance of distinguishing between exiting and reentering.

Although this distinction between exiting and reentry is assumed in the more common differentiation between treatment and rehabilitation, the failure to distinguish among these activities programmatically (for example, by having separate treatment and rehabilitation programs) or operationally (by specification of desired outcomes or goals for each type of intervention) has had profound and unfortunate consequences in the field of drug abuse. The most troublesome of these consequences has been the shared designation of diverse intervention strategies as drug abuse treatment modalities. Not only are the differences among such modalities so extreme that giving them a common name defies credibility, but using the same evaluative criteria to compare their efficacy is, at best, inappropriate. Considering the differences among detoxification, outpatient counseling, methadone maintenance, and residential therapeutic communities, for example, on what rational basis should each of them be expected to achieve the same results?[4] Clearly, each of these treatment modalities is oriented toward facilitating addicts' exit from one or another aspect of their drug involvement, but each has different goals in this regard and none of them focuses necessarily on reentry per se.

From the above points we derive the following propositions as the first steps toward a systematic model of addict aftercare:

(1) Aftercare is distinguished from treatment by its explicit focus on reentry.

(2) Eligibility for aftercare is established when a former addict has begun exiting from a career path of drug involvement (regardless of the means by which this exit is initiated).

(3) Aftercare services include any intervention—educational, supportive, or therapeutic—the intent of which is to encourage or enable a former addict to secure or maintain a meaningful bond to the conventional society.

(4) In contrast to treatment, which may be considered complete when an addict has exited from active drug involvement, the duration of aftercare should extend until the former addict has secured a stake in conventional society that will allow him to resist an expectable range of temptations.

(5) The evaluative criteria used to judge the efficacy of drug abuse treatment should focus only on exiting or disengagement from drug involvement. Aftercare should be evaluated on the basis of criteria pertinent to achievement and maintenance of reentry.

In effect, all of these propositions rest on the distinction between exiting and reentry and on the assumption that exiting and reentry are (relatively) discrete processes, each with its attendant difficulties. By assigning to treatment the role of assisting addicts to exit from the world of drug abuse and to aftercare the role of assisting them to reenter conventional society, we have attempted to free the concept of aftercare from the conceptual pitfalls that arise from traditional definitions which focus primarily on aftercare's temporal relationship to treatment services (Pittel, 1979). In this manner we have also attempted to draw a finer distinction between treatment and aftercare than is typical of other writings in the field, and have suggested that each should be evaluated in terms of criteria specific to its respective goals.

Finally, we argue that successful reentry is not achieved until former addicts have acquired positive ties to conventional society that they are unwilling to sacrifice by returning to the world of drugs. And from this perspective we have suggested that the widely accepted tripartite model of success (based on a tough-minded view of drug abuse) slights significant process goals. To put it differently, we believe that the abilities of the former addict to function effectively in the "straight" world, and to derive satisfaction from these unaccustomed activities, must be given equal weight as evaluative criteria lest their importance be ignored. Toward that end, we turn next to consider a social-psychological perspective for conceptualizing reentry goals in terms of well-functioning.

REENTRY GOALS: WELL-FUNCTIONING PERSONS

To date, the concept of well-functioning and other important ideas and findings in social-psychological research on adjustment, coping and well-being have not played central roles in the analysis of drug treatment issues. Instead, the focus has been chiefly on bio-medical issues (National Institute on Drug Abuse, 1975), and to lesser degrees on macrolevel social issues (Levin et al., 1975), and microlevel psychological issues (Chein et al., 1964; Kandel, 1978). In this section we draw upon concepts and findings from five separate but related areas of activity in social-psychological research to develop a conceptual guide for understanding addict reentry and mapping out goals of successful reentry. These five areas are: person-environment fit models; patterns of adjustment and coping; social cognition and motivation; psychological well-being, including satisfaction and happiness; and life-span development.

Person-Environment Fit

At the core of the person-environment fit model (French et al., 1974; French and Kahn, 1962) are the concepts of subjective and objective assessments, demands, and supplies. Subjective assessments are how the persons view themselves (self-concept) and their environment. Objective assessments, on the other hand, are those views of the persons and their environment as seen by an "external neutral judge" or "generalized other." Demands consist of the persons' needs (or wants and desires) and the environmental requirements to satisfy such needs. Supplies are the persons' resources and the environmental opportunities that can potentially be used to satisfy their needs. The degree of fit (adjustment) is then determined by the congruence of subjective and objective assessments of demands and supplies of the persons and their environment. Because the person-environment fit model is dynamic, the parameters of congruence can change from situation to situation and from time to time.

The relevance of these concepts for defining reentry goals is threefold. First, successful reentry is a delicate balance between objective fits and subjective evaluations of such fits. Thus, data on job status without complementary information about perceptions of job status can be misleading as a criterion of adjustment. Second, if a course of aftercare intervention which develops personal skills (objective resources) is to be successful, it should include not only skill-specific training, but also components which realign both the client's self-perception (recognition of new skills) and his perception of the environment (for example, alteration in the pervasive attitude which is reflected in the statement: "They won't hire me even if I'm qualified for the job [because I'm an addict] ."). Third, reentry is most likely to be successful in conditions where both the client's and the program's (or agency's) subjective views of the nondrug world are in close agreement with objective demands and resources. For example, reentry failure or setbacks may be inevitable in those situations where clients' expectations regarding an employment position are clearly in conflict with their educational background, as well as in those cases where an aftercare program attempts to place clients in work situations which require adequate transportation and clothing (which most work situations do) when the clients have neither. In summary, the person-environment fit model underscores the significance of a dual perspective (subjective and objective) and the dynamics of demand and supply in formulating reentry goals.

Patterns of Adjustment and Coping

Moving into the arena of social-psychological studies of coping and adjustment (Monat and Lazarus, 1977; Lazarus, 1966), we find several concepts of direct relevance for understanding the former addict's struggle with adopting a conventional life-style. Similar to the person-environment fit model, the emphasis here is on the interface of the person with his environment. Of particular importance is the relationship between stress and coping, or the ability to adapt to difficult conditions. Stress is defined in terms of physical, psychological, and social pressures on the individual. Coping, adjustment, and adaptation (concepts often used interchangeably) are described as strategies (styles) or dispositions which usually take the form of either direct actions (flight or fight behavior) or palliative modes (relief of the emotional aspects of stress).

The dialectic between stress and coping is viewed as a continual process consisting of four phases: stress definition, selection of coping response, mobilization of coping resources, and consequent results—reduction, maintenance, or increase in stress. Stress varies in severity according to its suddenness of onset, its duration, and the timing. The timing factor denotes the importance of stress in terms of its juxtaposition with the susceptibility of the individual; for example, the influence of stress is often exacerbated during periods of grief or when numerous life-style changes have occurred. Solutions to stress (coping styles) vary in their efficacy and all have their cost. For instance, some solutions may even be iatrogenic in the sense that short-term adaptation is deleterious to the long-term well-being of the individual. Well-functioning persons usually have a range of coping skills and strategies in their adaptational repertoire which can be implemented depending on the nature of the stress. Finally, it is important to recognize that often the most successful coping style is anticipatory rather than reactive.

These concepts and findings supply six insights into formulating a social-psychological model of addict aftercare. First, many addicts have survived under very stressful conditions and thus have developed specific coping strategies which are, undoubtedly, of highly variable quality. Thus, in designing an effective aftercare model, we can potentially learn a great deal about these individuals by examining their already existing coping strategies. The products of this examination could then serve to redefine reentry tasks in terms of reapplying or transferring established coping styles to nondrug world stresses rather than defining reentry solely in terms of learning new coping strategies. Second, stress is self-defined and each solution to stress brings its own stress. Thus, just as some of the physical and psychic costs of coping in the drug world are hypertension and depression, there will be costs to the former addict in coping with the stresses of a conventional life-style. Successful aftercare intervention will help prepare clients for such costs. Third, aftercare should include broad-based training for competencies in the defining and solving of problems, in addition to training for task-specific skills. Fourth, positive movements toward reentry goals as a result of aftercare are more likely to endure if they follow a process of slow and steady change rather than sudden and sharp shifts. Fifth, planned changes during critical periods, such as the first few months after giving up heroin, are often the most important, yet the least likely to succeed. And finally, successful reentry, like adaptation, requires coping with chronic problems, and thus is a continual process, not an achieved status. Hence, evaluators of aftercare programs should not rely too heavily on status indicators measured at any one point in time.

Social Cognition and Motivation

Theories of social cognition and motivation provide us with four concepts relevant to the analysis of aftercare reentry goals: causal attributions (Jones et al., 1971; Harvey et al., 1976; Weiner and Kun, 1976), internal versus external generalized expectancies (Rotter, 1966), delayed gratification (Mischel et al., 1972; Mischel and Gilligan, 1964), and competency motivation (White, 1974). Like the basic ideas discussed above in the person-environment fit model and patterns of coping and adjustment, the commonality in these four concepts is their focus on the relationship between subjective and objective conditions. Causal attributions are those processes whereby persons make judgments (evaluations) from evidence about the relationships between causes and effects. Findings from attribution research show considerable variation in the structure and accuracy of causal judgments. These results have direct implications for understanding journeys through reentry pathways. Specifically, a major obstacle to achieving reentry goals may be clients' malfunctioning causal schemata, which lead to inaccurate causal attributions, which in turn may result in inappropriate attitudes and behavior. For example, an aftercare client who attributes his lack of friends to universal prejudice against him, rather than to his paucity of interpersonal skills, is not likely to take a reentry pathway that will foster his development of friendships.

The concepts of internal-external generalized expectancies (I-E) and delayed gratification both focus on control issues. The I-E dimension indicates the degree of perceived control in personal and political situations, whereas delayed gratification is the ability to control immediate behavior in the service of longer-term goals. As with causal attributions, variations in perceived I-E control and delayed gratification are related to environmental cues. That is, appropriate degrees of perceived internal control and delayed gratification are facilitated by supportive characteristics of the environment. The applicability of these concepts to aftercare issues is obvious: the probabilities of successful reentry are substantially increased if the former addict can develop appropriate expectancies regarding control and can adequately delay gratification. For example, to the extent that an aftercare client realizes he can control his financial situation (through proper budgeting) and that he can minimize impulsive spending, his chances for financial security are increased.

The concept of competency motivation is based on the observation that a primary determining factor of behavior is the attainment of environmental mastery. The perception of competency, which stems from such mastery, develops from rewarding experiences and the consensual validation of others. Thus, if reentry tasks offer opportunities for environmental mastery, then there will be chances for the aftercare client to develop a sense of competency (and likewise competency motivation) in the pursuits of the nondrug world. The growth of competency is, of course, dependent on the delicate balance between new challenges and consequences of previous experiences.

Analyses of Well-Being

Our fourth area of interest, studies of satisfaction and happiness (Minor et al., forthcoming; Bradburn, 1969; Campbell et al., 1976; Andrews and Withey, 1976), contributes three ideas useful for constructing a conceptual framework of aftercare which specifies reentry goals in terms of the well-functioning person. In contrast to the social-psychological concepts described above, which have been taken from relatively well-developed theoretical models, the ideas in this area are direct products of research findings. The first idea is that well-being (report of overall satisfaction and happiness) is composed of two independent dimensions: positive affect and negative affect. Ratings of well-being appear to be a balance of the two dimensions, and thus, information about only one dimension of affect (either positive or negative) is not sufficient for determining overall well-being. The relevance of this idea for an aftercare model is twofold: (a) most reentry goals can be analyzed from this perspective of a balance between positive and negative dimensions; and (b) too much emphasis should not be placed on only one dimension in the evaluation of overall reentry progress. A second idea is that neither positive nor negative subjective evaluations are directly linked to objective conditions. Again the concept of balance comes into play in that subjective evaluations are thought to be a balance between expectations (aspirations) and perceptions of current status which are based on personal history. The implications of this idea are in agreement with those mentioned previously in the discussion of the person-environment fit model: objective indicators of reentry progress and goals may not agree with the client's perception of such matters. And long-term adjustment will be in jeopardy to the degree that there are discrepancies between subjective evaluations and objective conditions. The third idea is that, for most subgroups, subjective evaluations of leisure activities and interpersonal relations (especially marital and family relations) are more important than subjective evaluations of work in determining overall ratings of life satisfaction. Although this idea stems from findings in nationwide household population surveys, we suspect that the relative importance of these life areas is similar in the subpopulation of addicts. If this assumption is correct, it suggests that specification of reentry goals should include consideration of leisure activities and interpersonal relations, and also that aftercare interventions into the domains of leisure and interpersonal relations may be as important (if not more important) to the client's well-being as interventions into work-related issues.

Life-Span Development

Our final perspective on the social-psychological analysis of reentry goals is from a life-span developmental viewpoint (Levinson, 1978; Neugarten, 1967). This viewpoint has at least five concepts which are useful to an aftercare model. First is the notion of a life cycle which has definable stages, each with its own developmental tasks. Second is the natural ordering of life stages where progression through any one stage is dependent on the resolutions of issues in prior stages. A third concept is that the resources and efficiency of coping strategies vary from stage to stage. Fourth, while the facade of problems which arise in the adjustment to developmental tasks can be transformed from one stage to the next, in many instances it reflects recurrent personal problems present throughout development. Fifth is the idea that overall adjustment is related to developmental synchronism ("in" versus "out" of phase)—that is, whether or not the person is addressing developmental tasks in the expected order and at the expected time in life.

Although there has been some application of these concepts to the field of drug abuse (e.g., Brill's [Brill, 1972; Alksne et al., 1967] discussions of the life cycle of addiction), in general, life-span developmental issues have been largely ignored in the areas of drug rehabilitation and aftercare. Yet, in our opinion, they are of direct relevance to the implementation of effective aftercare. For example, in setting up reentry goals it is necessary to respect the variability and influence of life stages and their sequence. Furthermore, in describing reentry pathways and goals, there must be consideration of both client's progress with current developmental tasks and the resolution of prior developmental tasks. In summary, recognition of life-span developmental issues widens the framework of an aftercare model and calls for a perspective in which the feasibility and relevance of reentry goals are evaluated in terms of the total life cycle instead of situation-specific problems.

Conclusion

In conclusion, a social-psychological analysis of reentry goals both broadens and sharpens the focus of an aftercare model. It portrays the aftercare client as interfacing with the environment, influenced by a personal history, and addressing developmental tasks in a life stage. The client is defining problems, attempting to mobilize coping resources, and struggling with solutions of varying efficacy. The degree to which the individual succeeds in reentry is dependent on the development of psychosocial competencies which are spawned from experiences of mastery over environmental challenges. In monitoring reentry progress and the attainment of reentry goals, this model suggests that we take a dualistic perspec-

tive, consisting of both objective indicators and their psychological equiva-
lents (subjective indicators). Similarly, a balanced view of positive and
negative components will give us the best estimate of overall well-functioning. Furthermore, reentry goals in the domains of leisure and interpersonal relationships are probably just as important as goals in the vocational
domain. Finally, well-functioning, as a reentry goal, refers to an adjustment process instead of an achieved status.

THE IMPORTANCE OF SOCIAL NETWORKS

A common thread throughout our patchwork of defining social-psychological reentry goals is the importance of social networks. Although there
have been some informal discussions of the interpersonal worlds of addicts
(Preble and Casey, 1972; Gould et al., 1974; Feldman, 1973; Waldorf,
1973), to our knowledge, there have not been any analyses conducted on
the formal properties of (former) addicts' social networks. Yet the conceptual richness and policy relevance of social network analysis in the aftercare area cannot be understated. The demonstrated utility of network
analysis for understanding issues in related fields, such as overall well-being
(Fischer, 1978), health promotion practices (Langlie, 1977), coping and
adjustment (Mechanic, 1974), and recovery from medical problems (Finlayson, 1976) gives ample evidence of its potential for yielding insights
into the processes of addict reentry. In this section we present a brief
overview of some key social network concepts that can be used in an
aftercare model, and then apply these concepts to the analysis of reentry
issues.

The origins of network analysis can be traced to Durkheim's classic
study of suicide (Durkheim, 1897). Although there has been a rather
lengthy history of small group research based almost entirely in laboratory
settings (Bales, 1970), only during the last two decades have there been
programmatic research efforts to examine the properties of naturally
occurring networks. Current work in social network analysis is so extensive
that illustrations of network studies can be found in such diverse areas as
anthropology (Boissevain, 1974; Mitchell, 1969), social ecology (Moos,
1976), social psychiatry (Horowitz, 1977), social psychology (Travers and
Milgram, 1969), sociology (Fischer et al., 1977; Leinhardt, 1977; Laumann, 1973), epidemiology (Berkman, 1977; Kaplan et al., 1977), and
mathematics—especially graph theory (Alba, 1973). Last year, a new
journal, entitled *Social Networks,* began publication in an attempt to bring

together articles on the wide range of network analyses. The recent growth of attention paid to network studies is a result of at least three factors: (1) the emergence of perspectives on social networks which transcends disciplines, that is, a cross-fertilization of ideas that is not commonplace in basic or applied research; (2) advances in the development of statistical techniques which increase the feasibility of conducting empirical analyses on network data; and (3) the increased accessibility to high-speed computers which allows for the handling and analysis of network data sets.

Most network studies can be characterized as focusing on either positional or relational issues (Burt, 1978). Positional studies (e.g., Burt, 1976; Kadushin, 1968; Coleman et al., 1966) examine the characteristics of patterns among relations between actors (persons) in a system (e.g., a politically elite group). Of particular interest in such investigations is the concept of "structurally equivalent individuals"—those individuals who occupy similar positions (have the same pattern of relations) in the network system. Relational studies, on the other hand, are interested in the characteristics of relationships among persons. This approach is best exemplified by traditional sociometric investigations where a person is asked to give names in response to questions (such as, "Who are your close friends?"), and such names are then analyzed like attributes of the person. Social networks examined in relational studies are commonly referred to as "ego-centric" networks, or "personal social" networks. Our discussion here is limited to network concepts from a relational perspective; however, we do make use of the idea of structural equivalence in examining the implications of the similarities in social networks across aftercare clients.

Personal social networks have two classes of properties: morphological and interactive. Morphological properties are the structural characteristics of the network, that is, the pattern of relations (links). Interactive properties, on the other hand, refer to the nature of the links. Four morphological and three interactive properties of networks are of direct relevance for an aftercare model. These are anchorage, reachability, density, and homogeneity; and directedness, intensity, and frequency, respectively.

Anchorage refers to the length and complexity of network links. Length is the distance of a path (number of links) from the person to a needed individual or group (e.g., a babysitter). Complexity is the number of alternatives/substitutes (e.g., the number of available babysitters) in the network. Reachability denotes the extent of access in the links; that is, the availability of key people in the network. Density indicates the degree of connectedness, the extent to which persons in the network are associated with each other. Thus, as Bott (1971) states, networks can be either closely knit (most persons are connected with each other) or loosely knit (few connections among persons). Homogeneity (also referred to as "the range") indicates the degree of similarity in attributes (such as values or education) of persons in the network. Directedness refers to the flow of interaction, for example, reciprocal or unidirectional. The intensity of relations refers to the strength of commitments, that is, the degree to which obligations are established. And finally, frequency indicates the number of times persons in the network visit or talk with each other.

In addition to these seven properties which have been previously identified and analyzed, we distinguish two other network characteristics that are useful in the analysis of aftercare issues. These are informal versus formal links, and personal versus organizational links. Informal links are those relations which develop out of day-to-day activities (such as friendships at work), whereas formal links are relations established from unusual (often involuntary) circumstances (such as an aftercare client's relations with a counselor in a drug treatment program). Personal links refer to those relations formed primarily on the basis of individual characteristics (such as interest in playing pool), whereas organizational links are those relations formed primarily on the basis of organizational membership or status in an agency (such as an aftercare client's relation with a clerk at the welfare department). Thus, although the organizational link is to a person, the nature of this link is relatively invariant across replacements of the person, in contrast to a personal link, which is more likely to be sensitive to replacements.

Before moving on to a network analysis of reentry issues, it is important to review three major functional chracteristics of social networks. First, social networks serve as reference points; they are the primary vehicles of identification with societal norms. In other words, networks are the cultural (or subcultural) anchors in one's psychosocial matrix of behavior; and as such, they serve the purposes of defining values, goals, and pathways to goals. A second function of social networks is feedback and regulation. Networks serve to guide thoughts and actions through the process of consensual validation, consisting of both positive and negative reinforcements. The third function is that of a coping resource. Social networks can play both protective and supportive roles in helping the person adjust to stress. Networks supply direct solutions to stress and also give openings for effective solutions. In serving this function, networks provide opportunities for mutual help-giving, and thus not only facilitate the implementation of cooperative coping strategies (i.e., the pooling of resources), but also impose demands of reciprocity.

In the above paragraphs we have given a brief sketch of the anatomy (structural chracteristics) and physiology (interactive and functional characteristics) of social networks. The application of these conceptual tools to an analysis of reentry issues focuses on three questions:

(1) What ar‹ the characteristics of aftercare clients' networks? How are these characteristics different from the properties of networks found in other subpopulations?
(2) What are the consequences of these social network characteristics for the reentry of addicts? Specifically, are there identifiable positive and negative dimensions which facilitate or impede successful reentry?[5]
(3) To what degree are the social networks of aftercare clients amenable to change, both natural and induced change? In other words, do networks change organically as reentry proceeds, and can aftercare intervention effectively bolster the positive (reentry facilitative) components and eliminate or minimize the effects of negative components.' '

The comparative aspect of the first question is impossible to address because of the paucity of normative data on network characteristics. Although there are some data from classic studies (mostly anthropological) such as Bott's (1971) and Stack's (1970), overall, no data exist on the general distribution of network properties.[7] Thus, we turn to assumptions and hypotheses about addicts' networks. Standard characterizations of the addict (Sutter, 1966) portray the individual as a social isolate who interacts with other people only for instrumental purposes (such as getting money for dope, scoring dope, and using dope). Thus, as this story line goes, the typical addict's network has few links, is homogeneous (most persons being involved with the drug scene), is more extensive than dense, and is structured around instrumental and informational characteristics rather than affective components. The veridicality of this portrayal cannot be assessed, although to be sure, it pays minimal attention to positive attributes of the addict's network.

Of particular interest to us, though, are the differences between networks of addicts and networks of aftercare clients (former addicts). Again there are no data available to formulate informed opinions on these matters; however, we expect differences might exist in such network characteristics as complexity, density, homogeneity, directedness, and in the balance of instrumental to supportive interactions. In other words, the former addict who seeks aftercare may have more substitutes in his network, more close relations, a larger ratio of nondrug to drug links, more experiences of reciprocal help-giving, and a greater emotional stake in friendships. The extent to which such patterns in the variability of network characteristics provide clues for the potential of reentry leads to questions about the consequences of social networks themselves.

Analysis of the consequences of social networks entails looking at the relative effects of different mixtures of network characteristics. Just as findings from studies on nonaddict groups show that network characteristics are differentially important depending on the issues (such as utilization of health services [Salloway and Dillion, 1973] versus getting a job [Granovetter, 1974]), we expect there to be variability in the significance of aftercare clients' network characteristics depending on the reentry issue. Thus, it is probably necessary to describe the reentry problem before assigning positive or negative valences to properties of the client's network. A final point is that the degree of similarity in network characteristics across clients (thus indicating structural equivalence) should provide insights into the commonality of reentry problems and the resources available to cope with such problems.

Questions about changes in networks are, of course, critical to an aftercare model. If assumptions about the influences of social networks are true, and observations about the distinct nature of addicts' networks are correct, then change in networks becomes a key goal and indicator of effective aftercare. Natural changes in networks may occur through the life cycle of addiction or when the addict becomes an aftercare client. To the extent that these changes increase the person's links to a nonaddiction life-style, they can be used as leverage in aftercare service delivery. Induced change methods (such as network therapy [Speck and Attneave, 1973; Rueveni, 1979] and family therapy [Stanton, 1977, 1978]) show potential for enhancing the quality of networks; however, we doubt that such strategies can have permanent effects unless they are relatively long-term interventions.

In summary, we suggest that network analysis, replete with sampling and measurement problems, is a fundamental part of effective aftercare. It provides a perspective of aftercare clients in their human contexts, and it recognizes the influences of these contexts on their thoughts and behavior. The examination of social networks addresses directly the conundrum of heroinism, that is, the fact that psychosocial bonds to the drug world are stronger than physiological bonds. To the extent that an aftercare client's network has positive characteristics which facilitate reentry, the prospects for long-term adjustment to a nondrug world are good. On the other hand, if the client's networks are overladen with negative characteristics which impede reentry, the probabilities of effective adaptation to a nonaddiction life-style are slim.

THE ROLE OF ASSESSMENT

The role of assessment in aftercare is fourfold. First is to provide an initial picture of the client which specifies needs, expectations, goals to be accomplished, and pathways to these goals. Second is to supply process information about the client that can be used for feedback to both the client and the program on reentry progress and the management of resources. Third is to yield outcome data that can be used to evaluate aftercare services. And fourth is to measure service delivery units which can be used to analyze the cost-effectiveness of the aftercare program. In this section we set aside the measurement of service delivery for discussion elsewhere, and focus only on the issues of initial assessment, process assessment and outcome assessment of the aftercare client. Our discussion of these issues is organized around two questions: What to measure?, and How to measure?

What To Measure

Following the perspective presented in the preceding pages of this chapter, we recommend that aftercare assessment should include social-psychological measures of the client interfacing with the environment (both physical and interpersonal). Table 9.1 presents an overview of such social-psychological measures. These measures reflect a dualistic (subjective and objective) approach to collecting data on the strengths and deficits of the client and his environment. The emphasis is on current functioning (although some personal history data with regard to life-stage tasks are called for) and everyday issues rather than abstract personality dimensions.

Given the paucity of systematic theory and observations on addict reentry and aftercare interventions, however, it is difficult to give specific recommendations for the content of an overall battery of initial, process, and outcome assessment items. The framework presented above is based on the few ideas discussed in the preceding sections of this chapter and certainly does not represent a fully developed aftercare model. Instead of attempting to expand this framework to cover the range of potential topics which could be included in various assessments, we turn our attention to some key issues in the process of deciding what to measure.

The primary issue in determining what to measure is the coordination of assessment with theory and application. Ideally, measures should be

TABLE 9.1: A Social-Psychological Profile of the Aftercare Client

Domain	Indicators
Exciting: Physical and psychological bonds to drug world	• engagement in drug behavior • reliance on drug-world solutions to problems • interpersonal links to drug world
Reentering: well-functioning and psychosocial competencies	• subjective and objective views of demands and supplies • stress • coping styles and strategies • problem defining and solving skills • causal attributions • internal/external generalized expectancies of control • delayed gratification • competency motivation • positive/negative dimensions of well-being • satisfaction with leisure and interpersonal relationships • resolution of life-stage tasks • developmental synchronism
Social Networks: structural, interactive, and functional characteristics of social relations	• anchorage • reachability • density • homogeneity • directedness • intensity • frequency • personal/organizational • informal/formal • identification • guidance/regulation • coping resources

well grounded in some theoretical framework and also reflect areas in which the aftercare program can do (is doing) something. Thus, measures with high theoretical value (e.g., those with extensive literatures) but low applicability (e.g., unrelated to aftercare services) are of minimal utility as are those measures with high applicability but low theoretical value. Optimal measures are those which lend themselves to direct application for the implementation and management of an aftercare plan and are also readily interpretable from theoretical and research perspectives.

A second issue is the comprehensiveness of assessment. This issue is best characterized in terms of the classic problems of determining the economic parameters of information in a clinical setting. On the one hand, there are the costs of an extensive assessment, which can be broken down into three broad areas: labor (usually counselor or research assistant time); opportunity costs (restriction of other activities); and incompatibility with the clinical process (i.e., assessment is not typically regarded as service delivery nor a rapport-building activity). On the other hand, there are the negative consequences of failing to collect critical information. Such consequences include having an insufficient data base for establishing and managing an intervention plan and understanding change in reentry progress and outcome. These concerns are endemic to all clinical efforts and thus require careful consideration by investigators and program personnel in the aftercare area. To our knowledge, there are no straightforward algorithms for weighing the relative costs and benefits of variability in the comprehensiveness of assessment approaches. We suggest, however, that enumeration of the costs and benefits of any chosen assessment approach will substantially enhance the quality of an aftercare program.

A third issue is the trade-off between nomothetic and idiographic assessment. Preference for nomothetic data is determined by the desired amount of pooling of data across clients for group analysis and comparisons among clients. Idiographic data are more preferable in circumstances where the orientation is toward case studies or statistical analyses within clients. Again, there are no hard-set rules regarding the relative quality of these approaches; however, investigators should be aware of the advantages and disadvantages of each. We suggest a flexible strategy which incorporates a healthy mixture of both types of data.

A final issue with regard to the question about what to measure is the degree of continuity in measures. There is often a propensity to drop measurements in areas as the content of these areas becomes of less concern clinically, that is, they are no longer presenting problems. Although this strategy has some merit because it minimizes redundancy and is responsive to shifts in clinical focus, in our opinion, it has two severe limitations. First, this strategy slights the importance of the maintenance of clinical goals and tends to be problem-oriented (focus on negative dimensions) rather than person-oriented (focus on both positive and negative dimensions). Second, a shift in measures decreases the opportunity for conducting time series analysis, the most powerful and informative methodology for examining changes in client progress and reentry status. Thus, we recommend that aftercare programs attempt to maximize the degree of continuity in the measures of their initial, process, and outcome assessments.

In summary, we advocate a social-psychological approach to aftercare assessment which encompasses exiting behavior, reentering behavior in terms of well-functioning indicators, and various characteristics of social networks. This approach focuses on the day-to-day functioning of the aftercare client in his social context. Although no specific recommendations can be made at this point with regard to an overall set of assessment items, we suggest that aftercare clinicians and investigators be familiar with key issues in making decisions about what to measure. These key issues are: the coordination of assessment with theory and application; the comprehensiveness of assessment; nomothetic versus idiographic types of data; and the continuity of measurement.

How To Measure

The complexities of deciding what to measure are usually only surpassed by the complexities of deciding how to measure. The translation of concepts into empirical indicators remains one of the major obstacles to the advancement of the social sciences (Fiske, 1978). Although there is a plethora of potentially relevant scales and assessment strategies (ranging from Moos's [Moos, 1974] and Craik's [1973] measures of environmental characteristics to Lazarus and Cohen's [1978] and the Dohrenwends' [1973, 1974] approaches to coping and stress measures), the fact remains there is generally no consensus about the acceptance of any standard set of measures for important social-psychological concepts. The methodology of measurement is particularly complex in applied settings, such as aftercare programs, because in addition to the measurement-theoretical issues of generalizability (which encompasses reliability and validity) and discrimination, investigators must deal with the issues of feasibility and applicability. In the remaining pages of this section we first review some measurement-theoretical principles useful in making decisions about how to measure aftercare concepts, and then focus on the demands of feasibility and applicability.

One of the fundamental principles in modern measurement theory is the notion of a multiple-indicator approach. The origins of multiple-indicator assessment can be found in Campbell and Fiske's classic paper (1959) on multitrait-multimethod methodology. The basic idea is to minimize the reliance on single indicators of key concepts when conducting empirical studies. Instead, investigators should attempt to maximize the number of indicators of single concepts and use convergent and discriminant validation (the degree to which indicators behave jointly or separately) as tools for interpreting findings.

A nice illustration of this methodology in an area closely related to aftercare is Bradshaw's (1972) analysis of the concept of social need. He first describes four different perspectives on the concept of social need: normative, felt, expressed, and conformative; then gives indicators for each perspective and discusses the various interpretations of discrepancies and congruences among the perspectives. Bradshaw's work, unfortunately, is only one of the few examples of multiple-indicator methodology in applied social research. Systematic accumulation of knowledge about addict reentry would be substantially facilitated if this methodology were used more frequently by aftercare investigators.

Subscription to a multiple-indicator approach brings to mind the issues of item sampling and representativeness. Here the psychometric properties of generalizability and discrimination come into play. That is, indicators should be chosen so as to be replicable and interpretable and, in the case of nomothetic data, also provide adequate variability. Appropriate deference should be given to indicators used in prior studies, but creative new measures should not be dismissed outright because of their lack of a legacy.

Two additional points require special attention in the final selection of items for aftercare assessment. The first is with regard to item wording. Current standards for most psychological assessment are based on a "straight" white middle-class terminology. It is unlikely that aftercare investigators will find such language completely adequate for their assessment needs. Given the importance of item wording (see Sudman and Bradburn's [1974] review of response effects), we suggest that aftercare investigators engage clients in the development of aftercare measures, and that a thorough pretesting be carried out before actual assessment begins. The second point is about the concreteness and timeframe in items.

Methodological research has demonstrated that the reliability of measurement is highly correlated with the specificity and the timeframe of indicators: the more specific and current the measure, the more reliable it is likely to be. Global measures with long timeframes may have some theoretical appeal, but they are invariably of poor measurement quality and thus of limited utility in aftercare assessment.

Decisions about the ways (modes) of collecting data go hand-in-hand with decisions about measures. There are four major modes of collecting aftercare data: (1) client self-report, (2) staff (usually counselor) ratings, (3) reports by other persons (such as friends and family members), and (4) observations (for example, video tapes of special counseling sessions such as family therapy). Each mode has its strengths and weaknesses in terms of reliability and feasibility. A review of the drug abuse literature indicates that almost all of the social-psychological data are collected via the self-report mode. We find this situation unfortunate because of the obvious limitations of self-report data; limitations which stem in part from the fact that such data are often generated under conditions in which the client can be negatively affected—such as terminated from treatment—by certain responses to evaluative questions. Again following the multitrait-multimethod logic, we recommend that aftercare investigators pursue a multiple-mode measurement strategy whenever possible. Convergence in findings across modes will increase the interpretability of the data, whereas divergence in findings across modes may produce evidence about the possible effects of method factors. Both kinds of information are useful in developing an effective aftercare assessment strategy.

Turning to the more practical issues of feasibility and applicability we face the question of the compatibility of assessment with clinical process. To address this question adequately requires examination of at least four points:

(1) the relative allocation of resources across clinical versus measurement activities;
(2) confidentiality and intrusiveness;
(3) timeliness, especially critical points; and
(4) contamination effects of assessment.

Each of these points is sufficiently complex and important to warrant lengthy discussion by itself. Our purpose here, though, is not to present an analysis of each point, but rather to expose aftercare investigators to these points which should play significant roles in most decisions about an assessment strategy.

The first point, briefly mentioned previously, refers to the economics of information. Decisions about this issue require careful thought about how much the program is willing to spend to find out "how well it is doing about what." To our knowledge, there are no optimal ratios of clinical to measurement costs; however, we suspect that drug abuse programs typically underallocate resources to assessment activities. The second point, confidentiality and intrusiveness, is a particularly vulnerable spot in aftercare and drug abuse assessment. Despite specific regulations on confidentiality procedures, aftercare investigators need to be continuously sensitive to this matter because of the type of data gathered and the often illegal nature of activities currently or previously engaged in by aftercare clients. Similarly, comprehensiveness and reliability in assessment must be carefully weighed against intrusiveness, especially when there is a likelihood of negative consequences for the client. Timeliness refers to the fact that a major role of assessment is to provide an ongoing empirical basis for decisions about aftercare plans. Thus, assessments should be scheduled to coordinate with the reentry management needs of the clinical staff. The final point, contamination effects of assessment, notes that feedback to the clinical staff (and client) does not always facilitate the clinical process. That is, certain negative (or positive) information about reentry progress can jeopardize the relationship between the client and program. For example, some aftercare programs will terminate clients who are placed on welfare because this behavior is viewed negatively, whereas other aftercare programs would deem such behavior as a positive sign of reentry progress. Hence, as a safeguard to minimize contamination effects, we suggest that clear statements be written about the clinical consequences of responses to measures before any assessment effort is undertaken.

In summary, there are several factors to be considered when making decisions about how to measure. These factors include both measurement-theoretical issues, such as generalizability, discriminability, and item wording; and practical issues, such as feasibility and applicability. We suggest that the optimal aftercare assessment strategy is a multiple-indicator multiple-mode approach that is compatible with the clinical process.

CONCLUSION: POLICY IMPLICATIONS AND SOME SUGGESTIONS FOR FUTURE AFTERCARE RESEARCH

In the preceding pages we have discussed some new and old ideas on the issue of addict aftercare. Our purpose has been to lay the groundwork for a social-psychological model that can be used for both understanding "heroinism"—the addict's compelling attachment to a way of life based in the world of drugs—and for designing effective human service programs to facilitate the former addict's reentry to conventional society. Our discussion has focused on four topics:

(1) the distinction between exiting and reentering;
(2) the conceptualization of reentering in terms of well-functioning;
(3) the concept of social networks and their influence on reentry; and
(4) theoretical and practical considerations in aftercare assessment.

In this concluding section we present the policy implications of our discussions of these four topics and point out some directions of future aftercare research.

The first, and perhaps most important, policy implication stems from the distinction between exiting and reentering. We have presented a perspective that calls for separating primary treatment activities and goals from aftercare activities and goals. We argue that primary treatment activities should focus on the goal of exiting from the drug world, whereas aftercare activities should focus on the goal of reentry. In this view, treatment goals are both limited and short-term, while aftercare goals are more expansive and long-term. Acceptance of this distinction would lead to systematic differences among programs in terms of their design and evaluation, depending on stated goals. This ideal situation would be in dramatic contrast to the current state of affairs where drug abuse programs are expected to achieve results that they are neither designed to accomplish nor able to achieve.

In terms of future research, the distinction between exiting and reentering suggests at least three directions. The first is to study how the processes of exiting and reentering influence one another. To date this has not been possible because most investigators have not differentiated between indicators of exiting and reentering in their measurements. A second direction is the investigation of how former addicts develop meaningful stakes in conventional society. There is currently a paucity of long-term prospective data from which to derive specific hypotheses about this issue because most demonstration, evaluation, and research projects have short funding cycles. Waldorf and Biernacki's ongoing study (1979) of the natural recovery process in addicts, however, should provide some useful guidance in this area. A third direction of research is the examination of the relative efficacy of various designs of aftercare programs. We are currently conducting a demonstration project based on experimental evaluation methodology which examines the differential effectiveness of three types of aftercare models: referral, advocacy, and direct services delivery. Similar demonstration projects which systematically vary other parameters of aftercare programs are also needed.

Our conceptualization of reentering in terms of social-psychological dimensions of well-functioning also has broad policy implications. It recommends that policy-makers view clients as persons first and addicts (or former addicts) second. In other words, we argue that the field of drug abuse (especially the aftercare area) should be brought back into the mainstream of social science theory, instead of maintaining its isolated posture by espousing special theories of addiction (which are usually based on medical models). To be sure, innovations in medical science have had a substantial positive influence on the understanding of the physiology of addiction, but we have doubts about the utility of a medical model for dealing with the broader problem of "heroinism." Thus, we argue that the same social-psychological principles govern the behavior of all persons, regardless of life-specific circumstances, and that these principles are the most appropriate for understanding long-term care issues. Knowledge of these principles would help aftercare programs better meet the needs of their clients.

The directions of future research in the well-functioning area are almost limitless. Numerous studies have investigated vocational issues, but there is almost no programmatic research in other important life areas, such as leisure and interpersonal relations. This situation again probably reflects the short-term perspective of both drug abuse projects and policy decisions. Yet, we suspect that the long-term success of reentry will depend more on well-functioning in these other life areas than on employment status. Thus, in our opinion, the long-range pay-off in aftercare research will be in global models of well-functioning rather than in area-specific findings.

Network analysis, a particularly important component of our social-psychological model of addict aftercare, has two major policy implications. First, differences in social networks between addict and nonaddict populations should supply good evidence about the etiology and maintenance of these contrasting social roles. To the extent that such differences can be translated into program design, these data could serve as the foundation for drug prevention programs. More germane to the current discussion, though, is the identification of network characteristics which facilitate or impede addict reentry. If such characteristics can be identified, they could provide the basis for network intervention strategies as part of an aftercare plan. Recent efforts in family therapy with addicts are illustrations of how network analysis can play a role in aftercare services.

With regard to future research directions in network analysis, the situation is similar to the well-functioning area. In other words, currently there is no systematic knowledge about the formal properties of addicts' (or former addicts') networks. Thus, studies are needed which would map out the networks, examine the consequences of network characteristics for reentry, and demonstrate the degree of change and potential for change in networks.

The policy implications of aftercare assessment are rather straight-forward. To the extent that aftercare investigators can gather generalizable data, conduct thorough analyses, produce accurate reports, and translate results into policy statements, it can be expected that empirical studies will play a critical role in the aftercare decision-making process. Lack of quality and relevance are, of course, the two most frequently cited reasons for dismissing empirical findings when making policy. We think that consideration of the assessment issues presented here (especially the multiple-indicator/multiple-mode measurement strategy) will enhance the quality and relevance of most empirical studies and thus increase their likelihood of having an influence on policy. Future research in aftercare assessment must attempt to bridge the ever-widening gap between developments in measurement theory and empirical applications.

In conclusion, the social-psychological model we have outlined here has the potential for catalyzing and guiding the growing interest in a human services approach to drug abuse treatment and rehabilitation. Without the guidance that such a model can provide, we fear that new programmatic efforts in this area will be inadequately planned and that the promise of aftercare will remain untested and unfulfilled.

NOTES

1. Perhaps one of the most enduring findings of laboratory psychology can help to explain the importance of these transitory opportunities: the powerful consequences of partial reinforcement schedules.

2. In deference to common usage we will henceforth use only the term "reentry" to refer to the process whereby former addicts acquire ties to conventional society. Nonetheless, we hold with our previous assertion (Pittel, 1974) that "entry" is a more apt term for a majority of addicts who have never enjoyed full membership in that society.

3. Meisenhelder (1977) has made a similar argument with regard to criminal offenders: disengagement or exiting from a previous pattern of behavior is seen as the last stage in a career of criminality. Criminals might be motivated to take this step by fear of punishment (e.g., imprisonment) or, as they mature, they may "become envious of conventional security and [begin] to define a settled life as rewarding" (p. 324). But in either case, exiting results from "an intentional and meaningful decision to leave [a] career in crime" (p. 325). The crucial factor is the former criminal's ability to find a meaningful role in conventional society. In Meisenhelder's words, "successful exiting ... includes the development of meaningful expressive attachments and behavioral investments that bind the individuals to conformity and that provide them with significant reasons not to deviate" (p. 325). And among these attachments and investments, the most important to the former criminals in Meisenhelder's study were a good and steady job and the ability to make new friends in "straight" society. Among former criminals whose exits were successful, "relations with individuals who espoused conventional ideals formed an essential part of the offender's emerging bond to the social order.... The formation of these relationships was referred to by the men as settling down. This generally included the acquisition, or reacquisition of a wife, other familial ties, or peer relationships with conventional others.... These relational ties provided ... both a resource for use when confronting exiting problems and a tie to conformity which could be lost if they returned to crime" (p. 327ff).

4. We have discussed elsewhere (Pittel, 1979) the corresponding confusion that results from this broad usage of "treatment" with respect to the definition of reentry and aftercare services.

5. Note that this question treats networks as exogenous variables.

6. Note that here networks are treated as endogenous variables.

7. Fischer and his colleagues (Jones and Fischer, 1978) have recently completed a household survey in northern California which includes a number of questions about network characteristics. Results from this survey should yield comprehensive information useful for comparative purposes.

REFERENCES

ALBA, R. (1973) "A graph-theoretic definition of sociometric clique." Journal of Mathematical Sociology 3: 113-126.

ALKSNE, H., LIEBERMAN, L., and BRILL, L. (1967) "A conceptual model of the life cycle of addiction." International Journal of the Addictions 2 (Fall): 221-240.

ANDREWS, F. M. and WITHEY, S. B. (1976) Social Indicators of Well-Being: Americans' Perceptions of Life Quality. New York: Plenum.

BALES, R. F. (1970) Personality and Interpersonal Behavior. New York: Holt, Rinehart & Winston.

BERKMAN, L. (1977) "Social networks, host resistance, and mortality: a follow-up study of Alameda County residents." Ph.D. dissertation, University of California, Berkeley.

BOISSEVAIN, J. (1974) Friends of Friends: Networks, Manipulators, and Coalitions. New York: St. Martin's.

BOTT, E. (1971) Family and Social Network (2nd ed.). New York: Free Press.
BOURNE, P. G. (1974) "Human resources: a new approach to the dilemmas of community psychiatry." American Journal of Psychiatry 131: 666-669.
BRADBURN, N. (1969) The Structure of Psychological Well-Being. Chicago: Aldine.
BRADSHAW, J. (1972) "The concept of social need." New Society 30 (May): 640-643.
BRILL, L. (1972) The De-addiction Process Studies in the De-addiction of Confirmed Heroin Addicts. Springfield, IL: Charles C. Thomas.
BROWN, B. S. and ASHERY, R. S. (1979) "Aftercare in drug abuse programming," in R. L. Dupont, A. Goldstein, and J. O'Donnell (eds.) Handbook of Drug Abuse. Washington, DC: National Institute on Drug Abuse and Office of Drug Abuse Policy.
BURT, R. S. (1976) "Positions in networks." Social Forces 55 (September): 93-122.
––– (1978) "Applied network analysis." Sociological Methods and Research (November): special issue.
CAMPBELL, A., CONVERSE, P. E., and RODGERS, E. W. (1976) The Quality of American Life. New York: Russell Sage Foundation.
CAMPBELL, D. and FISKE, D. (1959) "Convergent and discriminant validation by the multitrait-multimethod matrix." Psychological Bulletin 56: 81-105.
CHEIN, I., GERARD, D. L., LEE, R. S., and ROSENFELD, E. (1964) The Road to H: Narcotics, Delinquency and Social Policy. New York: Basic Books.
COLEMAN, J. S., KATZ, E., and MENZEL, H. (1966) Medical Innovation. Indianapolis: Bobbs-Merrill.
CRAIK, K. H. (1973) "Environmental psychology," in Annual Review of Psychology. Palo Alto, CA: Annual Reviews.
DOHRENWEND, B. P. (1974) "Problems in defining and sampling the relevant populations of stressful life events," in Dohrenwend, B. S. and Dohrenwend, B. P. (eds.) Stressful Life Events: Their Nature and Effects. New York: John Wiley.
DOHRENWEND, B. S. (1974) "Life events as stressors: a methodological inquiry." Journal of Health and Social Behavior (June): 167-175.
Domestic Council Drug Abuse Task Force (1975) White Paper on Drug Abuse: A Report to the President. Washington, DC: U.S. Government Printing Office.
DORUS, W., SENAY, E. C., and JOSEPH, M. L. (1977) "Evaluating service needs in drug-abusing clients." Presented at the National Drug Abuse Conference, San Francisco, May.
DUPONT, R. L. (1978) "The drug abuse decade." Journal of Drug Issues (Spring).
DURKHEIM, E. (1897, 1951) Suicide. New York: Free Press.
FELDMAN, H. (1973) "Street status and drug users." Society 10: 32-38.
FINLAYSON, A. (1976) "Social networks as coping resources: lay help and consultation patterns used by women in husbands' post infarction career." Social Science and Medicine 10: 97-103.
FISCHER, C. S. (1978) "The social contexts of personal relations: an exploratory network analysis." Working Paper No. 281, Institute of Urban and Regional Development, University of California, Berkeley.
FISCHER, C. et al. (1977) Networks and Places: Social Relations in the Urban Setting. New York: Free Press, 1977.
FISKE, D. W. (1978) Strategies for Personality Research. San Francisco: Jossey-Bass.
FRENCH, J.R.P. and KAHN, R. L. (1962) "A programmatic approach to studying

the industrial environment and mental health." Journal of Social Issues 18: 1-48.
FRENCH, J.R.P., RODGERS, W., and COBB, S. (1974) "Adjustment as person-environment fit," pp. 316-333 in G. Coelho, D. Hamburg, and J. Adams (eds.) Coping and Adaptation. New York: Basic Books.
FREUDENBERGER, H. J. and PITTEL, S. M. (1979) "The challenge of re-entry: problems and prospects," in K. Blum, S. J. Feinglass, and A. H. Briggs (eds.) Social Meaning of Drugs: Principles of Social Pharmacology. New York: Basic Books.
FRIEDMAN, L. N. (1978) The Wildcat experiment: An early test of supported work in drug abuse rehabilitation. Washington, DC: National Institute on Drug Abuse Services Research Monograph Series (DHEW Publication No. 79-782).
GOULD, L., WALKER, A., CRANE, L., and LIDZ, C. (1974) Connections: Notes from the Heroin World. New Haven, CT: Yale Univ. Press.
GRANOVETTER, M. S. (1974) Getting a Job: A Study of Contacts and Careers. Cambridge, MA: Harvard Univ. Press.
HARVEY, J. H., ICKES, W. J., and KIDD, R. F. [eds.] (1976) New Directions in Attribution Research. Hillsdale, NJ: Lawrence Erlbaum Associates.
HOROWITZ, A. (1977) "Social networks and pathways to psychiatric treatment." Social Forces 56 (September): 86-105.
JONES, E. E., et al. (1971) Attribution: Perceiving the Causes of Behavior. Morristown, NJ: General Learning Press.
JONES, L. and FISCHER, C. (1978) "A procedure for surveying personal networks." Sociological Methods and Research (November).
KADUSHIN, C. (1968) "Power, influence and social circles: a new methodology for studying opinion makers." American Sociological Review 33 (October): 685-698.
KANDEL, D. B. (1978) Longitudinal Research on Drug Use. Washington, DC: Hemisphere.
KAPLAN, B. H., CASSEL, J. C., and GORE, S. (1977) "Social support and health." Medical Care 15 (May, supplement): 47-58.
LANGLIE, J. K. (1977) "Social networks, health beliefs, and preventive health behavior." Journal of Health and Social Behavior 18 (September): 244-260.
LAUMANN, E. O. (1973) Bonds of Pluralism: The Form and Structure of Urban Soial Networks. New York: Wiley Interscience.
LAZARUS, R. (1966) Psychological Stress and the Coping Process. New York: McGraw-Hill.
––– and COHEN, J. (1978) "The uplifts scale, the hassles scale (process), and the hassles scale (trait)." Unpublished document, University of California, Berkeley.
LEINHARDT, S. (1977) Soial Networks: A Developing Paradigm. New York: Academic Press.
LEVIN, G., ROBERTS, E. B., and HIRSCH, G. B. (1975) The Persistent Poppy. Cambridge, MA: Ballinger.
LEVINSON, D. J. (1978) The Seasons of a Man's Life. New York: Alfred A. Knopf.
MECHANIC, D. (1974) "Social structure and personal adaptation: some neglected dimensions," in G. Coelho, D. Hamburg, and J. Adams (eds.) Coping and Adaptation. New York: Basic Books.
MEISENHELDER, T. (1977) "An exploratory study of exiting from criminal careers." Criminology 15 (November): 319-334.

MINOR, M. J., BRADBURN, N., and SCHAEFFER, N. C. (forthcoming) "The structure of life satisfaction: a comparative analysis across social groups," in A. Szalai, and F. Andrews (eds.) Comparative Studies of Life Quality. Beverly Hills: Sage Publications.

MISCHEL, W., EBBESEN, E. B., and ZEISS, A. (1972) "Cognitive and attentional mechanisms in delay of gratification." Journal of Personality and Social Psychology 21: 204-218.

MISCHEL, W. and GILLIGAN, C. (1964) "Delay of gratification, motivation for the prohibited gratification, and responses to temptation." Journal of Abnormal and Social Psychology 69 (4): 411-417.

MITCHELL, J. C. [ed.] (1969) Social Networks in Urban Situations—Analysis of Personal Relationships in Central African Towns. Manchester: Manchester Univ. Press.

MONAT, A. and LAZARUS, R. [eds.] (1977) Stress and Coping: An Anthology. New York: Columbia Univ. Press.

MOOS, R. (1974) Evaluating Treatment Environments: A Social Ecological Approach. New York: John Wiley.

——— (1976) The Human Context: Environmental Determinants of Behavior. New York: John Wiley.

National Institute on Drug Abuse (1975) Findings of Drug Abuse Research. Washington, DC: National Institute on Drug Abuse, Monograph Series.

NEUGARTEN, B. L. [ed.] (1967) Middle Age and Aging. Chicago: Univ. of Chicago Press.

NEWMAN, R. G. (1979) "Detoxification in the treatment of narcotic addicts," in R. L. Dupont, A. Goldstein, and J. O'Donnell (eds.) Handbook of Drug Abuse. Washington, DC: National Institute on Drug Abuse and Office of Drug Abuse Policy.

PITTEL, S. M. (1974) "Addicts in wonderland: sketches for a map of a vocational frontier." Journal of Psychedelic Drugs 6: 231-241.

——— (1975) "An assessment strategy for supported work." Unpublished manuscript.

——— (1976) "Addict aftercare needs and services." Unpublished manuscript.

——— (1978) "Addict aftercare: essence or afterthought?" Contemporary Drug Problems (Winter): 491-514.

——— (1979) Community support systems for addict aftercare. Washington, DC: National Institute on Drug Abuse, Research Monograph.

———, DAKOF, G., FOSTER, T. L., and HEJINIAN, C. L. (1979) "Re-entry concerns of incarcerated substance abusers." American Journal of Drug and Alcohol Abuse 6: 59-71.

PITTEL, S. M. and FOSTER, T. L. (1970) "The Oregon re-entry program: a comprehensive plan for delivery of treatment and rehabilitation services to substance dependent correctional clients." Unpublished manuscript.

PREBLE, E. and CASEY, J. J. (1972) "Taking care of business: the heroin user's life," in D. E. Smith, and G. R. Gay (eds.) It's So Good Don't Even Try It Once. Englewood Cliffs, NJ: Prentice-Hall.

ROTTER, J. B. (1966) "Generalized expectancies for internal versus external control of reinforcement." Psychological Monographs 80 (609): 1-28.

RUEVENI, U. (1979) Networking Families in Crisis: Intervention Strategies with

Families and Social Networks. New York: Human Sciences Press.

SALLOWAY, J. C. and DILLION, P. B. (1973) "A comparison of family networks and friend networks in health care utilization." Journal of Comparative Family Studies 4: 131-142.

SPECK, R. V. and ATTNEAVE, C. L. (1973) Family Networks. New York: Vintage.

STACK, C. B. (1970) All Our Kin: Strategies for Survival in a Black Community. New York: Harper & Row.

STANTON, M. D. (1977) "The addict as savior: heroin, death, and the family." Family Process 16 (June): 191-197.

––– (1978) "The family and drug misuse: a bibliography." American Journal of Drug and Alcohol Abuse 5 (2): 151-170.

–––, TODD, T. C., HEARD, D. B., KIRSCHNER, S., KLEIMAN, J. I., MOWATT, D. T., RILEY, P., SCOTT, S. M., and VAN DEUSEN, J. M. (1978) "Heroin addiction as a family phenomenon: a new conceptual model." American Journal of Drug and Alcohol Abuse 5: 125-150.

SUDMAN, S. and BRADBURN, N. (1974) Response Effects in Surveys. Chicago: Aldine.

SUTTER, A. G. (1966) "The world of the righteous dope fiend." Issues in Criminology 2: 177-222.

TRAVERS, J. and MILGRAM, S. (1969) "An experimental study of the small-world problem." Sociometry 32 (December): 425-443.

WACKER, N. and HAWKINS, J. D. (1978) "Verbal performances and addict conversion: toward a linguistic understanding of the successes and failures of therapeutic communities." Unpublished manuscript.

WALDORF, D. (1973) Careers in Dope. Englewood Cliffs, NJ: Prentice-Hall.

––– and BIERNACKI, P. (1979) "Natural recovery from heroin addiction: a review of the incidence literature." Journal of Drug Issues 9 (2).

WARD, H. (1973) Employment and Addiction: Overview of Issues. Washington, DC: Drug Abuse Council.

WHITE, R. W. (1974) "Strategies of adaptation: an attempt at systematic description," in G. Coelho, D. Hamburg, and J. Adams (eds.) Coping and Adaptation. New York: Basic Books.

WEINER, B. and KUN, A. (1976) "The development of causal attributions and the growth of achievement and social motivation," in S. Feldman and D. Bush (eds.) Cognitive Development and Social Development. Hillsdale, NJ: Lawrence Erlbaum Associates.

PART V

CLIENT ADVOCACY

10

ADDICTS' RIGHTS AND ADVOCACY INITIATIVES

DEBORAH HASTINGS-BLACK

INTRODUCTION

Drug abusers have rights as citizens and as clients of the drug abuse treatment system. These rights apply to the care and services they receive from clinics and to the treatment they receive in the community. They include, for example, rights to due process, to certain standards of care, and to access to services, benefits, housing, and employment. Many of those involved in the drug abuse treatment field, clients and staff alike, are not aware of these rights. Consequently, services and benefits essential to the long-term rehabilitation of drug abusers remain unavailable. If the necessary supports in the community, such as training and employment, are not available to clients, the progress made within treatment cannot be expected to be sustained.

Indeed, treatment itself will have limited appeal if opportunities for a "better life" in the community are not perceived as realistic alternatives after treatment. Thus, access to such opportunities should be viewed as vital components of the treatment and rehabilitation process.

In an era that has seen the legitimization and growth of the consumer and civil rights movements, it is surprising that there has been no comparable effort to establish and protect the rights of drug abusers. Through well-organized campaigns combining legislation, litigation, negotiations, and creative public relations, the rights of many—including minorities, women, welfare recipients, the elderly, and the disabled—have been successfully established.

There are a number of factors which might explain why no addicts' rights movement per se has developed. Some pertain to the nature of the relationship between drug abusers and the treatment field; others pertain to the status and condition of the drug abusers themselves. First, for example, much of the impetus for the client/patients' rights movement in the mental health field evolved from a concern for the individuals' right to freedom and basic civil rights. It was argued that if persons with mental disabilities were to be denied their liberty through commitment to institutions, they had a right to appropriate treatment for their condition (*Wyatt v. Stickney*) and to the least restrictive form of treatment (*Welsch v. Likens*). In the drug abuse field it is not generally thought that freedoms of persons in treatment are jeopardized. Unlike many mental health patients, the majority of drug abusers in treatment are enrolled in community-based, outpatient clinics, not large restrictive institutions. If they find the services unsatisfactory, they are free to leave. Indeed, in 1978 for clients in federally funded treatment, the average length of stay in outpatient drug-free treatment was 23.9 weeks and for residential drug-free it was 15.9 weeks (National Institute on Drug Abuse, 1979). There are obvious exceptions to this, such as the restrictions imposed on clients enrolled in civil commitment programs and those in treatment under court order. Also, though clients in methadone maintenance are certainly free to leave the program, their "freedom" to do so is confounded by their dependence on methadone.

Second, the relationship between drug abusers and treatment programs differs from the relationship between the mentally disabled and the mental health institutions. Many drug programs are managed or largely staffed by ex-addict former clients, thus somewhat diffusing the distinction between clients and staff. Indeed, it could be said that both clients and staff have a vested interest in preserving the existing drug abuse treatment system since it is one of the major sources of employment for ex-addicts.

Third, treatment providers do not regard drug abusers as handicapped persons in need of protection and care in the community as patients are often viewed by mental health professionals. Thus, securing access to education, training, and employment services in the community is not considered a major responsibility of treatment staff. Drug abusers are thought capable of negotiating for such services on their own.

Fourth, unlike many of those with obvious physical or mental handicaps, the drug abusers' status or condition is not immediately apparent. Their goal is to become indistinguishable from their nondrug-abusing peers. They have little to gain from revealing their drug abuse histories through participation in clients' rights activities. To do so they expose themselves to hostility and resistance as a result of the perceived dual handicap of a psychological disorder and a criminal background. The greatest residual problem of drug abuse is the stigma.

The events surrounding the promulgation of regulations for Section 504 of the Rehabilitation Act of 1973 illustrate clearly the deep-seated prejudice that exists toward drug abusers and the lack of advocates or spokespersons to speak on their behalf. Hearings were held in 1976 across the country to receive comments on the draft regulations establishing procedures to insure that qualified handicapped persons are not discriminated against by recipients of federal funds in their access to services, benefits, and employment. The interests of the traditional handicapped groups were well presented at each hearing. And, at each hearing strong objections were voiced on including drug abusers under the definition of handicapped.[1] Handicapped groups and service providers alike did not want to afford drug abusers the same protections provided all other persons with recognized physical or mental impairments. There was no organized representation of the interests of addicts. It was a highly emotional issue. Somehow drug abusers were considered unworthy of the protections since their impairments were viewed as self-inflicted and their actions as criminal. In fact, so controversial was the issue that the Secretary of the Department of Health, Education, and Welfare sought the opinion of the Attorney General before finally deciding to retain addicts under the scope of the Section 504 protections.

It is clear that for former drug abusers to be integrated into the community, they need access to services, benefits, and employment to which they are entitled. Though drug abusers currently have rights to such access, the drug abuse field does not appear to be taking advantage of some of the techniques available for exercising them. This chapter will review some of the mechanisms which currently exist within the drug abuse field for protecting the rights of addicts in their pursuit of appropriate treatment and rehabilitation services. Where appropriate, reference will be made to recent developments within the mental health field which have implications for drug abuse and suggestions will be made for further action.

PATIENTS' RIGHTS IN THE MENTAL HEALTH FIELD

Developments in the mental health field provide a background for understanding key issues in the patient/clients' rights movement. Morton Birnbaum, an attorney and physician, is considered the first to have focused attention on the rights of mental health patients in an article in 1960 in the *American Bar Association Journal* on the right to treatment (Birnbaum, 1960). Philosophical discussions followed between those in the legal profession concerned about individual liberties and the quality of life and those in the mental health profession concerned about humanizing treatment. Many of those involved were also involved in the civil rights movement and brought to bear on behalf of patients the same legal tools which had proven successful in civil rights. Professional associations, such as the American Psychiatric Association, and the American Civil Liberties Union, joined with concerned citizens and patients to bring law suits to focus on the most egregious abuses, namely the denial of constitutional rights within mental health institutions.

For example, procedures for committing and retaining individuals were challenged (*Lessard v. Schmidt; Hawks v. Lazaro*); the appropriateness and quality of care was questioned (*O'Connor v. Donaldson*); and certain rights of individuals within institutions were established (*Souder v. Brennan*). The landmark court decisions of the early 1970s have required a major reexamination and overhaul of the way in which mental health patients are treated.

The Response

Many of the court decisions require the upgrading of services, the provision of treatment through the least restrictive community-based care and the deinstitutionalization of patients. However, there is now concern that if the resources are not available in the communities to provide the necessary outpatient care and supports, the mentally disabled will be as abused within the communities as they were within the restrictive institutions (Kirk and Therrien, 1975; Aviram and Segal, 1973; Arnoff, 1975; Allen, 1974; Turner and TenHoor, 1978). There is also concern that with the rapid developments in mental health law, neither patients nor mental health professionals are fully aware of the implications of the rights and obligations which are being established. Consequently, state legislatures, professional organizations, and patients' rights organizations are developing different mechanisms for informing both clients and staff of the rights of the mentally disabled and techniques for protecting those rights.

FORMAL SYSTEMS FOR THE PROTECTION
OF PATIENTS' RIGHTS

The formal systems for protection range from networks within the state mental health or public welfare departments, to separate organizations directly responsible to the governor or programs administered by the state courts or public defenders. Some focus on the mentally disabled and mental health services exclusively, while other states have established offices of patients'/recipients' rights or patient/consumer advocacy programs.

As one might expect, the programs vary according to their mandate, organizational location and staffing. Some are heavily oriented toward litigation, while others focus on negotiation and advocacy. The systems in three states illustrate the impact of the different approaches.

New York Mental Health Information Service

The Mental Health Information Service (MHIS), created in 1964, operates as an arm of the New York state court system. It is responsible for informing institutionalized patients of their rights, for presenting to the court a summary of all relevant material on every mental health case heard, and if requested, for representing patients at the hearings. MHIS has four divisions deployed throughout the state, one for each of the four judicial areas. Two of the divisions are predominantly staffed by lawyers; two by social workers. As might be expected, the two divisions with lawyers are very heavily involved in legal proceedings and those with social workers focus on nonlegal advocacy and representation of client interests (Stone, 1975).

New Jersey Division of Mental Health Advocacy

The Department of the Public Advocate was established in 1974 as an independent agency in New Jersey to help individuals who are "disenfranchised, institutionalized, and/or puzzled" by governmental rules and regulations and to make government more responsive to the individual. The department includes an Office of the Public Defender which handles cases for indigent individuals charged with criminal offenses, for jail and prison inmates and for juveniles in child abuse or neglect proceedings; Divisions of Public Interest Advocacy, Rate Council, Citizens Complaints and Mental Health Advocacy. The Division of Mental Health Advocacy has two principal functions. First, it provides legal assistance to indigent clients on issues concerning admission, retention, or release from mental institutions. Second, it handles class action suits on behalf of mental health clients. The division is staffed by mental health professionals who conduct investigations and negotiate the settlement of conflicts out of court whenever possible; and attorneys who handle litigation. The division has been involved in successfully negotiating issues in the community on behalf of former mental health clients such as the revocation of a driver's license and the provision of psychiatric benefits to members of Health Maintenance Organizations (Van Ness and Perlin, 1977).

Michigan Office of Recipient Rights

An Office of Recipient Rights (ORR) was created within the Michiga Department of Mental Health in 1975. It provides for "rights advisers" in all 23 state institutions. Unlike the systems in New Jersey and New York, the emphasis of the program is not on litigation. Instead, administrative procedures are provided for protecting the civil, treatment and environmental rights of clients which are specified in the state mental health code. All providers of mental health services are required to establish straightforward procedures for informing clients of their rights and for reporting, investigating, and correcting violations. The rights advisers work within each agency to implement the program. They are accountable to the director of their agency but report regularly to the ORR on their activities and cases. Problems are referred to lawyers for legal action when issues cannot be resolved within the department (Coye, 1977).

PATIENTS' RIGHTS GROUPS AND ADVOCACY

Systems for the protection of the rights of the mentally disabled within the community are not as well-developed and tested as the institutional protections. However, certain features of the different existing programs can be combined to meet the needs of clients in the community. One configuration suggested would combine the established institutional protections with community advocates, legal advocates, and an ombudsman.

This combination acknowledges the need for representatives within the mental health institutions to help resolve internal grievances; for advocates to work on behalf of clients to secure services and benefits within the community; for legal representation for clients both within institutions and in the community when negotiations fail; and finally, for an ombudsman to review and investigate the functioning of the system as a whole and to make recommendations for corrections to the system (Wilson et al., 1977).

The citizen advocates can be volunteers or paid professionals; they can be employed by the treatment provider institution or associated with a consumer or patients' rights office outside the mental health system. The legal advocacy can be provided by attorneys within the mental health system, within another state agency, or through the Legal Services Corporation. The ombudsman can be sponsored by the city or state and should have sufficient authority to cut across bureaucratic divisions and to be able to make his or her recommendations for corrections to the highest appropriate level within the government.

Within the National Institute of Mental Health there is a Patient Rights and Advocacy Program to focus attention on the rights of the mentally disabled and to encourage the development of mental health advocacy by treatment providers, consumers, the judiciary, and the government. The program has sponsored symposia on the subject and published monographs with practical, legal, and philosophical reviews of patients' rights and advocacy. The program has an ad hoc advisory group of ex-patients who serve as NIMH consultants to advise on program plans, legislation, and regulations (Kopolow, 1979). NIMH is also funding the National Paralegal Institute to provide advocacy training to mental health professionals.

In 1978, the President's Commission on Mental Health recommended that each state have a bill of rights and advocacy system for the mentally disabled similar to that required for the developmentally disabled by the Developmentally Disabled Assistance and Bill of Rights Act 1975, which established protection and advocacy systems in each state. It also recommended that the Legal Services Corporation be required to represent the mentally handicapped more adequately (President's Commission on Mental Health, 1978).

Another technique for protecting the rights of patients is the creation of patients' rights groups. Many such groups, composed of volunteers, ex-patients, and patients, exist in communities to deal with local issues. Their goals are usually to provide mutual support to each other, to share information on patients' rights issues, information on the availability and nature of mental health treatment and alternatives, and to educate the public on mental health issues (Chamberlin, 1979).

On the national level, there is the National Committee for Patients' Rights composed of a coalition of service providers, patients, former patients, lawyers, and concerned citizens. It was created in 1975 to bring a cross-section of perspectives to bear on the issue of the rights of the mentally disabled and to create a bridge between the service providers and the patients. The committee of 20 members includes representatives from the National Council of Community Mental Health Centers, the National Mental Health Association, the Mental Health Law Project, the National Institute of Mental Health (NIMH), the National Association of Social Workers, the American Bar Association, the New Jersey Division of Mental Health Advocacy, and representatives from local patients' rights groups, such as the Mental Patients' Liberation Front. Members from governmental or service provider organizations do not formally represent their organizations but rather participate as individuals while those from local patients' rights groups do represent their organizations. The committee was originally supported with funds from NIMH, the National Mental Health Association, the Mental Health Law Project, and other private foundations. The funds primarily provided for travel for the representatives of the patients' rights groups to the committee meetings which were held every other month. The other committee members would donate their time and provide space for meetings and all the necessary backup services, such as typing and coordination.

Over the last few years the committee has provided a forum for the discussion of major patients' rights and advocacy issues ar has assured the injection of the patients' perspective in the formulation of mental health policy. For example, the committee conducted a survey of legal mental health advocacy across the country, it has reviewed and commented on all major federal legislation and regulations of significance to the mentally disabled, and it has contributed to the education of the public on mental health issues through the sponsoring of panels on patients' rights at professional meetings, such as those of the American Bar Association, the American Psychiatric Association, and the American Psychological Association.

The committee is now preparing models for advocacy initiatives. Unfortunately, however, its future is in doubt since its grant funds have expired, and it is currently searching for other sources of funds (Chamberlin, 1979; Kopolow, 1979).

What Rights?

Combining the original concerns about conditions within institutions with the concern for adequate care within the community, the following rights have evolved as the backbone of the mentally disabled patients' rights movement:

(1) The right to be treated with dignity and respect;
(2) the right to be free from unnecessary hospitalization;
(3) the right to be free from unnecessary treatment;
(4) the right to information about treatment;
(5) the right to confidentiality;
(6) the right to quality care;
(7) the right to access to needed services;
(8) the right to participate in treatment decisions;
(9) the right to redress for grievances; and
(10) the right to a patient advocate (Sadoff and Kopolow, 1977).

Many of the issues which prompted the establishment of rights in the mental health field also confront drug abusers in search of appropriate treatment and rehabilitation services. In the drug abuse field some issues pertain to conditions and procedures within the drug programs; others concern services and relationships within the community. They are both relevant to a consideration of drug abusers' rights since the rehabilitation process involves drug treatment services, such as counseling and methadone, in combination with an array of other community-based social, vocational, legal, medical, and financial services. From the perspective of the drug abuser, the treatment program services and the community-based services and benefits are interwoven, and thus any initiatives to protect the rights of drug abusers cannot focus on one without the other.

The drug abuse rehabilitation issues most frequently articulated are:

(1) The need for formal treatment program procedures for the redress of grievances;
(2) the need for formal procedures for handling involuntary termination from treatment;
(3) the need for client access to treatment records and information on medication;
(4) the need for client participation in treatment decisions;
(5) the need for protection of client confidentiality;
(6) the need for methadone clinic hours to accommodate the work hours of employed clients;
(7) the need for payment of clients for work within treatment programs;
(8) the need for established procedures for the use of clients' benefits, such as welfare funds or food stamps, for the treatment program;
(9) the need to permit continuous methadone treatment while on travel;

(10)   the need for drug programs to establish formal liaisons with other
       community service providers to insure access to benefits, housing,
       education, and employment; and
(11)   the need to address the particular needs of women, minorities,
       and youth in treatment (Civil Liberties Union of Massachusetts,
       1975).

Initiatives to address some of these issues in the drug abuse field are
discussed below.

THE STATUS OF ADDICTS' RIGHTS INITIATIVES
IN THE DRUG ABUSE FIELD

Though no "movement" exists currently, some issues listed above and
aspects of the rights of drug abusers are being addressed through regulations, program procedures, legal and advocacy services, and clients' rights
groups.

Laws and Regulations

Both the Federal Funding Criteria (FFC) (21 CFR 1402), which establish minimum standards of care for federally funded treatment programs,
and the Standards for Drug Abuse Treatment and Rehabilitation Programs,
which establish the optimal standards required to attain accreditation from
the Joint Commission on the Accreditation of Hospitals (JCAH) (Joint
Commission, 1975), require procedures for the protection of clients' rights
and establish the treatment programs' obligation to secure access to
community service on behalf of their clients. Both require the provision of
supportive services, such as educational, vocational, or legal services, to the
extent that they are related to the clients' treatment. If the service cannot
be provided by program staff, they are required to be provided through
formal arrangements with community agencies.

However, the requirements concerning the rights of patients are much
less strongly stated. Both sets of standards address the issue of termination
of treatment and discharge. The FFC require that clients receive written
notification of changes in treatment or termination and establish that they
have the right to have the decision reviewed "in accordance with procedures for that purpose." The JCAH standards require that, where programs
have discharge policies, they should have written procedures which define
the types of infractions which would lead to discharge; who is authorized

to discharge clients; how clients would receive prior notification; and the nature of the review and appeal mechanism, *if any*. Ironically, though the criteria and standards were obviously developed for the ultimate benefit of clients, throughout there are no references to clients' rights per se or requirements for participation of clients in clinic policy-making or procedures. The methadone regulations have the same limitations. In fact, it is only the proposed revised methadone regulations (Narcotic Treatment Program Standards, 1977) which have yet to be approved, which require written policies and procedures for involuntary termination to protect the clients' rights to due process.

By contrast, the regulations (42 CFR 2) designed to protect the confidentiality rights of drug abusers in treatment are considered a model in the field of patients' rights. They establish the procedures for protecting the confidentiality of clinic records and clients' identities. They indicate the conditions under which certain information can be released and provide strict penalties for violations of the regulations. Well-respected and effective as they are, they too present problems. Many clients, treatment providers, and criminal justice professionals do not understand them. For example, in the area of community linkages, where there is a need for treatment program staff to establish relationships with employers or other service providers, confusion as to what client information can and cannot be shared often results in a breakdown of communications and a denial of the services or benefits. The regulations do allow for the sharing of certain client information if, in the judgment of staff, it would benefit the client. Sometimes, for fear of the penalties for the improper release of information, programs err on the side of caution and refuse to release information. Treatment staff have to balance their responsibility for protecting the confidentiality of their clients with their obligation to act as advocates in the community to secure needed services.

The National Institute on Drug Abuse (NIDA) recognizes the problems with the interpretation of the regulations and provides technical assistance, training and seminars on the subject. Also, a layman's technical assistance handbook on the regulations is being prepared.

The most recent and far-reaching protections are those provided by the Rehabilitation Act which prohibit discrimination against the handicapped. The implementing regulations establish that qualified individuals may not be denied, on the basis of a handicap, services, benefits, or employment for which they are eligible (45 CFR 84). This means that in addition to guaranteeing access to federally funded community services for qualified drug abusers, drug treatment programs are now obliged to accept for services eligible handicapped individuals. The regulations also contain a provision (§ 84.53) implementing section 407 of the Drug Abuse Office and Treatment Act of 1972, which prohibits hospitals or outpatient facilities from denying general medical, emergency, or treatment services to drug abusers or alcoholics.

In some states which have already established regulations or programs for the protection of patients' rights, and where the state drug abuse treatment programs are administered by the public health or mental health agencies (Georgia, Minnesota, South Carolina, Wisconsin), drug abusers, as patients of the state programs, are covered by the protections (National Institute on Mental Health, 1978).

In Michigan, the Office of Substance Abuse Services within the Department of Public Health has been mandated by state law to promulgate "recipient rights rules" by October 1979 (Michigan Public Health Code section 6231). That office is currently considering various models for the implementation of the rules.

Program Procedures

Certain practices have been developed within some programs to involve clients in clinic policy-making and to establish procedures for involuntary termination.

The New York City Methadone Maintenance Treatment Program developed procedures for patient termination in 1974. Grounds for termination were established along with procedures for notification and appeal. After initial staff apprehension, the system was accepted by patients and staff as not too burdensome, fair, and in fact, an improvement in clinic management (Stone and Karten, 1978).

A similar system was instituted by Boston City Hospital which stipulated that termination would be justified if a client's behavior threatened the continued operation of the clinic or if it were destructive to patients' treatment. The termination procedures provided for written notification, hearings, and representation by counsel (Patch and Raynes, 1975). Boston City Hospital also has client councils, elected by clients to serve as ombudsmen within the clinics. They attend weekly staff meetings, disciplinary hearings, and hiring interviews. They comment on program policies (Renner, 1979).

These systems reflect the programs' commitment to formal client participation in clinic procedures and recognition that clients have rights which the programs are obliged to respect and protect.

Services

Services which relate directly to the ability of clients to exercise their rights in the community include the legal assistance of the Legal Action Center and the travel assistance to methadone clients provided through TRIPS ("Treatment, Referral, Information and Placement Services").

The Legal Action Center is a public interest law firm, supported in part by NIDA, based in New York City, focusing on legal services and law reform litigation to expand the rights of former drug abusers. It provides free legal advice to drug abusers and treatment programs on the rights of drug abusers and provides assistance to selected clients in court and administrative proceedings. Its efforts are concentrated on test cases which have the potential for widespread impact on addicts' rights. Though with its limited resources it cannot provide individualized legal services to clients on a large scale, it does provide assistance to other attorneys whose clients may benefit from its expertise.

Over the last six years the Legal Action Center has handled cases involving discrimination against former drug abusers in its efforts to secure professional licenses, employment, custody of children, and access to services. Through litigation it forced the United States Postal Service to revise its eligibility criteria to allow for the employment of former drug abusers. It also handled the now famous case *Beazer v. New York City Transit Authority* in which the exclusion from employment of individuals on methadone maintenance was challenged. (This case and others are discussed in detail in the following chapter, "Discrimination Against the Former Addict: 'Legal' Prescriptions.")

TRIPS was established in 1975 by the Special Action Office for Drug Abuse Prevention to identify programs which would be willing to provide methadone to methadone maintenance clients on travel in different cities. The TRIPS office acts as a broker between the client's regular program and the participating program in the city the client will visit, making arrangements, for example, for the correct methadone dosage to be made available to the client on a regular basis for the duration of his or her visit. In a five-month period in 1978, TRIPS provided placement services to over 1,700 clients. In addition to the travel service, TRIPS, now funded by NIDA, issues a newsletter, *TRIPS Travels,* with information on issues of importance to methadone clients and programs such as the status of the methadone regulations, congressional hearings, legislation, and new programs. It also acts as a hotline and clearinghouse on methadone issues.

ADDICTS' RIGHTS GROUPS

The Committee of Concerned Methadone Patients and Friends

The Committee of Concerned Methadone Patients and Friends, Inc. (CCMP) was established as a nonprofit tax-exempt group in 1974 in New York City with plans to build an organization that could lobby on issues of importance to methadone patients both within the drug abuse treatment system and in the community. It had a twelve-member board of directors and four executive officers. The CCMP set as long-term goals the promotion of a patients' Bill of Rights, the establishment of a political base that would allow it to support, in local elections, candidates sympathetic to the needs of methadone patients, and the placement of CCMP patient and staff representatives in every methadone clinic in the city.

By 1976 the members reported, as some of their major accomplishments, that they had organized a voter registration drive among methadone patients, provided consultation to federal, state, and local health and drug abuse organizations on the needs and demands of methadone patients, persuaded a New York City library not to purchase an educational film which presented a distorted view of methadone maintenance, and that they had been influential in resolving to the satisfaction of the patients a controversy over methadone dosage formulation (Oracca, 1979).

Since then CCMP has acquired a membership of 700, established annual dues of $15.00, and has created the following six subcommittees to focus on specific issues: political action, peer support, women's issues, legal action, fund raising, and public relations. A core group of approximately 200 patients are active in the committee. A general meeting with an average attendance of 80 is held monthly in a borrowed classroom or rented church. At the general meetings presentations are occasionally made by invited speakers such as the Director of NIDA, current issues of significance to methadone patients are reported on, and the membership is invited to suggest issues which should be researched, such as certain treatment program practices or employment problems. The issues needing further research are referred to the appropriate subcommittee and are reported on at a later general meeting. Executive meetings are also held once a month to consider the issues raised in the general meeting, to plan later meetings, to plan fund-raising strategies, and other general business. In addition, CCMP presented a workshop on clients' rights at a recent New York drug abuse conference.

Without any full-time paid staff, however, the committee finds itself unable to concentrate on many broad issues requiring long-term planning and continuous work. Instead, it is constantly pulled into crisis situations involving clients' disputes with their treatment programs over termination procedures, dosage levels, etc. In such cases, members of the organization provide support to the methadone patient by interceding on his or her behalf with the clinic administrators or borrowing attorneys from public interest groups when legal assistance is necessary.

Recently a decision was made by CCMP to form a new patients' rights organization with a membership expanded to include patients and administrators from drug-free clinics including Daytop, Reality House, and Project Return. This was prompted by the recognition that although there remain deep-seated philosophical differences between the drug-free and methadone communities, they share many of the same patients' rights issues. With an expanded membership and larger resources they hope to be able to address in greater depth long-term issues, such as those involving national drug abuse policies and government regulations. The new organization is still in the planning phase and has yet to be incorporated, to be named, to appoint officers, and to establish a specific charter. It is expected to be formally established in spring 1979. Both the original CCMP and the new organization include program administrators and staff as members. The members feel that the concerns of the patients will be best served with a broad representation of interests in the organization itself (Oracca, 1979).

Addicts' Rights Organization (ARO)

In 1970, at the instigation of a social work student working at the Philadelphia Community Legal Services, the Addicts' Rights Organization (ARO) was created with a membership of ex-addicts and clients in treatment. Over four years, a core membership of three-five committed individuals kept the organization alive.

During that time two major accomplishments were reported. The first involved the treatment of addicts in area hospitals. Hospitals were reporting overdose cases to the police. A few agreed to end that practice, but refused to publicize the agreement for fear of being inundated with addicts. ARO called for a meeting with area hospital representatives and invited the press, which prompted 15 hospitals to agree publicly not to report overdoses to the police and to provide regular medical and detoxification services to addicts. The second issue involved the treatment of prisoners. ARO filed a successful law suit on behalf of addicted prisoners which established their right to methadone detoxification services (Wenk, 1975).

Considerations in Establishing
Addicts' Rights Initiatives

Ideally, the drug abuser is not the client of a single program, but is rather a consumer of services from a number of community agencies. Thus a broad consumer's rights approach, instead of a narrow patient's or client's rights focus, is needed to be most responsive to the concerns of drug abusers. A coordinated strategy is called for with contributions from addicts' rights groups, drug treatment programs, concerned citizens, the legal community, the states, and NIDA.

Addicts' Rights Groups

The perspective of the consumer, the drug abuser, should be kept central when developing addicts' rights strategies. Addicts' rights groups can identify the issues that are of most concern to their membership, including those pertaining to treatment and those involving the community. The groups can be composed of clients from one treatment program or of clients and former clients from a number of programs in the community. They can include friends, concerned citizens, program staff, and attorneys.

To encourage the creation of groups and to help sustain them, treatment programs could establish client councils, as was done in Boston, to formalize the role of clients in the policy-making and procedures of the clinics. Initially such groups would probably focus primarily on treatment program issues, but as they evolved and became accepted by staff and clients, they could focus more largely on community issues. As they became more active in the community, the members could serve as excellent examples of capable individuals, thereby helping to dispel the myths and stigma that plague former drug abusers.

Treatment Programs

The treatment programs' commitment to addicts' rights could be demonstrated through the development of a Bill of Rights for clients which would establish the rights of clients in treatment, the obligations of the program and staff, and procedures for implementing the provisions. Included should be a clear explanation of the programs' responsibility for securing access to community services and benefits. Some programs have well-developed formal arrangements with other community agencies for providing educational, vocational, or legal services to their clients. Others do not, either because they handle such issues on a case by case basis or because they view such services as ancillary and beyond the central responsibility of the program. Some may establish linkages with essential community agencies, but to insure that the clients actually secure the services in a timely fashion, and that they continue to receive them once they have left treatment, goes beyond the scope of what many programs can provide. With rapidly growing costs and shrinking resources it is unrealistic to expect treatment programs to invest extensively in providing access to those services they regard as ancillary.

This is where volunteers, acting as citizen community advocates on behalf of clients and former clients, could be invaluable in cutting through the red tape of bureaucracies to help drug abusers secure the services and benefits to which they are entitled. The advocates could either operate on behalf of individual clients or on behalf of the class of drug abusers as a whole. They could be sponsored and trained by the drug treatment program, by the addicts' rights groups or by an outside communitywide agency. Their work should be coordinated within the community so as to avoid duplication of effort and unnecessarily antagonizing the community agencies. Treatment programs or city coordinating agencies could also create an ombudsman and invest in that individual the authority to negotiate within the treatment community on behalf of clients and to bring to the administrators for resolution all issues that could not satisfactorily be negotiated between staff and clients.

Legal Services

For a rights initiative to be taken seriously, there has to be a legal component. Unfortunately, without the threat of litigation, some agencies will continue to deny appropriate services and benefits to drug abusers. Some treatment programs do make legal services available to their clients for assistance in handling pending criminal and civil matters which adversely affect the clients' ability to participate in treatment. However, in many instances the lawyers providing such assistance are also the attorneys for the program. This situation presents the potential for conflict of interest. For example, in a situation where a client has a disagreement with the clinic over procedures or with other community agencies which the clinic does not wish to challenge, drug abusers need to have available independent legal assistance to represent their interests. In most communities there exist local legal aid programs or offices of the Legal Services Corporation responsible for providing assistance to the poor. Often, however, they are not familiar with the complicated issues involving discrimination against drug abusers, and they are hesitant to handle such cases. Training in such issues could be provided to legal aid attorneys by NIDA, the states, or the Legal Action Center, and the center could serve as an ongoing technical assistance resource.

As the application of the Section 504 regulations to the protection of the rights of drug abusers are interpreted by courts across the country, and as other legal developments occur, it will be important to have a clearinghouse that local attorneys can turn to for the latest information. The Legal Action Center could serve as such a clearinghouse.

In addition to the need for legal advocates at the local level, there will continue to be a need at the national level for the review of state and federal laws and regulations to insure that the rights of drug abusers are being respected. Major class action cases, such as *Beazer,* will need to be brought to correct violations and establish rights. Since such cases can take years to be resolved, a commitment will have to be made on the part of the drug abuse community to provide the necessary resources to sustain attorneys or groups such as the Legal Action Center for the duration of such cases.

Drug Abuse Single State Agencies

The single State agencies can do much to promote addicts' rights. They can help to foster the creation of clients' or addicts' rights groups; they can require, through their licensing authority, that treatment programs establish a Bill of Rights with appropriate implementation provisions; they can sponsor community/client advocates to help drug abusers secure community services; they can serve as a clearinghouse on information pertaining to the legal rights of drug abusers as consumers, clients, patients, and citizens within their states; they can encourage the development of legislation establishing the rights of drug abusers; they can serve as watchdogs to insure that the needs of drug abusers are addressed by other state agencies, such as those providing vocational, employment, or housing services; they can use, to the fullest extent possible, the existing state programs for protecting the rights of individuals, such as those in Michigan and New Jersey; they can create an ombudsman office to review the status and resolve problems of drug abusers within the state networks of treatment and other community agencies; and they can provide training to treatment program staff, community advocates, and other agency staff on the rights of drug abusers.

National Institute on Drub Abuse (NIDA)

On a national scale NIDA could address all of the issues suggested for the single state agencies. In addition, it could provide legitimacy to a "movement" on addicts' rights through formal recognition of the existing clients' rights groups and the solicitation of their comments on policies, procedures, and regulations; through the encouragement of the creation of more such groups; and through the consideration of addicts' rights issues in program guidelines, regulations, and state plans. NIDA could provide education to the public and formal training to the states, programs, and community agencies on addicts' rights issues. Finally, NIDA could develop and share new knowledge on the subject through the sponsorship of research and demonstration studies (Scallet, 1978).

In summary, no matter how many laws exist to prohibit discrimination and establish rights, former drug abusers will continue to be denied access to community services and benefits essential to their long-term rehabilitation unless coordinated advocacy initiatives to protect and promote their rights are developed at the local and national levels. In some areas the tools are already in place and simply need to be applied more aggressively on behalf of drug abusers. In others, models from other fields are available to be adapted to meet the needs of the drug abuse community.

NOTE

1. "Handicapped person" is defined as "any person who (i) has a physical or mental impairment which substantially limits one or more major life activities, (ii) has a record of such an impairment, or (iii) is regarded as having such an impairment" (45 CFR 84).

REFERENCES

ALLEN, P. A. (1974) "Consumers' View of California's mental health care system." Psychiatric Quarterly 48: 1-13.
ARNOFF, F. (1975) "Social consequences of policy toward mental illness." Science 188: 1277-1281.

AVIRAM, U. and SEGAL, S. P. (1973) "Exclusion of the mentally ill: reflection on an old problem in a new context." Archives of General Psychiatry 29: 126-131.

Beazer v. New York City Transit Authority, 299 F. Supp. 1032 (S.D.N.Y. 1975) affirmed 558 F. 2d. 97 (2d Cir. 1977).

BIRNBAUM, M. (1960) "The right to treatment." American Bar Association Journal 46: 499.

CHAMBERLIN, J. (1979) Chairperson, National Committee on Patients' Rights. Personal communication, April.

Civil Liberties Union of Massachusetts (1975) "Clients' rights in drug treatment program regulations." Draft prepared for Massachusetts Division of Drug Rehabilitation, December.

Confidentiality of Alcohol and Drug Abuse Patient Records, 42 CFR 2.

COYE, J. L. (1977) "Michigan's system for protecting patients' rights." Hospital and Community Psychiatry 28 (May).

Federal Funding Criteria, Drug Treatment Services and Central Intake Units, 21 CFR 1402.

Joint Commission on Accreditation of Hospitals, Accreditation Council for Psychiatric Facilities (1975) Standards for Drug Abuse Treatment and Rehabilitation Programs. Chicago.

KIRK, S. A. and THERRIEN, M. (1975) "For their own benefit: mental health myths regarding community treatment." Presented at the 102nd Annual Forum of the National Conference on Social Welfare, San Francisco, May 12.

KOPOLOW, L. C. (1979) Chief, Patients' Rights and Advocacy Program, Financing Branch, Division of Mental Health Service Programs, Mental Health Care and Service, National Institute of Mental Health. Personal communication, April.

Lessard v. Schmidt, 349 F. Supp. 1078 (E.D. Wis., 1972).

Narcotic Treatment Program Standards and Methadone in Maintenance and Detoxification, Notice of Intent and Proposed Rule (1977) Federal Register 24, 208.

National Institute on Drug Abuse, Division of Scientific and Programmatic Information (1979) CODAP (Client Oriented Data Acquisition Process). Unpublished tabulation.

National Institute on Mental Health (1978) Symposium on Safeguarding the Rights of Recipients of Mental Health Services, October 1977. Washington, DC: U.S. Government Printing Office.

O'Connor v. Donaldson, 95 S. Ct. 2486 (1975).

ORACCA, J. (1979) Committee of Concerned Methadone Patients and Friends. Personal communication, April.

———, CATTES, D., and PATTERSON, D. (1978) "Our history and future," in Critical Concerns in the Field of Drug Abuse. New York: Committee of Concerned Methadone Patients and Friends.

PATCH, V. and RAYNES, A. (1975) "Patients' rights and involuntary termination of methadone maintenance treatment," in E. Senay, V. Shorty, and H. Alksne (eds.) Developments in the Field of Drug Abuse: Proceedings of the National Association for the Prevention of Addiction to Narcotis, 1974. Cambridge, MA: Schenkman.

President's Commission on Mental Health (1978) Report to the President from the President's Commission on Mental Health, Vol. 1. Washington, DC: U.S. Government Printing Office.

RENNER, J. (1979) Program Director, City of Boston Drug Treatment Program, Boston City Hospital. Personal communication, April.

SADOFF, R. L. and KOPOLOW, L. E. (1977) "The mental health professional's role in patient advocacy," in Mental Health Advocacy: An Emerging Force in Consumers' Rights. Washington, DC: HEW, National Institute of Mental Health (HEW Publication ADM 77-455).

SCALLETT, L. (1978) "Advocacy is a loaded word," in Symposium on Safeguarding the Rights of Recipients of Mental Health Services, October 1977 (HEW, Public Health Service). Washington, DC: U.S. Government Printing Office.

Souder v. Brennan, 367 F. Supp. 808 (DD.C. 1973).

State ex rel Hawks v. Lazaro, 202 S. E. 2d. 109 (W. Va. Supp. Ct. App. 1974).

STONE, A. A. (1975) Mental Health and Law: A System in Transition. Washington, DC: HEW, National Institute of Mental Health, Center for Studies of Crime and Delinquency (HEW Publication ADM 75-176).

STONE, B. and KARTEN, S. (1978) "Appeal board hearings for patient in terminations from treatment in methadone maintenance clinics," in A. Schechter, H. Alksne, and E. Kaufman (eds.) Drug Abuse: Modern Trends, Issues and Perspectives (Proceedings of the Second National Drug Abuse Conference, New Orleans). New York.

TURNER, J. C. and TenHOOR, W. J. (1978) "The NIMH Community Support Program: pilot approach to a needed social reform." Schizophrenia Bulletin 4, 3.

VAN NESS, S. C. and PERLIN, M. L. (1977) "Mental health advocacy: the New Jersey experience," in Mental Health Advocacy: An Emerging Force in Consumers' Rights. Washington, DC: HEW, National Institute of Mental Health (HEW Publication ADM 77-455).

Welsch v. Likens, 373 F. Supp. 487 (D. Minn. 1974).

WENK, J. R. (1975) "Addicts in the consumer movement: Philadelphia's Addicts' Rights Organization," in E. Senay, V. Shorty, and H. Alksne (eds.) Developments in the Field of Drug Abuse: Proceedings of the National Association for the Prevention of Addiction to Narcotics, 1974. Cambridge, MA: Schenkman.

WILSON, J. P., BEYER, H. A., and YUDOWITZ, B. (1977) "Advocacy for the mentally disabled," in Mental Health Advocacy: An Emerging Force in Consumers' Rights. Washington, DC: HEW, National Institute of Mental Health (HEW Publication ADM 77-455).

Wyatt v. Stickney, 325 F. Supp. 781 (M.D. Ala. 1971), 344 F. Supp. 1341 (M.D. Ala. 1971), 344 F. Supp. 373, 387 (M.D. Ala. 1972).

11

DISCRIMINATION AGAINST THE FORMER ADDICT
"Legal" Prescriptions

THE LEGAL ACTION CENTER

INTRODUCTION

As everyone involved or interested in treatment of drug addiction recognizes, treatment of the physical and psychological dependence on the addictive drug is only part of the effort the addict must undertake to begin his or her successful reintegration into society. The former addict often faces barriers in obtaining housing, employment, the licensure or bonding required to pursue certain occupations, insurance, financial credit, and assistance from social benefit programs. These barriers are caused by discrimination practiced by both governmental and private agencies, programs, and employers.[1]

Quite often, those who try to assist the former addict obtain employment or benefits and services become frustrated because they feel they have only the tool of persuasion to use in surmounting the barriers of discrimination. While just a few years ago persuasion was the only way to

AUTHOR'S NOTE: The Legal Action Center is a public interest law firm in New York with a commitment to eliminating artificial barriers to resocialization faced by persons with histories of substance abuse.

convince a reluctant agency, program, or employer to accept a former addict, recent legal developments provide rehabilitation professionals with new tools to overcome discrimination against the former addict.

This chapter is designed to inform professionals in the drug rehabilitation field—be they planners or practitioners—of these new legal developments. It is not to be expected that after reading this chapter nonlawyers will be able to dispense completely with the need to seek professional legal advice.[2] However, quite often uninformed nonlawyers are not equipped to recognize "legal" issues and problems which confront them. Information about new developments in the law will assist drug rehabilitation professionals—planners and practitioners—in recognizing problems with which the law has begun to deal so that they can provide their clients with access to the new legal tools to overcome discrimination.

LEGAL ISSUES AND ANTIDISCRIMINATION EFFORTS

The primary advances in the law prohibiting discrimination against former addicts have been in the area of employment. Development in the area of employment law has occurred for two reasons. First, a body of law has developed in recent years prohibiting irrational employment discrimination against other groups—such as minorities and women—which could, by analogy, be used to argue that discrimination against former addicts was also irrational and illegal. Second, rehabilitation experts and interested lawyers believed that the barriers faced by the former addict seeking employment were key to the struggle to reintegrate him or her more completely into the social fabric.

Clearly, advances in the area of employment discrimination are important, for the employment barrier is the major problem faced by most former addicts. A voluntary association of businessmen committed to rehabilitation efforts recently reported that for every five companies in which it attempts to place a recovered drug addict, it is able to open up only one job.[3] Close to 70% of former opiate abusers are unemployed at the conclusion of their treatment.[4] Since there are not sufficient numbers of lawyers available to assist former addicts in challenging the discrimination they meet in seeking employment, it is vitally important for the nonlawyer rehabilitation professional to become aware of the arguments available to former addicts and the contexts in which they can be used. And while the "law" affecting discrimination against former addicts in other areas is not as well developed, the treatment professional should be aware of the areas in which lawyers are beginning to push for new rulings and the arguments they are utilizing.

What follows is a description for the nonlawyer rehabilitation professional of the issues and concepts involved in recent developments in the law prohibiting discrimination against the former addict. Section A sets forth the current state of the law concerning employment discrimination against the former addict. Section B goes on to describe legal issues and concepts in other areas of discrimination against the former addict. Because a high proportion of ex-addicts are also ex-offenders, Section C outlines the law relating to discrimination on the basis of criminal history.

A. Employment Discrimination and the Former Addict

Lawyers have used several legal concepts to argue that employment discrimination against former addicts is illegal. The first of these is based upon the United States Constitution. The rest are based upon statutes passed by the Congress, regulations issued by federal agencies, and, in some cases, laws passed by the states.

The Constitution: Equal Protection and Due Process. The Fourteenth Amendment requires each state to provide its citizens the equal protection of the laws, and it forbids each from taking its citizens' life, liberty, or property without due process of law. These expansively worded guarantees have had their primary applications in condemning racial discrimination and providing certain uniform minimum protections to persons accused of crimes in the society.

A person's equal protection and due process rights are not limited to these contexts, however. The draftsmen framed these constitutional guarantees in open-ended language in order to protect the citizenry against governmental overreaching in any sphere. In these broad principles lay the possibility of protecting former addicts against discrimination by government employers.[5]

The Equal Protection Clause places a limit on the kinds of classifications a government can make in writing laws or regulations and setting policies. Where special considerations, such as race discrimination, are not involved, the fundamental requirement of equal protection is that every classification must bear a "rational relationship" to some "legitimate governmental interest." That is, if government is going to treat one group of persons differently from another, the classification must serve some government policy in a reasonable way. Moreover, that government policy must be one in which government has a legitimate concern, such as the health or safety of the citizenry.

Along these same lines, courts have long interpreted the Due Process Clause to mean that government cannot treat its subjects "arbitrarily" or "irrationally." This principle too requires government at a minimum to provide some reasonable explanation for the actions it takes.

Out of these broad doctrines of constitutional law arose the specific question: Does a government policy of flatly refusing to hire former addicts rationally serve any legitimate governmental interest?

There is as yet no clear answer. The Supreme Court of the United States, reversing two lower courts, recently held, in *New York City Transit Authority v. Beazer,*[6] that a blanket policy of excluding *current* methadone patients from a group of jobs a substantial number of which are hazardous may be unwise, but is not so irrational as to be unconstitutional. The basis of the Court's decision was that since a substantial number of methadone patients do not succeed in treatment, a policy of individualized consideration would be less certain and more costly than a policy of total exclusion. A majority of the Court (five justices) did not consider whether it would be legal to exclude former methadone patients, or persons who had completed or were currently in drug-free treatment, but did indicate that an exclusion of such persons "would be harder to justify."[7] Three other justices thought that such a policy would be unconstitutional, and one justice expressed no opinion on this point. It is not clear from the *Beazer* opinion whether it would be unconstitutional to exclude methadone patients from a group of jobs none of which were safety-sensitive.

Although there is no clear mandate from the Supreme Court, other courts throughout the country have begun to condemn irrational discrimination against former drug abusers. In one case a federal court of appeals ruled that the federal government could not legally dismiss a product inspector at an army arsenal merely on the basis of his conviction for off-duty possession of amphetamines, barbiturates, and marijuana.[8] The court found the dismissal arbitrary because the employer had shown no reasonable connection between the employee's conduct and impairment of the efficiency of the government agency's operations. A federal district court in Florida ordered a state civil service board to hire a qualified applicant for a clerk's position who had been refused a position because of a single incident of marijuana use in the six months prior to her application. The court found a constitutional violation because there was no rational connection between the marijuana use and the applicant's fitness to perform the duties of a clerk.[9] Similarly, a New York State court ordered the reinstatement with back pay of a typist for the New York City Transit Authority who had been dismissed because a lab report resulting from a voluntary physical examination had concluded that methadone had been present in her urine. The woman had performed her clerical duties at the Transit Authority satisfactorily for two years. The state court concluded that the dismissal had been unconstitutional, and it ordered her reinstated with back pay.[10]

Because it is often difficult to prove that there is no rational relationship between an employer's policies and its legitimate interests in safety and efficiency, and because the equal protection clause applies only to public employers, other tools with which to protect the employment rights of former drug abusers merit attention.

The Rehabilitation Act of 1973. The Rehabilitation Act of 1973, as amended in 1978,[11] holds great potential as a weapon with which to fight discrimination against the former drug abuser in a variety of contexts, including, but not limited to, employment.[12] The act prohibits discrimination against "handicapped persons" and applies to private employers who contract with the federal government, all enterprises and institutions that receive federal financial assistance, and the federal government itself.[13] Federal revenue-sharing legislation[14] also applies the ban on discrimination against handicapped persons to all local and state governments that receive revenue-sharing funds.[15] The 1978 amendments to the act make clear that "handicapped persons" protected against discrimination include drug addicts and alcoholics.[16] Accordingly, the Rehabilitation Act and the revenue-sharing legislation appear to provide an important alternative for future challenges to discrimination against former addicts in the wide range of employment and government benefits controlled by enterprises and agencies subject to the legislation. Indeed, one lower federal court has relied on the Rehabilitation Act to condemn Philadelphia's refusal to hire any former addict for any city job. The court ruled that former addicts, including current methadone patients, were entitled to individualized determination of their qualifications.[17]

The Rehabilitation Act offers much that the Constitution cannot. First, while it does not apply to all private employers, it does apply to the huge share of the private sector connected to the federal government through contracts or financial assistance. Second, the act provides a more affirma-

tive, specific command than the "rational relationship" test, requiring that
an employer against whom a claim of discrimination is lodged show that
the claimant's current use of alcohol or drugs prevents that individual from
performing the duties of the job in question or constitutes a direct threat
to the property or safety of others.[18] The act applies to presently handicapped persons, formerly handicapped persons, and persons who are
regarded as handicapped.[19] Thus the act will protect present addicts,
former addicts, and persons thought by an employer to be presently or
formerly addicted, so long as they are otherwise qualified for employment.

The act prohibits discrimination in all terms and aspects of employment. Moreover, the legislation and the related regulations which have
been issued by various federal departments require an employer to make
reasonable accommodations to an individual's handicap. These affirmative
commands go further than the Equal Protection and Due Process Clauses.
The regulations implementing the act make very clear that all employment
criteria that would tend to screen out handicapped persons must be shown
to be job-related if they are to be maintained. These specific commands
and the clear congressional intent to protect handicapped individuals,
including former addicts, from employment discrimination should prove
more persuasive to courts than the bare "rational relationship" constitutional test. While the Supreme Court has stated, in *Beazer* and elsewhere,
that substantial deference to the government as employer is due when its
policies are challenged under the "rational relationship" test, no such
deference is due when a court is asked to implement Congress's affirmative
command to eliminate discrimination on the basis of handicap in the
Rehabilitation Act.[20]

The Civil Rights Act of 1964. There is another legal theory which may,
in certain circumstances, be used to challenge flat refusals to hire former
addicts by both public and private employers. This theory rests on the fact
that the population of addicts and former addicts contains substantially
greater percentages of black and Hispanic persons than does the population at large. For example, of those admitted in 1977 to federally funded
drug treatment programs in New York for heroin abuse, 85% were black or
Hispanic and 14.3% were white, so the disparity from the general population is quite substantial.[21]

Title VII of the Civil Rights Act of 1964 prohibits racial discrimination
in any form by employers, both public and private. The federal courts
have interpreted that statute to condemn more than intentional race
discrimination. Under the decision of the United States Supreme Court in

Griggs v. Duke Power Co.,[22] an employer is guilty of illegal discrimination if it adopts an eligibility criterion which, however neutral it may appear, operates in fact to exclude racial minorities from employment at a rate that is disproportionate to the percentage of minority group members in the general population from which the employer's work force is drawn.

An example may help explain the theory. In *Griggs* the employer required all employees to have a high school diploma, a requirement that on its face has nothing to do with race. If high school diplomas were dispersed evenly throughout the population, one would expect the racial makeup of the group that could not meet the employer's requirement to be the same as the population at large, say, 80% white, 15% black, 5% Hispanic. However, because of the historic denial of equal educational opportunities to racial minorities in the United States, high school diplomas are not dispersed evenly. Many fewer black and Hispanic persons possess them than they would under an even distribution. As a result, a high school diploma requirement will result in the denial of employment to a disproportionate number of minority group members.

This "disproportionate impact" on racial minorities constitutes illegal racial discrimination under Title VII. Only if "business necessity" requires use of the particular employment criterion that is creating the disproportionate impact, will the employer be allowed to continue that use. Courts very rarely have found this "business necessity" test to have been met.

The question is thus posed for anyone who wishes to challenge an employer's flat refusal to hire former heroin addicts: could such a policy be shown to have an illegal "disproportionate impact" not justified by any "business necessity"? Again, the answer is not clear.

Title VII of the Civil Rights Act of 1964 and the "disproportionate impact" theory apply to both public and private employers. The theory was presented as an alternative ground for attacking the Transit Authority's exclusionary policy in *Beazer.* While a majority of the Justices of the Supreme Court found that the policy did not violate Title VII, it did so primarily because it was not satisfied that the statistics available in that case established that the policy had the required disparate impact on minority applicants. Three justices disagreed. In another case it might be possible to get racial/ethnic data about actual applicants rejected because of their addiction histories, or evidence that former addicts were deterred from applying because they knew of the employer's policy.

State Laws. Many states prohibit discrimination against "handicapped" or "disabled" persons in a variety of contexts. These statutes could be of use in challenging discrimination. Rarely, however, do such statutes cover addicts or former addicts explicitly, presenting a threshold issue which may require advocacy before the responsible administrative agency, if not before a court.

B. Discrimination Against Former Addicts in Areas Other than Employment

Unfortunately, employment is only one of many areas in which the former addict faces discrimination. Also unfortunately, the law in these other areas remains somewhat undeveloped. What follows is a brief foray into some of these other areas to outline what they are and the arguments being developed by lawyers to combat discrimination.

Insurance. The Center for Public Representation in Madison, Wisconsin has recently confirmed the existence of a pattern of which most rehabilitation professionals have long been aware: the widespread refusal by health and life insurers to write policies for persons with a history of drug abuse, particularly heroin addiction.[23] NIDA statistics show that 69% of persons admitted to treatment for opiate abuse have no health insurance coverage; 67% of persons admitted to treatment for all forms of drug abuse are similarly unprotected.[24]

Translating the theories used against employment discrimination to this context will require some hurdling, however. Where insurance is provided by the employer under a group plan, the Rehabilitation Act may prohibit discrimination in insuring those employees who have addiction histories. When an individual purchases insurance directly from the insurer, however, the Rehabilitation Act would not appear to apply. Moreover, the Constitution places no limitations on this wholly private contract. However, state laws frequently require the official in charge of regulating the insurance industry to approve an insurer's policies and their terms before they may be issued. The Constitution might require this state officer to withhold approval of any policies discriminating against former drug abusers. Moreover, relief may be available under the many state statutes that prohibit insurance companies from discriminating in premiums on the basis of classifications that cannot be actuarially justified. However, these possibilities have not yet been tested.

Housing. Discrimination in housing should be readily susceptible to attack under existing legal theories, at least in the public sector. Both the constitutional "rational relationship" test and the Rehabilitation Act apply to eligibility criteria for public housing projects. The rational relationship test may be a viable weapon for attacking policies excluding former addicts from these projects; the same questions left unanswered in the employment area by the *Beazer* decision remain unanswered here. In any case, the Rehabilitation Act will prohibit discrimination against former addicts in housing projects receiving federal funds.

Education. Discrimination in access to education in the form of refusal to admit a former drug addict to schools should be susceptible to various attacks, again depending upon whether the educational institution is state-run or private. Discrimination by state-run institutions may be vulnerable to a challenge under the constitutional "rational relationship" test; discrimination by institutions, public or private, which receive federal financial assistance should be vulnerable under the Rehabilitation Act.

Credit. Discrimination in access to credit is probably vulnerable to legal attack only to a limited extent. Institutions providing credit are usually privately run, do not receive governmental financial assistance, and are therefore not subject to the requirements of the Constitution or the Rehabilitation Act. However, some states have laws prohibiting discrimination in relation to credit on the basis of disability.[25] If "disability" is interpreted to include drug dependence, then addicts or former addicts would be protected by such laws. Moreover, there are laws and regulations which permit the credit-seeker to see his or her credit file and correct misinformation. This sometimes provides an avenue for a former drug abuser to obtain the credit he or she seeks.

Various Government Benefits. Both the constitutional "rational relationship" theory and the Rehabilitation Act protect the former addict from discrimination in the provision of various government services and benefits.[26] The scope of the Rehabilitation Act in this regard is quite wide for, as mentioned above, it applies to the large portion of the private sector connected to the federal government through contracts or grants of financial assistance. Through federal revenue-sharing legislation the prohibition of discrimination against "handicapped" persons—including former drug abusers—also extends to all local and state governments that receive revenue-sharing funds.

C. Discrimination Against Ex-Offenders

Employment opportunities for former drug abusers will not open up in a substantial fashion until efforts to root out irrational discrimination against persons with criminal records also make headway. This tandem results from the well-documented fact that so many former drug abusers also have arrest and/or conviction records. A recent report indicated that up to 60% of the people entering the municipal, county, and state criminal justice systems are drug abusers.[27]

In a series of decisions during the 1970s, the courts have ruled that an employer's flat refusal to hire ex-offenders, without regard to any specific connection between the nature of an individual's past offense and the nature of the position for which he or she is applying, is illegal. In condemning these exclusionary ex-offender policies, the courts have employed the same legal theories discussed above in connection with discrimination against former addicts. That is, courts have found that such exclusionary policies bear no rational relationship to the legitimate interests of a government employer and therefore violate the Equal Protection and Due Process Clauses of the Fourteenth Amendment. Similarly, the decisions have recognized that such policies have a "disproportionate impact" on racial minorities and, unjustified by "business necessity," therefore violate Title VII of the Civil Rights Act of 1964, whether those policies are maintained by public or private employers.

Illustrative of the constitutional rulings and most recent in this line of cases is *Smith v. Fuessenich*.[28] There the court held that a rule disqualifying all felony offenders from licensure as private detectives and security guards violated equal protection.

Smith illustrates another important aspect of the legal effort to open employment opportunities to ex-offenders and former drug abusers. *Smith* challenged the government in its capacity, not as employer, but as dispenser of occupational licenses. The frequently antiquarian and hypercautious policies and practices of occupational licensing agencies pose a large stumbling block to this effort, for the denial of a license often frustrates not only the applicant for licensure, but also a private employer who has assessed the applicant and, whether for reasons of social conscience or simply out of a desire to bring aboard a good employee, is ready and willing to hire the applicant if only he could obtain a license. Indeed, the President's Commission on Law Enforcement and Administration of Justice recognized a decade ago that many if not most disabilities and disqualifications in the area of the employment of ex-offenders result from the actions of various occupational licensing agencies, rather than directly from the conviction.[29]

Even more strongly than in the context of public employment eligibility criteria, it has long been recognized that equal protection and due process require that any qualification for an occupational license imposed by government "must have a rational connection with the applicant's fitness or capacity" to perform in the occupation.[30] Beginning with this legal standard, which was announced by the United States Supreme Court, the court in *Smith* had no difficulty in finding unconstitutional the exclusion of all felons from licensure for a particular line of work. The court recognized that state law gathers a broad range of conduct within the definition of felonious behavior, including conduct of no relevance to employment as a private security guard. Importantly for those concerned with the rehabilitation of ex-offenders, including the former drug abusers that fall within that class, the *Smith* court also found the blanket felon exclusionary rule unconstitutional because of its failure

> to consider probable and realistic circumstances in a felon's life, including the likelihood of rehabilitation, age at the time of conviction, and other mitigating circumstances related to the nature of the crime and degree of participation.[31]

While the lower federal courts have not viewed favorably all claims of employment discrimination against ex-offenders, *Smith* is one of several recent decisions in which the Equal Protection and Due Process Clauses condemn policies automatically denying licensure or public employment to all applicants for a particular license or job who had been convicted of a felony or of any criminal offense. A federal district judge in New York held invalid the refusal of the state civil service to consider an individual with three convictions for employment. A three-judge district court in Iowa similarly condemned a state rule disqualifying all felony offenders from civil service.[32] Exclusionary policies based on arrest records, where the applicant has never been convicted of a criminal offense, are also obviously invalid under these cases.

As in the area of discrimination against former drug abusers, the constitutional rulings striking exclusionary bans against ex-offenders do not affect private employers who are unwilling to hire ex-offenders. Again, the only avenue of relief against private personnel policies excluding ex-offenders without regard to individual qualifications has been the "disproportionate impact" theory of Title VII of the Civil Rights Act of 1964. The overrepresentation of racial minorities among the population that passes through the criminal justice system cannot be gainsaid. Given this fact, numerous federal courts at both the district and appeals level have held that a private employer cannot consider an applicant's arrest record at all and can only consider a conviction record insofar as it, along with all the other qualifications of the applicant, directly relates to the demands of the particular job sought.[33]

Unfortunately, no analogue to the Rehabilitation Act provides protection to the ex-offender. However, various states have enacted legislation protecting ex-offenders against discrimination. New York, for example, now prohibits private and public employers and licensing agencies from denying employment or licensure on the basis of an individual's criminal offenses unless

> (1) there is a direct relationship between one or more of the previous criminal offenses and the specific license or employment sought; or
> (2) the issuance of the license or the granting of the employment would involve an unreasonable risk to property or to the safety or welfare of specific individuals or the general public.[34]

The legislation lists several factors the employer or licensing agency must consider in making the above determination, including the circumstances of an individual's offenses and evidence of rehabilitation.

Finally, the Civil Service Reform Act of 1978 protects against employment discrimination by the federal government on the basis of a criminal record. That act prohibits the federal government from rejecting an applicant or disciplining an employee on the basis of conduct which does not adversely affect that individual's performance or the performance of others.[35] While the act permits the government to take into account a person's criminal convictions, the legislative history of the act makes it very clear that Congress intended the government's discretion to be strictly limited. Only criminal conduct that is related to the person's duties or job performance, or to the performance of others, may be taken into consideration.[36]

D. Covert Discrimination

Mention should be made at this point of a type of discrimination other than absolute exclusionary policies such as those involved in cases like *Beazer* and *Smith*. As legislatures and courts continue to declare blanket exlusionary policies barring employment of *all* ex-offenders, *all* felons, *all* former addicts or the like illegal, it can be expected, from the history of legal challenges against other forms of discrimination, that employers will adopt personnel policies that require individualized consideration of applicants but that these policies will not necessarily change the underlying reality of hiring practices.

Unfortunately, this "covert" type of discrimination is more difficult to combat. The courts have consistently stated that employers may consider a record of drug abuse or of criminal convictions insofar as they directly relate to the qualifications for the job in question. While undoubtedly sound as a theoretical matter, such statements create a practical loophole which, combined with the tendency toward superficial accommodation to changes in the law, could limit the actual change effected by the Rehabilitation Act or by decisions such as *Smith.*

This prospect will require vigilant attention to the process of defining precisely when and how a record of prior drug abuse or criminal conviction may legitimately be said to relate directly to the qualifications of a particular job. For example, will a conviction for possession of heroin be considered job-related when a rehabilitated ex-addict/ex-offender applies for employment in a school drug prevention program? This sort of question will require further attention if the gains registered against flat exclusionary bans are to be secured.

The command of the Equal Protection and Due Process Clauses that public employment criteria must be rationally related to the particular demands of the jobs sought provides some basis for expecting that the courts will keep the discretion permitted public employers in their "individualized consideration" of former drug abusers and ex-offenders within reasonably narrow bounds. However, it must be noted that the "rational relationship" test is a very flexible one, as the Supreme Court has recently emphasized, under which substantial deference is due to the governmental policies under challenge.

Similar concerns apply to the licensing area. In fact, occupational licensing agencies present a special problem of covert discrimination. While many licensing agencies in the past have maintained explicit policies precluding former drug abusers and ex-offenders from licensure, many others have achieved the same result through application of vague "good character" requirements. A determination of "good character" is so subjective as almost to be unreviewable. Moreover, agencies frequently deny licensure with little opportunity for the applicant to confront whatever evidence may have troubled the agency or to present evidence in his or her own behalf.

These specific problems in occupational licensing are fortunately subject to specific legal attack. The Supreme Court has long held that before an occupational licensing agency excludes someone from the practice of a profession, the Due Process Clause requires the agency to provide certain procedural protections, namely, notice and an opportunity to respond to

the charges. The former addict or ex-offender may insist on some opportunity to present evidence on his or her behalf before licensure is denied.
The Due Process Clause also forbids undue vagueness in statutes and
regulations. An applicant is entitled to know something more specific
about the requirements for licensure than that he must have "good
character."

THE ROLE OF THE NONLAWYER

Having concluded the description of the law relating to discrimination
against the former drug abuser, one may ask: What can the nonlawyer do
to help effectuate the law and advances in it? The answer is, many vitally
important things.

Legal Education of Drug Treatment Personnel

Rehabilitation professionals and treatment personnel are, with their
clients, closest to the problems of discrimination which can be challenged
in the courts. Their "legal" education must be attended to by planners and
program managers. Unless people on the "front lines" can identify problems which can be handled by "the law," most often those problems will
not be handled by the law.

For example, statutes such as those protecting ex-offenders against job
discrimination are not self-executing. Indeed, American legislatures have
historically responded to social problems by passing legislation declaring
them illegal. Such statutes are high sounding and by themselves cost
nothing, but without substantial effort by those whose interests are
protected by the legislation, they will achieve nothing. The same applies to
the Rehabilitation Act: Its important provisions will mean nothing unless
those who counsel and assist former addicts are informed about what they
mean for their client group. Thus, the first thing for treatment personnel
to do is to educate themselves and to spread the word about the various
legal tools for responding to various types of discrimination encountered
by former drug abusers.

Communication with Other Professional
Groups, Government and Private Agencies

Quite often advances are slowed because those with the power to bring
about changes lack the necessary knowledge. For example, lawyers who
might be interested in championing the cause of the former addict may be

unaware of some of the types of discrimination being suffered or the extent of certain types of discrimination. Often before lawyers can go into court to challenge discriminatory practices, they must be able to document the scope of the problem. This requires communication from drug treatment professionals who may have the necessary information readily available.

Sometimes discrimination is practiced through ignorance. Lack of knowledge about drug abuse and rehabilitation can mean employer reluctance to "take a chance." In addition, lack of knowledge about various legal provisions prohibiting discrimination against former drug abusers can mean continued discrimination. Treatment personnel should be equipped to "educate" and negotiate with individuals and agencies who have the power to hire or not to hire the former drug abuser seeking employment or to provide or not to provide him or her with benefits or services.

Similarly, it has long been suspected that discrimination against former addicts in the provision of insurance might be affected by an effort at "education" and negotiation by persons equipped with a knowledge of the effect a history of addiction has on a former abuser's health, life expectancy, and other insurable interests.

Finally, communication between program personnel and governmental agencies responsible for enforcement or oversight of laws prohibiting discrimination based on race or disability should prove useful in keeping bureaucrats in touch with the problems faced and advances made by former addicts.

Informational Access and Accuracy

One way to protect against covert discrimination against former drug abusers and ex-offenders is to restrict the information about drug abuse and criminal history to which an employer or licensing agency has access.

A host of state and federal laws restrict the release of juvenile offender convictions, youthful offender adjudications, arrests followed by certain dispositions deemed favorable to the accused, and similar records. In practice, however, employers regularly make unduly broad inquiries and these records are not so carefully guarded. Vigilance is needed to enforce the requirements of these statutes.

Similarly, federal statute and the regulations of the Department of Health, Education and Welfare require drug treatment programs to maintain the confidentiality of their patients' records.[37] Information can be released to prospective employers only with the consent of the person in treatment, and then only if the treatment program determines that the prospective employer will not use the information as a basis for discriminating against the former drug abuser. The same is true for inquiries from prospective insurers and other third persons. It should also be noted that the Rehabilitation Act contains restrictions on preemployment inquiries into handicaps, including addiction. By federal regulation, a recipient of federal financial assistance (as distinct from a government contractor) cannot make any inquiry about a person's handicaps or even conduct a physical until *after* the organization has determined that the person is otherwise suitable for hiring. Clearly one way those in the drug rehabilitation field can help former abusers is to keep program personnel fully informed of their obligation to protect the confidentiality of persons in drug treatment.

Another way to protect the former drug abuser or ex-offender from discrimination is to insure that the information that the employer has received is accurate. All too often the "record"—whether of treatment for drug abuse or of involvement with the criminal justice system—which reaches the prospective employer is frighteningly distorted. An example taken from a case now pending in federal court is illustrative of the problems created by the present lack of proper procedures to ensure the accuracy of criminal records.

The plaintiff in that suit is a young man who had, while a college student, worked temporarily in a post office. He stole some envelopes containing a small amount of cash and was arrested by postal inspectors. He pleaded guilty to embezzlement and was sentenced to imprisonment for one year, twelve days (six weekends) of which were to be served in jail, the remainder of the sentence being suspended so he could finish his education. He was also placed on probation for two years, but was discharged early from probation and, pursuant to the federal Youth Corrections Act, his conviction was set aside. He graduated from City College *magna cum laude* and Phi Beta Kappa and went to work for a bank as a clerk. In the first year, while still on temporary status, he received promotions to cost analyst and then to performance analyst. He was about to be given a permanent position when the bank, pursuant to a routine check, obtained his identification record from the FBI. The young man had informed the bank that he had a youth offender conviction which had been set aside, and bank personnel had told him that if this fact were confirmed by the FBI, his conviction would not bar him from employment. The FBI record, however, contained two entries, creating the impression that the young man had been convicted of two different crimes, and made no mention of the fact that he was sentenced as a youth offender or that his conviction had later been vacated. He was fired by the bank and was unable to obtain other employment for two years.

While the young man in the example was forced to seek help from a lawyer, quite often inaccuracies can be cleared up by treatment personnel or by the former drug abuser or ex-offender himself. Thus, for example, one can obtain a copy of the official court record indicating the charges filed against a person on a given date and the disposition of each charge. Most often such "disposition slips" as they are called are more accurate than the information contained in other sources to which the employer has access and can nip in the bud difficulties the job-seeker may face. Treatment personnel can also be of obvious assistance in clearing up any inaccuracies about a job applicant's history of drug abuse.

Enforcement of record-keeping requirements and insurance of the accuracy of information disseminated are important for limiting all types of discrimination against drug abusers. The harmful effects of unwarranted dissemination of information and dissemination of inaccurate information reaches beyond the area of employment to the areas of housing, education, credit, insurance, and access to various government benefits.

Communication with the Client Group

Program personnel can provide an important communication service to former drug abusers in two ways. First, they can educate them about their legal rights and how best to obtain them. Second, they can, through their daily contact with clients and with client organizations, maintain a flow of communication from the client group to other professional groups and government and private agencies.

CONCLUSION

In the past few years, important strides have been made in the law protecting the former addict. Much work remains to be done, however. Without constant vigilance on the part of the drug abuse treatment professional, without communication among professional groups concerned with reintegrating the former addict into society, without efforts to educate and negotiate with those who can deny the former drug abuser jobs and benefits, the barriers which presently stand in the path of the rehabilitated addict will remain and his or her "treatment" will be incomplete.

NOTES

1. Former addicts also often face discrimination because of their membership in other groups against whom discrimination is practiced. Thus, the former addict who is also black, Hispanic, female, or an ex-offender may suffer discrimination for multiple reasons.

2. For a helpful "how to" manual in the area of combating employment discrimination against the former addict, see *Employment Discrimination and How to Deal With It: A Manual for People Concerned with Helping Former Drug Abusers* by the Legal Action Center, published by the National Institute on Drug Abuse.

3. See *Addiction and Substance Abuse Report*, Vol. 9, No. 3 (March 1978): pp. 2-3.

4. National Institute on Drug Abuse, *Statistical Series: Quarterly Report, Provisional Data July-September 1977* 22 (1978) (CODAP data, 3d quarter 1977); National Institute on Drug Abuse, *Statistical Series: Quarterly Report April-June 1976* (CODAP data for all 1975 and first two quarters 1976).

5. The Constitutional guarantees of equal protection and due process place limits on what action governments can take vis-à-vis individuals; they do not place limits on the action individuals—or private businesses—may take against other individuals.

6. 47 U.S.L.W. 4291 (March 20, 1979).

7. Ibid. at 4292 n. 3.

8. *Young v. Hampton*, 568 F. 2d 1253 (7th Cir., 1977).

9. *Osterman v. Paulk*, 387 F. Supp. 669 (S.D. Fla. 1974).

10. *Matter of Spruils*, New York Law Journal, March 15, 1978 (App. Div.).

11. 29 United States Code § 791, 793, 794, as amended by the Rehabilitation, Comprehensive Services and Developmental Disabilities Amendments of 1978, P.L. 95-602.

12. For a discussion of the other contexts in which the Rehabilitation Act may be available to protect the former addict, see pp. 278-279 below.

13. The Drug Abuse Office and Treatment Act of 1972 also prohibits discrimination in federal employment based on drug history. It provides: "No person may be denied or deprived of Federal civilian employment [other than with national security agencies] or a Federal professional or other license or right solely on the ground of prior drug use." [21 United States Code § 1180(c) (1)].

14. 31 United States Code § 1242.

15. The revenue-sharing legislation does not merely prohibit discrimination, but provides the sanction of termination of funding to agencies found to be in violation.

16. Rehabilitation, Comprehensive Services and Developmental Disabilities Amendments of 1978, P.L. 95-602, Section 122(a) (6) (C), amending 29 United States Code § 7 (6).

17. *Davis v. Bucher*, 451 F. Supp. 791 (E.D. Pa. 1978).

18. See note 16.

19. Ibid.

20. It should be added that while the Rehabilitation Act makes clear that a handicapped individual has a right not to be discriminated against, it does not make clear whether the individual has a right to bring a lawsuit on his or her own behalf when he or she falls victim to illegal discrimination other than in federal employment

or whether enforcement of the Act is to be left entirely to the federal government. A majority of courts have found that, at least as against recipients of federal financial assistance, an individual victim of discrimination may bring a private lawsuit. There also exists a question whether the individual will have to exhaust administrative remedies within the agency that provides the federal financial assistance before he or she can proceed with his lawsuit. It is noteworthy that the revenue-sharing legislation explicitly provides for a private right of action and strictly limits the amount of time an individual must give the administrative agency before resorting to court. 31 United States Code § 1244.

21. National Institute on Drug Abuse, *State Statistics, 1977,* Statistical Series E, No. 8 (1978): Table 3, p. 203.

22. 401 U.S. 424 (1971).

23. Center for Public Interest Representation, *Availability of Health and Life Insurance for Persons with a History of Mental Illness, Alcoholism, Drug Abuse or Criminal Record* (November 1978).

24. National Institute on Drug Abuse, *Statistical Series: Quarterly Report, Provisional Data July-September 1977* 12 (1978) (CODAP data).

25. E.g., New York Executive Law § 296a.

26. The questions about the utility of the "rational relationship" theory raised by *Beazer* also apply here. See above.

27. *Drug Abuse Treatment and the Criminal Justice System: Three Reports* 4 (NIDA; 1977).

28. 440 F. Supp. 1077 (D. Conn. 1977) (three-judge court).

29. President's Commission on Law Enforcement and Administration of Justice, *Task Force Report: Corrections* 32, 91 (1967).

30. *Schware v. Board of Bar Examiners,* 353 U.S. 232, 239 (1957).

31. 440 F. Supp. at 1080.

32. *Carr v. Thompson,* 384 F. Supp. 544 (S.D.N.Y. 1974); *Butts v. Nichols,* 381 F. Supp. 573 (S.D. Iowa 1974).

33. See, e.g., *Green v. Missouri Pacific R.R.,* 523 F. 2d 1290, 1293-95 (8th Cir. 1975); *Gregory v. Litton Systems,* 316 F. Supp. 401, 403 (C.D. Cal. 1970), *aff'd,* 472 F. 2d 631 (9th Cir. 1972).

34. N.Y. Correction Law § 752.

35. 5 U.S.C. § 2302(b) (10).

36. H.R. Cong. Rep. No. 95-1717, 95th Cong., 2d Sess. 131 (1978), *reprinted* in [1978] U.S. Code Cong. & Ad. News 4594.

37. 42 C.F.R. Part 2.

ABOUT THE AUTHORS

REBECCA SAGER ASHERY received her doctorate degree in Social Work from Catholic University in 1976. She is a Public Health Advisor at the National Institute on Drug Abuse in Rockville, Maryland. Her background includes child welfare, manpower development, genetic counseling, and family therapy as well as drug abuse. She recently coauthored a chapter on aftercare issues for the nationally sponsored *Handbook on Drug Abuse.*

BARRY S. BROWN is the Chief of the Services Research Branch of the National Institute on Drug Abuse. His work in the field of aftercare with drug abusers dates back to his brief, but heady, success in establishing a Narcotics Anonymous Group in the U.S. Penitentiary in Terre Haute, Indiana. After an abortive effort to develop a self-help group in association with his work at the District of Columbia's Narcotics Treatment Administration, he has wisely restricted his efforts in this field to writing and research.

JAMES M. N. CH'IEN is a doctoral candidate at the Harvard School of Public Health, Department of Behavioral Science. His main research interest lies in the cross-cultural application of the self-help concept and the organization of mutual support networks to facilitate the integration of detoxified or treated drug addicts into the community as productive members. In 1967 he was instrumental in the founding of the Alumni Association of the Society for the Aid and Rehabilitation of Drug Abusers in Hong Kong. He was also the founding chairman of the Neighborhood Advice-Action Council which spearheaded grass-roots community development and neighborhood self-help in the city of Hong Kong. After serving as NAAC chairman for ten years, he is now its Vice President. During 1973-1975, he was the President of the Hong Kong Social Workers Association. He also served as consultant and advisor to the U.N. Fund for Drug Abuse Control, World Health Organization, Colombo Plan, and other international bodies.

STEPHEN E. GARDNER is currently with the National Institute on Drug Abuse, where he has been with both the Services Research Branch and the Prevention Branch in the Division of Resource Development. He has a doctorate in social work from Catholic University, a masters in Social Work from Marywood College, and a bachelors degree in Anthropology from the University of Pennsylvania. Dr. Gardner has previously written a manual for use of volunteers in corrections programs. Prior to coming to the National Institute on Drug Abuse, Dr. Gardner was a research consultant at the Institute for Urban Affairs, Howard University, and taught at Catholic University.

DEBORAH HASTINGS-BLACK is Chief of the Supportive Services and Evaluation Section of the Services Research Branch at the National Institute on Drug Abuse. Her career in drug abuse began with her work in the Congress for the House Select Committee on Crime, followed by the Special Action Office for Drug Abuse Prevention. Her recent writings include the coauthoring of a chapter on vocational rehabilitation strategies for drug abuse clients.

J. DAVID HAWKINS received his Ph.D. in Sociology from Northwestern University. He is currently Research Assistant Professor, School of Social Work, and Prevention Specialist, Center for Law and Justice, University of Washington. His research interests center on the ways in which formal social policies affect the abilities of informal interactional systems to socialize and constrain their members.

TOARU ISHIYAMA is presently Deputy Commissioner-Regional, Division of Mental Health, Ohio Department of Mental Health and Mental Retardation. He is also an Associate in Psychology, Case Western Reserve University, Cleveland, Ohio. He is a Fellow in the American Psychological Association with focused interest in the areas of psychopathology and community mental health.

DOUGLAS M. KERR received his doctorate in Psychology from the University of Michigan in May, 1978. His principal interests in the mental health and substance abuse fields are the utilization of paraprofessionals, primary prevention strategies, and program evaluation research. In addition to his involvement with the project described in the present volume, Dr. Kerr is a Lecturer in the Community Psychology Program of the University of Michigan, and is coauthoring a book on system diagnostic and intervention techniques to deal with practical/political obstacles in the implementation of program evaluations.

MICHAEL J. MINOR received his Ph.D. from the University of Chicago in December 1977. He currently teaches at the Wright Institute and is a Research Psychologist at the Pacific Institute for Research and Evaluation. In addition to working as Research Director on the California Connection aftercare project, he is also Director of an evaluation study examining the effectiveness of the California Women's Commission on Alcoholism's primary prevention program on fetal alcohol syndrome. His major areas of interest are the social psychology of health, survey research methodology, and the experimental evaluation of social programs.

STEPHEN M. PITTEL is currently Director of the California Connection—a demonstration research project on addict aftercare funded by the National Institute on Drug Abuse through Pacific Institute for Research and Evaluation. He is also a Professor of Psychology at the Wright Institute and Director of the Berkeley Center for Drug Studies. After receiving his doctorate at the University of California at Berkeley in 1964 he taught at the University of Wisconsin for three years. He has also been on the faculty of the University of California and at San Francisco State University. Beginning with a five-year longitudinal study of psychedelic drug users, he has worked primarily in the field of substance abuse for the past twelve years. Since 1972 his work has focused on the reentry problems of addicts, alcoholics and other disadvantaged groups, and on the delivery of aftercare services.

M. DUNCAN STANTON, Ph.D. is Director of the Addicts and Families Program, and a senior staff psychologist at the Philadelphia Child Guidance Clinic. He is also Associate Professor of Psychology in Psychiatry at the University of Pennsylvania School of Medicine. His clinical and research experience in drug abuse dates from 1969 when he was a psychologist in Vietnam. Since 1971 he has performed family treatment with drug abusers, beginning research in this area in 1972. He is a consultant to the White House Office of Drug Abuse Policy and the National Institute on Drug Abuse. A Diplomate in Clinical Psychology of the American Board of Professional Psychology, he has fifteen years of clinical experience, ten years of which have involved family and marital treatment. Since receiving his doctorate from the University of Maryland he has published over fifty scientific and professional papers and chapters, including a book (in press) on the family treatment of drug addiction.

EILEEN WOLKSTEIN has a Ph.D. in Vocational Rehabilitation and has
been working in the field of rehabilitation for fifteen years. She has been a
vocational counselor, supervisor and administrator. For nine years she was
the Director of Vocational Rehabilitation for the Methadone Maintenance
Treatment Program, Beth Israel Hospital, New York. She has published
numerous professional articles, lectured, served as an adjunct professor,
and consulted on numerous drug addiction related projects and committees. She is currently in private practice as a vocational consultant.

KENNETH WOLF received his Ph.D. from Wayne State University in
1976. He has been working in the field of substance abuse for eight years
on international, national, state, and local levels. He is currently Director
of Multi Resource Corporation, a research and treatment organization in
Detroit, Michigan, as well as principal investigator on a National Institute
on Drug Abuse grant using companionship therapy with heroin abusers in
community settings.